6

Mr. M.P. Grace our first President and Landlord

Porters Park Golf Club

A Centenary History

By

John F. Moreton

Grant Books, Worcestershire 1998

ISBN 0 907 18628 9

Acknowledgements

Porters Park Golf Club wish to thank all those involved in the production of this Centenary History. Thanks are due to Peter Fry, author of *The Whitcomes – A Golfing Legend* (Grant & Hobbs 1994) for permission to reproduce the song by the Western Brothers and for details of Eddie's career. John Stobbs kindly gave permission to quote from his article on Brian Chapman in *Golf World,* October 1962. William Notley created the current course map and Tony Jennings and Juliette Anthony provided sketches from around the course. Older members contributed reminiscences which have been incorporated into the story and the National Golf Clubs Advisory Association and the English Golf Union were most helpful in providing information.

Typeset in 11 on 13 point New Baskerville
and produced in Great Britain by
Hughes & Company
Kempsey, Worcestershire

Designed and published by
Grant Books
The Coach House, Cutnall Green
Droitwich, Worcestershire WR9 0PQ

Porters Park Golf Club

A Centenary History

Published in a limited edition of 750 copies
of which the first 55 are the
Subscriber's Edition

Copy No:

Contents

Foreword

By
Nigel Notley
Centenary Captain

W<small>E CAN</small> all be extremely grateful to those founder members who had the foresight to seek golfing land in Hertfordshire and create this wonderful course that we all enjoy at all times of the year. Good golfing land is rare, but our course lends itself so naturally to the contouring that we can be thankful that we have not had to invest the millions that would now be required to lay out a championship course. We must also be thankful to those members who have painstakingly agreed leases with successive landlords until, finally, Paul Orchard-Lisle was able to deliver the freehold of the course to us and put us in control of our own destiny.

When we started the research for the club history in 1991, with Malcolm Reid, it quickly became evident what an immense influence he had had on this club since the war, not just as the stalwart of junior golf for the English and Hertfordshire Golf Unions but also in the development of the course, its membership and finances, and in promoting it to leading golfers on a national scale. Malcolm was able to fill most of the gaps in our historical knowledge from the date he first set foot on the course in 1927. It is a great shame he did not quite make it to the Centenary to be able to read John Moreton's extraordinarily vivid account. I know he would have approved.

This book, however, runs deeper than a mere historical record. It is evident how those early members wanted this club to develop, their keen interest in the parkland, the competition on which they personally thrived, and also their pleasure in seeing the top golfers of their day compete over our course. Within financial reason they ensured that the clubhouse facilities were comfortable and they never lost sight of the opportunity to enjoy each other's company, as a group of like-minded people. This is the Porters Park tradition.

There are also serious lessons to be learned. I am convinced that no member acting on behalf of this club has given anything but one hundred per cent effort but not all decisions have proved to be in the club's best interest and who can tell if what we currently do will be perceived, in years to come, as having been for the general good. I hope this book will aid those in the decision process to steer a wise course and keep us from the rocks!

As to the future, we should remember that we cannot assume that golf will remain in demand, that there will be a never-ending stream of new members and societies to subsidise our fees. The membership is ageing and we had temporarily neglected the juniors who will ultimately be our lifeblood. The welcome increase in junior members this year may well solve our problem. I know we will give them every support and encouragement and take it with good grace when they start to dominate our competitions! I hope also that we will move forward as one club without the ever-increasing need for expanded Rules and Regulations. Let's play our golf, be courteous to our fellow members and guests, try to put something back into the club and live up to the wonderful legacy of our first hundred years.

Nigel Notley
Porters Park
November 1998

Author's Preface

IFIRST met Malcolm Reid in 1993 at a meeting of county junior golf delegates, shortly after taking over that role for the Worcestershire Union of Golf Clubs. I was immediately impressed by the quiet authority which he imposed on the meeting, by his deep knowledge of the game and his tremendous enthusiasm for junior golf. We met subsequently at tournaments such as the Peter McEvoy Trophy and the Carris Trophy and it was flattering to be recognised by such a doyen of the organisation of junior golf. It has subsequently been a great privilege, indeed, a duty, to be able to enter some of "my boys" in the Reid Trophy. When the invitation to write the history of Porters Park Golf Club was offered it was impossible to refuse. Malcolm had recently died and I was conscious of the loss at national level. The first meeting with Nigel Notley and Campbell Boal confirmed that I had been correct in accepting the invitation and when I was finally able to play the course in that illustrious company, confirmation became dedication to the cause. I only hope the reader will consider it was worth the effort. Both gentlemen have been of immeasurable assistance and inspiration. Nigel set me on the right lines about the development of the course and Campbell regularly unearthed valuable material at Colindale and from local sources. He has also contacted older members, some of whose reminiscences have enabled me to enliven this history. Fionnuala Smith and Angela Davis researched the history of the Ladies' section. I cannot thank them enough. I hope that these pages will help older members relive happy memories and that younger members will realise the difficulties the club has overcome successfully through one hundred years and two world wars so that they can enjoy the magnificent golf course they have inherited and the congenial atmosphere in the clubhouse.

Prologue

At the end of the nineteenth century Radlett was a small village of no great antiquity on Watling Street, the old Roman road which, it is believed, followed the course of an even older road. The population in 1891 was 541 souls who were nevertheless served by the Midland Railway, for the station was opened in 1868. Lying in a valley in a once heavily wooded area, on a bed of sands, clays and pebbles, between London clay and the chalk which forms the Reading Beds, the village was surrounded by substantial properties, many of which had long and interesting histories.

John Le Porter owned the park known as Porters in 1340, Geoffrey Porter in 1391. The fourteenth century manor Sherlands was renamed Randolphs in the sixteenth century before it acquired the name Aldenham Lodge 200 years later. The Monastery of St Albans owned Newberries which once held the cherishable name Bonesbushes before becoming the more prosaic Organ Hall. This was the manor house for the village and originally the profits were for the benefit of the sacrist and infirmerer of St Albans Abbey.

The famous architect, Nicholas Hawksmoor, lived at Porters in 1728. The mansion was rebuilt several times and presumably he had much to do with that. He also assisted in relieving smallpox victims in the district to the sum of sixteen shillings per month.

A distiller and maltster, John Mason purchased Porters and Aldenham Lodge in 1748. The Lord of the Manor of Weld, which appears to have been absorbed into the estate, he was a keen gardener and something of a scholar, writing a supplement to Dr. Johnson's dictionary. His most celebrated work, though, was his *Life of Richard, Lord Howe*. Mason died in 1750, leaving two sons, John and George. The property devolved upon the latter and George sold Porters to Lord Howe in 1772. Although a great name in naval history, it is his development of the house and estate which is more pertinent to our story. He fitted a library "resembling in shape and arrangement the cabin of his flagship, and was able to resume his march and countermarch in comfort."

Lord Howe caused Radlett Lane to be built, linking Shenley with Watling Street, giving some of his land for the purpose, and paid for the construction of the bridge over the brook. Late in the nineteenth century, when Mr. P.M. Grace resided at Porters, the great cricketer W.G. Grace came to lay out a cricket pitch there. It is too much of a coincidence not to assume that they could have been related. When Grace sold Porters to Mr. C. Raphael, this gentlemen improved the pitch and built a pavilion. He was the last private owner of the mansion, for after a disagreement with other stately home owners, the irascible Mr. Raphael sold Porters to the Middlesex County Council for use as a hospital.

While Mr. Grace owned Porters, Mr. H.J. Lubbock dwelt at Newberries, where he played golf in the groun   and, as Squire, took a great interest in the village cricket team. Another private golf course lay in the grounds of Aldenham Lodge, home of Mr. Charles T. Part D.L. He was a great benefactor of the village of Radlett, erecting in 1884 the first shop which he ran with his bailiff, attaching a men's club room and a post office. Later a branch of his bank was incorporated, opening twice a week, before Barclays took it over in 1908. His son Alec was the first managing director of the Hertfordshire Public House Trust. Mr. Part senior sold Aldenham Lodge to a builder so that high class houses could be built in the beautiful parkland.

With two golfers playing on their private greens in the immediate vicinity and an extremely attractive park about which the golf architects of the day might have been tempted to say "was designed by providence to be a golf course", all that was needed was a man of enthusiasm, vision and energy to suggest that Porters become just that.

In the 1890s that man arrived. His name was Dr. Ross Smyth.

Dr. R.V.B. Smyth

C.T. Part

Chapter One

The Origins of the Club

THE HUGE expansion of golf in the closing decade of the last century and the beginning of the present one was partly due to the realisation that pleasant exercise was beneficial to good health. As an advocate of this premise, Dr. Smyth of Shenley was able to persuade one of his patients, a Mr. M.P. Grace of Porters, the mansion outside the village, that his park would be the ideal location for a golf course. Permission was granted and Dr. Smyth and a few friends laid out an inexpensive course, which nevertheless bore some similarity to the present layout of Porters Park Golf Club.

When a group of London professional and businessmen sought a venue for a formalised golf club within easy reach of the city and close to a railway station, Radlett, on the Midland Railway, with apparently small existing courses in the vicinity, seemed a good choice. Members of Colney Heath seemed dissatisfied with their course and when Mr. Grace had responded to overtures from the City and from his neighbours, they were permitted to join the new club without paying an entrance fee. So, by the end of 1899 the newly formed Porters Golf Club had sixty members, including Mr. Grace, who was elected the first President, and his three daughters.

Mr. C.T. Part became the first captain and when the first secretary, Mr. Barre Goldie, resigned after only six months in office, Dr. Smyth took over the minute book. He remained in office for five and a half years before resigning due to the pressure of the work involved. Dr. Ross Vincent Beatty Smyth, who was born in Strabane, Co. Londonderry, in 1860, a highly qualified practitioner and a graduate of Dublin University, had taken on a number of public appointments in addition to his general practice, including surgeon to the South Division of the Metropolitan Police. Having gained his M.D. in 1886, he worked in the Rotunda hospital in Dublin for eight months, married Emily Sutcliffe of Naas and immediately moved to Shenley in 1887. Mrs. Smyth also figured prominently in the early days of Porters Golf Club.

The minutes of the first committee meeting, held on 7th April 1899, show that a course was ready for play and that sufficient paid-up members had been recruited for the club's first monthly medal to be held the following week.

Mr. Grace had agreed the terms of the lease for the land, initially for seven years with the option to terminate it within three. This was presented to the committee by Mr. Grace's lawyer, C.G. Kekewich, who was also on the committee and became the club's solicitor. The whole arrangement seems to have been very amicable for Mr. Grace also subscribed £25 towards the costs of founding the club and Messrs. Part and Lubbock advanced similar amounts. Mr. Kekewich practised in St Albans and was a relative of the Hon. Justice Sir Arthur Kekewich, who was captain of West Herts in 1897. He had already been the first president of Woking Golf Club, a well-known recreation ground for members of the Bar, and was one of the first true golf addicts. Sir Arthur converted his billiard room into a putting green and padded the walls so that he could practise his driving indoors.

A professional, Arthur Long, had already been engaged and as one of his duties was to sell whisky and other beverages to the members, the first minutes record the supply of whisky to the professional. They also listed the club's own rules for play.

In 1888 the Royal and Ancient Golf Club had added a provision to the rules of golf to permit clubs to frame their own local rules and the conservation conscious committee of Porters Golf Club lost no time in doing so.

1. No play allowed out of a gorse or other bush, but to be lifted and dropped behind in a penalty of one stroke.(sic)
2. Ball driven into bush to be dropped within one club length, opposite where it went in, on the same side and loose (sic) one stroke.
3. Ball driven into a pond whether lost or not is to be dropped on the side farthest from the hole.
4. If ball picked out of a bunker to be dropped in the far side of the bunker can be teed & loose 2 strokes.

Caddies were not permitted on Sundays, nor was the professional allowed to play on a Sunday or before 2.00 p.m. on weekdays, before which time he was required to work on the links. In return for this he was to receive £1 per week, a free house and coal and could charge two shillings per round when playing with a member. He was also "allowed" to supply luncheons and teas "at the published price".

The entrance fee and first year's subscription for gentlemen amounted to £5, ladies and minors paid £2, and as a number of members joined towards the end of the year, they paid £3.10s. as entrance fee and half subscription.

Messrs. Part and Thomas and the honorary secretary were appointed green and handicapping committee "and their duties shall be to look after the proper keeping and improvement of the links and to handicap the members of the club". The secretary was authorised to offer Long a further shilling per week to "have the putting greens clean and in playing order on Sundays" but this work had to be done before 9.00 a.m. It also indicates that the course was at least partially grazed; however, the two holes made on the land of the Model Farm were to be mown. This land was leased to the club by a Mr. Tayler, who in turn leased the land from Mr. Grace. We shall return to Mr. Tayler in due course because refusal of his application to the club to allow the grass to grow on this part of the course led to a sequence of events beneficial to the club.

Members continued to join the club, among them family groups and a considerable number of young or unmarried ladies. A number of prizes were donated for a variety of competitions organised in 1900.

At the first Annual General Meeting held on 3rd May 1900, Mr. Kekewich resigned from the committee but was re-elected and the balance sheet was presented in which the costs of laying out the links were published: a figure of £87.7s.1d. up to 31st March 1899, demonstrating that a course had been laid out prior to the first committee meeting.

Two days after the A.G.M. it was proposed at a committee meeting to issue debentures for the erection of a new clubhouse, acceptance of which was facilitated by Mr. Grace's agreement to extend the lease to fourteen years. However, he subsequently reconsidered this, and having already extended the lease from six to ten years, felt that it should remain so. Nevertheless, the committee went ahead with plans to commission architects and builders for the proposed new clubhouse.

Each £10 debenture would bear 4% interest, payable yearly on the first day of July, the club retaining the option to pay off as many debentures as it wished at any time, with interest to date. The scheme proved popular, for by the end of June 1900 promises to take up sixty-two of the sixty-five debentures had been received.

Mr. Angus D. Ross was the architect who successfully tendered a design for the clubhouse, another shrewd move by the committee as it transpired that Mr. Ross did not charge for his time in designing and supervising the work. He was accordingly invited to become an honorary member of the club, which also offered to pay the expenses he incurred on his many visits from London to the site. It could be assumed from his name that Mr. Ross was a Scot and therefore quite likely to be a golfer and very appreciative of the honour accorded him.

The estimate received from Messrs. Boff of £482 was accepted for the building and heating of the new clubhouse, less £32 for bath, lavatory and drainage. Mr. Ross was asked to obtain from Boff the cost of fitting the lavatory with running water, drainage but *no* bath. The committee then felt able to apply for a loan not exceeding £800 to pay for the work and proceed with the debenture issue.

3

Another example of the fair-mindedness and shrewdness of the committee was the return of £4 to the landlord as the Inland Revenue had not taxed the club on the previous year's income. In return Mr. Grace dealt summarily with Mr.Tayler, the tenant of the Model Farm who had tried to prevent the greenstaff cutting the grass on the two holes on his land leased from Mr. Grace. Having been informed by the secretary that the grass must be cut, Tayler gave the club notice to quit his land. Mr. Grace retaliated quite splendidly by giving Tayler notice to quit thereby saving the two holes for the club.

A suggestion to provide stabling for horses was shelved as the committee was not agreed upon the use of the old shed on the links being suitable for this purpose. However, a shed to house an earth closet and urinal was proposed and to be constructed beside the clubhouse at a cost not exceeding £10. At the same meeting (24th November 1900) it was decided to ask the professional if he and his wife would be willing to undertake the cleaning and maintenance of the new clubhouse as well as supplying the refreshments according to the tariff of prices the committee would draw up and approve.

The Longs accepted and the necessary furniture, cutlery, crockery and napery were purchased. Cleaning and other materials were to be provided by the club, but the Longs were expected to make good any breakages. So, by 1901, the members could enjoy a luncheon of cold meat, potatoes and pickles, or salad, bread, butter and cheese, for one shilling and nine pence. If they required a cooked lunch, a day's notice would produce, for two shillings and sixpence, steak or chops with potatoes etc., bread, butter and cheese. Bread, butter and cheese were available for either six or nine pence; tea, bread, butter and cake, sixpence; and "ditto with bread and jam, eight pence". The tariff also listed alcoholic and soft drinks, a large whisky costing sixpence and a large brandy eight pence. A pint of ale cost sixpence, cigars the same and cigarettes one penny. A caddie could purchase a lunch of bread and cheese for three pence.

Subsequent inspection of the facilities about to be offered led to a review and some of the china, glass and cutlery was returned to the supplier in exchange for cheaper items. Furniture was obtained on approval including armchairs, two tea-tables "and any other necessaries requisite for the comfort of the clubhouse". The premises were further brightened by a picture, *The Sabbath Breakers*, presented by Mr. G.W. Jones.

Boffs were also asked to quote for a shed measuring seven feet by five, containing two compartments, door, windows and a paved floor, and finished to the same standard as the clubhouse; a cold water cistern and twenty-four lockers. That these were necessary was due to the fact that the majority of the members at this time travelled from London, St Albans and neighbouring towns rather than Radlett.

The Midland Railway was approached and asked to consider the proposal that a train should be provided leaving Radlett at 6.00 p.m. on Sundays, terminating at St Pancras. Cab fares to and from the station were to be posted in the clubhouse to facilitate the use of this. Unfortunately the immediate response was unco-operative. The railway was more helpful in 1902 when Mr. Haws was able to negotiate reduced railway fares for members travelling to Radlett for the purposes of playing golf. It should be remembered that railway companies of the time were keen to promote travel to golfing destinations, which featured on many of their posters, and a number of clubs, such as Denham, actually had their own platforms (indeed, Denham still has). The great James Braid would never have laid out so many courses as he did but for the vast rail network. The railway was finally prevailed upon to provide a Sunday service in 1903, a train departing St Albans at 5.20 p.m. and stopping at all intermediate stations, including Radlett, en route to Moorgate Street. The committee passed a vote of thanks to the manager of the Midland Railway. It is not known what provision was made for the many members who lived in St Albans.

The balance sheet at the A.G.M. of 1901 showed a balance in hand of £29.2s.7d., the building and furnishing of the clubhouse having cost £590.10s.10d. Visitors' green fees had already produced £24.9s.0d. and were the main topic of discussion at the meeting. It was proposed that gentlemen and ladies pay one shilling per round or part of a round on weekdays and two shillings and sixpence at weekends and bank holidays. Visitors could also pay five shillings for seven consecutive days' play, once a year. Members could compound this for visitors staying with them on payment of £1. An amendment put by A.F. Part and seconded by D.C. Part proposed that the fee should be one shilling on all days except competition days, but this was defeated.

It has been noted that a considerable number of the club's members were ladies and it was proposed to obtain plans and estimates for a small clubhouse for the ladies. Boff's estimate of £58 was rejected at the next meeting but deferred for further consideration. This duly happened a fortnight later when the secretary was authorised to spend £60 on the construction of the ladies' pavilion. Five more debentures of £10 would be issued to defray this cost. It was then proposed to turn the existing ladies' room into a bar and smoke room and install lockers in the saloon which then housed the bar. A closet then had to be built "for the convenience of the lady members" and an oil stove provided for their further comfort. This in turn led to the ladies' and minors' entrance fee being raised to £3, and the purchase of a table, chairs and cutlery for the ladies.

The club continued to expand. It has been demonstrated that it was popular with visitors and in November 1901, it was decided to limit the number of gentlemen members to 200, the ladies to 50. The gentlemen's entrance fee was increased to £7. Mr. Ross was to be invited to design a new locker room, to be attached to the present clubhouse, with room for "about fifty lockers". "The best sort of linoleum" was to be purchased to cover the floors of the clubhouse.

Tayler having vacated the farm, Mr. Grace now offered the club a lease on eight and a half acres at a rent of £17 per annum, with one year's notice on either side to terminate the agreement.The offer was accepted, with effect from 25th December 1901.

Mr. Ross' design for the new locker room had been received by the time the committee met again. The estimated cost was £127, including heating and fifty-six lockers. Although the design was approved, the secretary was instructed to write to Mr. Ross to enquire into the probable extra cost of making the locker room two feet larger each way. However, if this could not be done without altering the proportion and aspect of the whole building the estimate supplied by Messrs. Boff of £115 should be accepted. To finance this, another ten debentures of £10 would be issued at the normal 4%. As eleven new members were elected at the same meeting, there would be no problem raising the money.

However, the club had not heard the last of Mr. Tayler, for he wrote to the secretary requesting a cheque for £5 and a further £10 for damage done by cutting the grass between the greens the previous September, when he had intended taking a crop of hay off the park. The club sent him £5 for the outstanding rent and admitted no further liability.

There can be no doubt that the club was being well run and soundly administered. In 1902, members were requested to pay their subscription direct to Barclays Bank and Bankers Order forms issued for that purpose. Mr. Haws was asked to look into the catering arrangements, and on the resignation from the committee of Mr. Robson, Major Creagh replaced him and immediately was elected the chairman of the house committee.

One of the first actions of this committee was to interview and appoint a new steward, Mr. J.J. Churchill, who with his wife would take charge of the clubhouse and cater for the members, subject to the club's satisfaction with his character. In return the Churchills received a salary of £50 per annum with free house, coal and light. Long, the professional, had his salary increased to £1.10s. per week but had to find his own house. A further financial reward came his way when he was appointed caddie master, taking one penny per round for himself from the fee of ten pence per round, seven pence per half round. Later in 1902 the club granted him further recognition by building a professional's shop, at a cost of £40, with a tool shed to be added at a cost no greater than £10.

Another important development in May 1902 was the election of Cecil Raphael, whose address was given as Porters, Shenley. He had moved into

Porters and later that year Mr. Grace's resignation as President and member was received with great regret and gratitude for all he had done on the club's behalf. Mr. Raphael became the club's new landlord and benefactor. Having sold Porters to Mr. Raphael, Mr. Grace left the county. The club lost no time in making the new landlord welcome. He became President in 1903 and soon began to make his mark, presenting a trophy later in the year. In January 1904 he agreed to extend the club's lease on condition that he be allowed to choose four members of the committee and that caddies be permitted to work on Sundays.

The club agreed to a lease of fourteen years, the first seven at a rent of £155 per annum, the next seven at £180. The landlord retained the grazing rights and the land in Home Farm. The membership continued to grow: when the number reached 200 anyone seeking election had to have the approval of the President. The ceiling for membership was raised to 250 and once the 200th member had been elected the subscription was raised to £5. The other notable change was that of the club's name, Park being added to Porters to give our present title. Some confusion had been caused by visitors thinking the golf club was for railway porters!

At the beginning of 1903 the club registered under the new Licensing Act. Despite the lack of members living in Radlett the club took up five shares in the Radlett Industrial Society Limited and further evidence of the club's encouragement of local development is to be found in the members' support, by signing a petition, for a scheme by the Hertfordshire Public House Trust Company to erect a hotel in Radlett.

Ernest S. Markham was elected a member in May 1903. His father was a founder member, having taken advantage of the offer to the Colney Heath members, and Ernest had the temerity to challenge the method by which the committee obtained the members' votes at the A.G.M. The committee was supported by the members, as well they might have been, for the balance sheet showed a healthy £304.18s.1d. at the bank. However, Ernest, or Bill as he was known, was to become an important figure in the growth of the club.

That the club was thriving could also be seen in the fact that the steward's

E.S. Markham

7

RADLETT, HERTS.

Particulars, Plan & Conditions of Sale

— OF —

The Radlett Park Estate,

COMPRISING ABOUT

100 VALUABLE & DESIRABLE

FREEHOLD PLOTS OF BUILDING LAND,

SITUATE ON THIS CHARMING ESTATE,

Suitable for the Erection of Good Class Residences.

Payment on the EASY PAYMENT SYSTEM, extending over Nine Years,
if desired.

Land Tax and Tithe Free.

Magnificent and Picturesque Timber included. Fifteen Miles from London on the
Midland Main Line, adjoining the PORTERS PARK GOLF LINKS.

For Sale by Auction, by

MR. WILLIAM YOUNG

IN A MARQUEE ON THE ESTATE,

On THURSDAY, MAY 30th, 1907, at 3.30 o'clock sharp.

Particulars, Plan and Conditions of Sale may be obtained of Messrs. HODDING,
JONES & CLARK, Solicitors, St. Albans, and of WILLIAM YOUNG, P.A.S.I., Auctioneer
and Surveyor, 4, St. Peter's Street, St. Albans.   (Telephone 1x St. Albans).

Gibbs & Bamforth, Ltd., Printers, St. Albans.

salary was increased to £60 per annum, in addition to the £5 beer allowance he received, though this had only been granted some time after Churchill's initial request. Clearly the steward and his wife were giving satisfaction and were given plenty to do by the members. A further increase of £12 was voted to them in April 1904, along with the provision of extra help on special occasions, which in its turn led, in October, to the engagement of a male servant and maid to assist them.

It is not surprising, then, that further extensions and improvements to the clubhouse were proposed, again funded by a further issue of debentures. However, these were changed to Annuity Bonds payable at the end of the extended lease; in other words, members would have to wait until 1923 before redeeming the bonds. Then a second debenture issue was launched to cover Boff's estimate of £1495 for these extensions. This estimate was accepted but the contract was not signed until the issue was completely subscribed.

Another call on the members' finances was made in September, when they were invited to sign a subscription list for furniture for the new extension. This cannot have met with a very enthusiastic response, because, although the secretary was empowered to purchase new tables and chairs the following month, in November a letter was sent to the membership requesting donations towards defraying the cost of the new items.

To maintain the credit balance of the club it was proposed that once 225 members had been elected the entrance fee would be increased from £7 to £10. That some members had strong views regarding the Sabbath became evident when it was felt necessary to make a rule forbidding the playing of cards in the clubhouse on a Sunday, though this was later amended to include only the public rooms. It was felt necessary to draw up a full schedule of House Rules and "other indoor games" fell under the same ban as playing cards. Visitors could not purchase intoxicating liquors unless twenty-four hours notice had been given, and members supplying their own wine and lunch were required to pay corkage and table charges.

The entertainment of the members was provided by a number of periodicals, including *The Field, The Illustrated Sporting and Dramatic News, Tatler, Graphic, Illustrated London News,* and, of course, *Punch.* Later the back numbers were donated to the local hospital.

All this took a toll on Dr. Smyth and he announced his resignation as honorary secretary with effect from the 1905 A.G.M. His resignation was received with regret and expressions of gratitude for all his efforts on the club's behalf. The committee then took an important step forward by deciding to employ a paid secretary to administer the club's affairs. The advertisement inserted in *The Field* and *Golf Illustrated* read:

"Wanted: a secretary for Porters Park Golf Club, Radlett, Herts, to reside in the neighbourhood. Must be well up in secretarial work and a good golfer. Apply by letter, stating age, experience and salary required to the Hon. Secretary."

At the Annual General Meeting Dr. Smyth was appointed by the President as his personal representative on the committee. The appointment of a paid secretary was sanctioned by the membership and Mr. W.O.F. Sergeant was duly confirmed in his post. Dr. Smyth was elected Captain for the year, a fitting reward for his labours.

Mr. Raphael thus held a strong influence on the club's development, his representative also being the Captain. The sheep which grazed the course belonged to the President and so when Mr. Richmond raised the possibility of removing them Mr. Kekewich advised the club very strongly that there were legal obstacles preventing this and it would cost them £50 in refunding grazing rights to Mr. Raphael, which the club could ill afford.

Mr. Richmond's next proposal was that the captain should be eligible for re-election at the A.G.M. and an Extraordinary General Meeting be called to vote on this. This meeting took place on 19th February 1909. The motion was passed unanimously, also the amendment of Rule No. 1, limiting gentlemen members to 250 and ladies to 70.

For the first time, in April 1909, membership was refused to an applicant, a Mr. Jacobs. His proposer was asked to withdraw the nomination but cannot have done so, for when the committee met in May they voted against Mr. Jacobs' election, having investigated his suitability for membership. Another applicant was refused election in October.

It was decided to print twelve copies of the new rules and regulations for the running of the club, which had been passed at the E.G.M. A proposal regarding the ladies' use of the course was raised at the A.G.M. in May, but as Mr. Skelton was not in attendance to propose it, it was set aside.

A letter asking for a donation to a proposed Men's Institute at London Colney invoked the club's involvement in the community. It was felt that although such a facility might be of benefit to the caddies, the making of

C.L. Richmond

donations was a matter of individual choice. Revd. Gotto offered to be responsible for the collection of any such donations.

A further request for financial assistance which came in December from the Carlisle and Silloth Golf Club, asking for a donation of one guinea to assist in meeting a demand from the Inland Revenue for payment of taxes due from the receipt of visitors' green fees, was met with more general approval. This was followed by a letter from the collector of taxes in St Albans asking for details of the club's repayment of borrowed capital and if the refunds had the tax deducted.

Further extensions to the clubhouse were proposed by the captain in June and tenders obtained, which were considered rather high. A subscription list was suggested to defray the cost. Despite a fire in the dressing room in March 1911, it was proposed to erect a shed for the greenstaff backing onto this room.

Although the Chairman reported to the members at the A.G.M. that the club was making steady progress, the first signs of dissent were making themselves felt. Mr. Richmond was obliged in June to request solidarity among the committee, as some of them had voted against proposed amendments to the club rules passed at the A.G.M., including members of the sub-committee which had drafted them. There had been instances of members breaking rules, for example a lady was found playing cards in the committee room one Sunday afternoon and another member had been observed bringing guests to play without obtaining a visitor's ticket. Whether these incidents prompted thirty-one members to write to the committee requesting an Extraordinary General Meeting to alter the club's rules yet again, or whether there were more general grounds for altering them, is not certain, but the meeting was duly convened on December 9th.

The changes demanded payment of visitors' green fees, restricting the number of lady visitors and stipulating their green fees.

The next important indication of the popularity of the club came at the committee meeting following the E.G.M., when it was proposed to open a waiting list for prospective members.

What may surprise the modern member more was the fact that electricity did not come to Radlett until 1913 and that the committee did not consider it worthwhile connecting the club to the supply at that time. It was much more positive in dealing with issues arising from the outbreak of the First World War.

The committee which sat on 26th September agreed, firstly, to dismiss the Austrian house boy, Hans Muller, and secondly, that dependents of any member of the club staff enlisting in the forces would receive allowances. The strongest action was the circular letter to all members:

Sir or Madam,

I beg to inform you that at a meeting of the committee, held on the 9th ult., the following resolution was passed, viz:-

"That members of German or Austrian origin be asked whether they have become British subjects by Naturalisation, and if so, to produce their papers to this effect."

It is the desire of the committee that such members not producing satisfactory papers should cease to enjoy the privileges of the club during the continuance of the war, and that members affected by the above resolution will at once give the information asked for to the secretary.

It is further resolved that a copy of this resolution be sent to every member of the club.

I am

Yours truly,

D.L. Cottam

Secretary.

In October it was agreed to respond to an appeal for clothes for Belgian refugees in France and an application for membership from a Mr. Roechling was held over. In November the secretary was instructed to ascertain the nationality of the husband of a Mrs. Goldberg who had been put up for membership. His inquiries must have proved satisfactory, as Mrs. Goldberg was elected the following month. She wrote back the following March declining membership because of the war. Meanwhile a cheque for £10.10s. had been sent to the Prince of Wales' fund and members joining the services had their subscription suspended for the following year.

Despite the war, competitive golf continued until 1916, when competitions were cancelled for the rest of the duration of the hostilities. Part of the course was used for cultivation, Mr. Raphael approving the planting of potatoes. It was felt that it would be difficult to retain the ground staff if they were not also employed in agricultural work. Mr. Raphael also built a soup kitchen at the gates of the mansion for the benefit of the local poor, but woe betide them if they stepped through the gate: Raphael once made children caught black-berrying on his land empty their jars and bags and return home chastened.

Wounded soldiers were entertained at a concert at the club, but the proposal to offer the clubhouse as a V.A.D. (Voluntary Aid Detachment) hospital was eventually rejected at an E.G.M., on the grounds that the club would not be able to honour its financial commitments to the debenture holders, the landlord and the surviving trustee and that this would result in the possible winding-up of the club. Additionally, other buildings in the area would be more suitable, both from the point of view of space and hygiene. Mr. Arthur Moore offered his house for use as the hospital. 150 members attended the meeting, which was held at the St Pancras Grand Hotel in London on 17th March 1917.

The entertainment of the wounded soldiers became a regular event; the officers of the Royal Fleet Auxiliary were offered a match with the club and members whose enlistment caused financial hardship were allowed to suspend their memberships. Some, including Capt. W.H. Bull, were killed in action. The number of provisional members awaiting membership was insufficient to make up the financial shortfall and the President was obliged to send the following letter to all members:

July 16th, 1917

Dear Sir or Madam,

The financial position of the club has been engaging the serious attention of the committee for some time past, and if the club is to be continued there is no doubt that substantial monetary assistance from members will be required in the immediate future.

The difficulty is entirely owing to the war, the annual income having suffered severely from :-

1) So many members serving at the front, and it not having been considered proper to insist on subscriptions being paid.

2) The increased cost of all kinds of labour.

3) The increased cost of all kinds of food.

4) The large decrease in the amount received from green fees.

5) Owing to the liquor restriction , the bar, which was a source of considerable revenue in pre-war days, is now almost non-productive.

It has therefore been decided to raise £1000, which amount it is hoped will carry the club well on to the end of 1919.

In view of the forgoing the committee will ask the assistance from all members of the club.

The list on the other side gives the names of the members who have already promised their support, and the Hon. Secretary will be very glad to know if you will allow him to add your name to it.

We should like to say that although the course has been kept up to the highest standard, every economy has been rigidly enforced in all departments.

The services of a paid secretary have been saved.

The club is very much indebted to the Hon. Secretary, Mr. C.L. Richmond, for all he has done for it.

Yours faithfully,
C.F.RAPHAEL,
President.

When it is realised that a large number of clubs failed to survive the war for similar reasons to those in Raphael's letter or because the land was not restored after agricultural use, the fact that Porters Park did survive indicates the quality and loyalty of the membership in responding to the appeal, and the good management of the club's affairs. Mr. Raphael also offered to reduce the club's rent by £20 per month.

1917 was a sad year in the club's history, for the deaths of Revd. Gotto, Mr. W.S. Wakefield and Dr. Smyth were recorded and letters of sympathy sent to the widows. All had served the club loyally for many years with enthusiasm, energy and a great deal of hard work. Dr. Smyth had suffered a long illness which, however, had only confined him to bed during the final weeks. Until then he had continued to care for his patients. The co-founder of the club had also played county cricket for Hertfordshire and was much mourned in the village. His son had leave from active service to attend his father during his last days. He also left two daughters.

Visitors "not of British nationality" gave cause for complaints about their behaviour and the captain promised to "take steps to have them informed of the etiquette of golf". It was also deemed necessary to place notices on the boundaries of the course advising strangers that the course was private property.

Further agricultural use of the course resulted in a very satisfactory hay crop in September 1918, twenty-seven tons having a value of £188. Large quantities of whisky had also been purchased, which, it was soon discovered, were being sold by the steward for members' use at home. As the steward had also invested in some sheep, his behaviour led to serious investigation and he was dismissed. The sheep were deemed the property of the club and it was reported at the house committee meeting on 2nd November that "they only awaited the attendance of the butcher".

The potato crop had also done well and after the club's requirements had been met the surplus was sold – to members. Porters Park was well placed to meet the challenge of post war living, but it seems the members were still unwilling to let bygones be bygones, for in 1919 it was proposed that unless persons of German, Austrian, Hungarian, Bulgarian or Turkish birth had served in the British Armed Forces, they were ineligible for membership. The war-time resignations had created vacancies but there was little problem in filling them, even with the above restrictions. Equally no person could be admitted as a visitor if they were ineligible for membership of the club. A separate guests' book was to be kept to regulate this matter. This, then, was the situation as the club approached an important decade in its history, the 1920s.

Porters Park, 1913

2nd Hole

Looking back from 7th Green

Sandpit guarding 8th Green

8th Hole

16

Original 9th Green

10th Tee, bunker to left of tee is adjacent to old 9th Green, the flag for which is just visible

Bridge to 14th Green. Note the depth of the brook, the pimples on the 15th and the bunkers on the 16th

Looking across from left of 18th Green to a green in front of pavilion

Chapter Two

The Development of the Course

PORTERS PARK has much for which to be grateful to Dr. Smyth. Not only did he act as honorary secretary and Captain in the formative years of the club, but his initiative created the golf course in the first place. A friend of, as well as, most probably, doctor to Mr. Grace, he was one of the first to see the potential for golf in the beautiful, wooded parkland of Porters.

It is clear that a course was ready for play when the first committee meeting was held in April 1899 as the first monthly medal was scheduled to take place the following week. It was quite common for a group of friends who wished to try golf as a means of exercise to lay out a few rudimentary holes wherever they could find suitable land and obtain permission to fashion greens and tees. As their enthusiasm and ability grew and more friends joined them, the need for a more formal course became apparent. Because the land was normally utilised for grazing, as it was at Porters, the need for mowing machinery was minimal, only greens being cut. There are still courses today, 100 years on, where the sheep keep the fairways down and gang-mowers are seldom seen [e.g. Kington, Herefordshire]. However, the club had stabling for a horse which pulled a "lawn-mower", which had to be returned to Ransomes for repair in March 1901. The horse was then employed in pulling a roller for a full week to level the ground on six holes.

Porters extended its course in September 1899 by laying out two holes on Model Farm, the site of the current twelfth hole, leased by Mr. Tayler from Mr. Grace. Their disagreements have already been noted. The farmer objected to the grass being cut as he wished to harvest a hay crop. The club stood their ground and the dispute was settled when Mr. Grace gave Tayler notice. These were replacement holes to improve the course. Eighteen holes were in play the following year when changes were made to the order of play.

The first tee was made to the left of the new pavilion, where the practice nets are now situated. The eighteenth green had been in this vicinity but was now moved in front of the pavilion. The first green was moved to the left and nearer to the second tee, which is the likely site of the present seventh tee. The old tee was moved nearer to the eighth green, now the sixth, although the original green on that site was not the swirling, layered green now in existence. The old thirteenth and fourteenth holes were to be combined into one hole and are the present fourth hole. The tee to the original seventeenth was moved nearer to the Radlett Road, was renumbered sixteen, and a hole measuring 130 yards was created. The altered seventeenth was a new hole with a drive over a pit to a new green near the old sixteenth green. This suggests that the direction of the original sixteenth hole was across and towards what we now know as the seventeenth green. There was also a suggestion to eliminate the cross-over on the third and fourth holes. Shared fairways and drives over preceding holes and greens were quite common on early courses. These old holes were on ground now largely occupied by the current seventh and eighth holes. The eighteenth was replaced completely, the tee being placed close to the existing seventeenth tee and "far back".

The ladies were given a separate course with new, red tee boxes in 1901.

The first local rules, protecting the gorse and the bushes, have been quoted in Chapter One. Further local rules passed in 1901 refer to a trench being cut along the front of the gorse on the second hole, the current seventh, and another guarding the green. A ball falling between these trenches was to be lifted and dropped on the side nearest the tee under penalty of one stroke. This rule was amended and a further local rule was made to cover rabbit scrapes:

"When a ball lies in a rabbit scratch on such part of the course being played, so that the shaft of the club can be placed across the centre of the hole without touching the ball, such ball may be lifted and dropped behind the hole *without penalty.*" This was later amended to include cart ruts and hoof marks.

In April 1903 a roller costing £8 and a mower costing £5 were purchased by the indefatigable Dr. Smyth. As early greens were usually cut out of the same grazing grass as the remainder of the course and relied on natural drainage, a roller was an essential piece of equipment. It was also necessary to keep sheep off the putting greens and it is clear from a minute of 5th September that these must have been fenced off:

"If a ball lying within four club lengths of the post guarding any of the putting greens is stymied by said posts the ball may be lifted and dropped on one side but not nearer the hole *without penalty.*"

At the same committee meeting the green committee was empowered to make the following alterations to the course. A new sixth hole of about 140-150 yards to be made with the green close to the original eighth green.

The Clubhouse 1902

This is broadly the short sixth as we now know it. A new seventh hole of about 520 yards, playing to the existing sixth green was to be created. This hole was probably played in the general direction of the current tenth, encompassing some land which is now the practice ground and eleventh hole. The seventeenth and eighteenth holes were to be made into one of about 420 yards, which is the present eighteenth hole. Although there is no mention of bunkers, in November it was proposed to purchase eighteen tons of seaside sand from Skegness. Previously sand was extracted from the pit at the current eighth hole, which, although not exhausted, was not of the same quality as the Skegness sand.

Ever on the look-out for improvement in the presentation of the course and its bye-laws, the green committee reworded some of the earlier local rules and added local rule no. 7:

"A ball played into any of the sheds or enclosures on the course may be lifted and dropped behind or to one side, but not nearer the hole being played. Penalty : one stroke."

An interesting minute in September 1904 recorded acceptance of an estimate of £6.15s.0d. "for constructing a bridge *half way across the pond* at the eighth hole". The original tee was somewhere in the wood between the current eleventh and thirteenth holes and the original eighth is undoubtedly part of the current thirteenth.

So far the layout and development of the course seems to have been the work of such dedicated men as Dr. Smyth and the green committee, but the first mention of an established architect being called in occurs in

21

December 1904 when the captain proposed to invite the great J.H. Taylor from Royal Mid-Surrey to advise on the general layout of the course and the formation of the bunkers, as some members had expressed some dissatisfaction with them. Taylor was at the height of his powers as a player and advised clubs on their courses, designing a number of worthy tests.

Taylor must have very busy because the professional who did come to offer his advice was Cuthbert Butchart, of the Highgate and East Finchley Golf Club. One of a family of golf professionals from Carnoustie, Butchart was a noted club-maker. Prior to his appointment at East Finchley he served at Royal County Down, where he laid out the second course. He later moved to Germany, where he designed a few courses and was a club professional. When the First World War broke out he was interned in a POW camp at Ruhleben for two years. In 1916 a five hole course was laid out, manufacturers sent equipment and seventy-three prisoners played golf. On his release he returned briefly to Scotland before moving on to America. He was head professional at Westchester Golf Club in New York but spent the winters in Florida, where he began making and selling wooden clubs bearing the family name.

He was engaged to make three bunkers on the course, between the eleventh and twelfth, twelfth and thirteenth, the current second, third and fourth holes, and the sixteenth hole.

The estimate of £15.10s.0d. for the labour involved was deemed satisfactory and Butchart's brief was extended to make further alterations, to be made ready for play by Easter. These consisted of a new summer green on the first hole, with new bunkers, if approved. The second and third to be made into one hole and rebunkered (this is now the seventh). A new third hole played to the old fourth green. This would be down the hill and up the slope to a green near the pit on the current eighth. A new tee and green for the fifth, which would be renumbered the fourth. This is probably the first attempt at the short hole which is now the ninth. The old sixth was to be renumbered the fifth and subsequently became the current tenth. A discussion regarding a new sixth hole with a green in a dell and a new seventh resulted in a postponement of that suggestion. Undoubtedly these proposed sixth and seventh holes were on land currently occupied by the eleventh hole but the eighth would be altered by moving the tee and the green.

The minutes confirm that the tenth green was to be made "cuppy and undulating". The secretary has here intermingled the new numbering with the old. We can deduce that the old ninth hole was played from adjacent to the site of the old eighth (current thirteenth) green down in the direction of the present fifth hole. The tenth green mentioned is therefore the previous eighth (now our short sixth). The eleventh green was altered in shape and is the second green as we now know it, although it is not clear whether the green was in front of or over the brook. The new twelfth green was to be on the side of a hill. This is the third green which has been recontoured subsequently to make the front slope less severe.

Bunkers were to be re-arranged on the thirteenth, the current fourth, and new tees built on the fifteenth. No reference is made in this section of the minutes to the fourteenth hole but we can assume that it is the present one. The bunker on the sixteenth was to be redesigned but subsequently all bunkering on this hole was removed. A new summer seventeenth green was made, which suggests that the siting of the new green was in a wet area which could not be used consistently through the winter. Finally the pit guarding the eighteenth green was to be "improved". There is little doubt that this is the pit on the right as we now know it, but evidence of a pond in that vicinity exists.

The suggestion to make three new bunkers had become a major project. Clearly the green committee had been thinking hard about the play on the course and it would seem fair to surmise that the standard of play at Porters Park was improving immeasurably. Messrs. Colebrook, Thomas and Rumsey were to instruct Butchart in his work and further refinements were made to the proposed changes.

Butchart's fee of £25 plus expenses added to the costs incurred and the work exceeded the planned budget but it was thought inadvisable to call an E.G.M. to sanction the extra costs, but to proceed as long as the alterations did not cost more than £300.

It is not known if Mr. Raphael suffered from golfers on his private property, but an "out of bounds" notice was put on his fence alongside the eighth hole (the current thirteenth). The sandpit on the fourth (present eighth) became ground under repair while it was being worked and further redrafting of local rules allowed players the option to play out of hedges, ditches and ponds or to take a drop under penalty, and stipulated procedure on the third, thirteenth and sixteenth holes (current eighth, fourth and sixteenth holes) in the event of a ball entering a ditch.

The green committee was still not satisfied with the order of play, however, and in June 1905 it was proposed to play the third hole from the old fourth tee nearest the clubhouse to a hole in the corner, i.e. down across the current seventh green area to a green at the left edge of the fairway in front of the brook. The old fourth (the "Pit hole") was to revert to the old tees. The Dell hole, which was then the sixth and is now the eleventh, should be played from a tee at the right hand corner of the fifth green (this is our current tenth hole but the green was set fifty yards back down the slope and to the left) provided the landlord consented to an oak tree being removed. The new seventh (twelfth), ninth (fifth) and seventeenth greens were to be abandoned as was the eighth hole (thirteenth) in its existing state, although it was recommended that the grass be cut back to the pond on the side nearest the tee. There is clear evidence here of significant restructuring of the holes which now comprise the twelfth and thirteenth, which was only satisfactorily resolved when land was bought in 1925, straightening the boundary and allowing the twelfth hole to be created in its present form. It is not surprising then, that it was also proposed to employ an extra boy to work on the course.

The fine-tuning of all these re-arrangements came at the meeting in November when the order of play was changed and several holes renumbered. [The first remained the same, the eleventh became the second, the twelfth became the third, the thirteenth the fourth, the ninth the fifth, the tenth the sixth, the second the seventh, the third the eighth, the fourth the ninth, the fifth the tenth, the sixth the eleventh, the seventh the twelfth, and the eighth the thirteenth, the other holes remaining the same.]

The following May the bogey of the seventeenth was reduced from 5 to 4. This same hole was to become the proposed site of an experiment by the head greenkeeper who wished to try out a worm-killer used at Totteridge Golf Club. The committee agreed on condition that it cost the club nothing in material or labour but when the time came Allom, the greenkeeper, decided that the sixteenth would be a better green to use as it was nearer to water. This was a long time before E.E.C. regulations on pesticides deprived greenkeepers of their more independent wiles.

Having exceeded their budget in 1905 it may not seem surprising that the secretary asked the green committee to consider turfing the sides of bunkers on the fourteenth, rather than using sleepers, as this would cost between £8 and £9. They agreed to "try turfing in the first place to see if it would stand."

Their next project was more ambitious and in April 1907 they presented a scheme for laying water to the greens at a cost not exceeding £500, the cost being £50 less if the twelfth green were excluded. The committee deferred the matter until it was felt that, because of the members' dissatisfaction with the condition of the greens, more urgent action was needed. A Mr. Macdonald of Harpenden was called in, who did not advocate watering as this led to worms, stating that the greens needed aerating with a fork, still the considered wisdom today. However, the committee felt that to improve the condition of the course water should be laid on, and to pay for it, needless to say, debentures would be issued. This was put to the membership at an Extraordinary General Meeting on 5th October 1907. Mr. Macdonald gave his opinion. Mr. Colebrook admitted the committee's awareness of the members' dissatisfaction and promised that the course would be improved on the greens, bunkers, and teeing areas and by introducing more hazards to make the course more interesting. It was agreed to leave the management of the greens to Mr. Macdonald and the motion to lay water on was withdrawn "in consideration of an expert's opinion having been since obtained".

At the committee meeting following the E.G.M. Mr. Macdonald was engaged by the club to carry out his scheme for improving the greens to the best of his ability and was asked to render a monthly account.

In attempting to fulfil their promise to the members to improve the course a new scheme for bunkering was discussed in December. Ten holes were to be affected, with some bunkers being reshaped and new ones, both large and small, being created. It was also suggested that the eighth and twelfth holes be scrapped and two new ones built, the first being about 450 yards long, with a tee near the existing twelfth tee and the green in the corner of the field near the haystack. The other hole would have a tee near this new green and play onto the twelfth green, giving a 150 yard hole. Macdonald was to be consulted for his opinion. Whatever that may have been is not clear, but a new hole was open for play on 22nd June the following year and despite Macdonald's expert opinion the committee had decided to lay water to the greens after all and was going ahead with the issue of debentures to finance it. They also decided it was time to approach the local council with a view to connecting the club's drains to the main sewerage system.

Once the water had been laid on and connected to the supply, hose was purchased for the purpose of watering the greens. The scheme had accrued extra charges because of the extra piping required to reach the eleventh green. Proposed changes to the course were discussed and the entire committee agreed to go onto the course to make a full inspection. The professional was called upon to make some small adjustments. Then the cesspool beside the fourteenth hole overflowed and Mr. Raphael instructed his gardeners to attend to the matter; all this suggests that the committee was less than happy with the greenkeeper's performance and in January 1909 he was given notice and J. Munt of the Mid-Surrey Club was appointed in his place, having been recommended as "quite competent to fill the position in every way". He received thirty-two shillings a week and was required to act as starter on Saturdays and Sundays. His working hours were to be 6 a.m. to 6 p.m. in summer, with half-an-hour for breakfast and an hour for dinner, and 7.30 a.m. to 4.30 p.m. in winter with one hour's break for dinner. He was required to stay until 10 a.m. on Saturdays and to have the tees and greens swept before play on Sunday morning. The caddie master's hours were similar but required him to stay until later in the summer.

A request from Radlett Cricket Club for the loan of the club's horse and roller every evening and on Saturday afternoons was turned down on the grounds that the horse was fully occupied on the golf course. The club did offer to sell a roller to the cricketers, though. The assertion about the horse was obviously true, because the following year £12 was spent on purchasing a black mare from Mr. Bradshaw.

A further business deal was made in November 1910, when the captain revealed that he had obtained the agreement of Carters Seeds to supply worm-killer at a reduced price of £9 per ton, in return for the results to be incorporated in Carters' advertising. Until then, the matter was strictly confidential!

That the course was becoming noticed by discerning golfers is evident from *The Evening Standard and St James Gazette* of 22nd July 1911, for none other than Bernard Darwin had favoured the course with a visit. Soundly beaten by "the Radlett Bogey", Darwin admitted to a gap in his golfing knowledge being filled. Unfortunately his attempt to describe the course is rather vague, although he found the park "wonderfully pretty" and the trees inspiring. He does describe the eighteenth in some detail, claiming it is a good last hole:

> "Passing by hedges, which are just hedges and nothing more, I came to the ponds, of which there are two … the green lies in a corner, flanked on the left by an impenetrable wood and on the right by the pond. The nearer one gets to the hole, the narrower grows the strip of turf and yet the ball must be hit strongly and boldly if one is to get a four instead of the dull though eminently respectable five which bogey allows himself. It is really a capital shot."

Sadly the pond has now been drained by the creation of another pond in the "impenetrable wood".

The sixth did not meet with the same approval, however:

> "The sixth is a really appalling hole to the complete stranger who has to play an iron shot up a hill, over a sea of gorse and undergrowth, at a fluttering flag which he can barely descry."

Darwin had been part of a society and seems to have been greatly amused by one of his partner's attempts to retrieve his ball from one of the ponds on the eighteenth. Subsequent writers were to give their opinions as Porters' reputation grew.

Two local rules were passed in the ensuing years, firstly that "a ball lying in the bushes or hedges of the banks of the brook may be lifted and dropped under penalty of one shot" and secondly, regarding grass in bunkers: "Grass does not form part of a hazard." This was adapted from the code in practice at Stoke Poges. Readers who wonder at the amount of clauses and sub-clauses in the modern rule book may now better comprehend why the Royal and Ancient seeks to cover every contingency in that august publication.

Because of the popularity of Sunday golf and the increased membership it was decided to permit the use of the tenth tee as a starting point, matches to alternate with those which had started from the first.

The war prevented further improvements to the course and as we have seen parts of it were used for agricultural purposes in order to retain the greenstaff. Potatoes and hay proved to be successful crops for the club, then as the war drew to its close, sadly the black horse had to be destroyed. The secretary was given permission to purchase a new one at a price not exceeding £80. He succeeded in buying one for £42 but after a few months was obliged to report that it was getting too old to work and another horse was purchased in a local sale for £22.1s.0d. The poor beast had probably been used in the first post-war improvements to the course when it was decided to lift the back of the first green and as far as possible level the final green. A new tee was made on the sixth – Darwin would surely have approved – to the left of the existing tees. More work for the horses was likely when the secretary was authorised to purchase a new 84" mowing machine for £170, subject to its suitability for the club's needs.

An aerial photograph of the course appeared in the *Evening News* of 16th October 1920, the first in a series, and clearly shows bunkers, trees, the brook and the pit. The caption describes Porters as "One of the most picturesque and best kept courses near London."

In November 1920, the Captain, Mr. Thomas, Mr. Markham and the secretary formed a sub-committee to discuss possible alterations for the improvement of the course. They must have been satisfied with it as it was, for their first recommendation to the committee in July the following year was for the adoption of R & A rules for the standard scratch score of the course, which was fixed at 77. This comprised figures of: 4,4,5,5,4,3,5,5,3 = 38 out and 5,5,3,5,3,4,4,5,5 = 39 home. The course layout was now, broadly, as we know it today.

A more encouraging outlook on the presence of children at the club manifested itself in May 1923 when it was agreed to lay out a few practice holes in the paddock (the practice ground to the left of the seventeenth) for the use of members' children who could play on payment of a one shilling green fee.

In the same month Mr. Raphael offered to sell the club the freehold land, comprising the course, buildings and timber, for £18,000. At an Extraordinary General Meeting held on June 23rd the membership expressed their sincere thanks for the offer but could not see their way to

PORTERS PARK GOLF CLUB,

RADLETT,

HERTS,

April, 1919.

DEAR MADAM,

The Committee have under their very serious consideration the future financial prospect of the Club. The position for the current year is fairly secure as the Committee have at their disposal the balance of the Special Maintenance Fund and an income from Entrance Fees from new members who are filling the number of vacancies, but after this year it is evident that the income from the subscriptions must be increased over the pre-war income by not less than £500 to meet the exceptional rise in the cost of labour, both on the Green and in the House, and the cost of all necessary materials for the upkeep of the Course, such as Machinery, Tools, Wormkiller, Horses and Horsekeep, etc., etc.

The Committee have decided that the only proper way to meet this additional expense is by raising the subscriptions, and they have decided that all gentlemen members elected to full membership shall pay an Annual Subscription of £7 and all ladies elected to full membership, £4.

In view of the fact that there are only a limited number of vacancies, this will not bring in anything like the amount which the Committee consider necessary. Under the Rules of the Club it is not possible to raise the Annual Subscription of existing members, but the Committee are of opinion that a great majority, if not the whole of the members, would voluntarily pay an increased subscription, and I am therefore instructed to ask you if you will be agreeable to pay an Annual Subscription of £4, commencing from the 1st January, 1920.

I should be obliged to you if you would kindly fill in the enclosed Postcard and return to me here.

Yours faithfully,

C. LENNOX RICHMOND,

Hon. Secretary & Treasurer.

accepting it. As a result, ownership of the estate passed to the Middlesex County Council, who in May 1925 agreed to straighten the boundary and provided an extra acre of land in the north corner by Monks Wood for £25, which enabled the new twelfth hole to be built.

The first visit by a professional golf course architect was recorded in November 1923, when a report on the greens by Mr. Reginald Beale and Mr. F.G. Hawtree was placed before the committee. This was to be circulated to the green committee. Beale was employed by Carters Seeds as an "in house" designer, while Frederick Hawtree was the founder of the famous dynasty of golf architects still practising today. With J.H. Taylor, he was responsible for many of the country's public courses and with Taylor founded the National Association of Public Golf Courses.

Unfortunately no record exists of their recommendations.

By the mid-twenties manufacturers were beginning to recognise the needs of golf clubs and that there was an expanding market for their products. On 12th September 1926, the green committee was given a demonstration by Shanks of a roller quintuple mower, pulled by a Pattison tractor. The results were so satisfactory that the committee agreed to the request to purchase the equipment and £210 was allocated for the mower and £165 for the tractor. Prompt cash payment the following January secured a 5% discount. It was not until 1937, however, that the old horse could be put

9th Green in its second location where the trees and water tank are now

out to grass, when another tractor and 5-gang mower were purchased. Another item of specialised equipment from Pattisons, a distributor for use on the greens, was ordered in July 1927. Extension wheels for use on the tractor in the winter were also purchased. Further items such as a fairway brush, to be pulled by the tractor, and mole draining equipment were added over the ensuing years as greenkeeping techniques became more sophisticated and mechanised.

In the same month the secretary was authorised to purchase wire netting for use in preventing balls being swept away in the brook when it was in flood.

At this time the club had a visit from A.C. Croome, the well-known golf writer, and the photographers Humphrey and Vera Joel of the *Morning Post*. Their attractive photograph spread right across the page on 6th August and was complemented by Croome's scholarly article, more serious than Darwin's of 1911 and daring to offer the club advice, for Croome felt it would be wrong to move the sixth green to eliminate a blind shot. He also advocated moving the ninth green twenty or thirty yards to the right to enable play to continue without endangering players on the tenth tee. He was very enthusiastic about the condition of the course and its powers of recovery from the heaviest rain.

The green committee examined the local rules again in 1927. Their deliberations met with approval, except that a ball lying in a rabbit scrape could not be lifted without penalty. The rules concerning lifting a ball from bushes and the brook were clarified. These rules were further redrafted in July 1932.

David Smith, a greenkeeper for twenty-five years, retired in 1928 and was presented with a chiming clock as a reward for his loyal service to the club. A shed was later provided for his colleagues to prepare dressing for the greens and they were given oilskins to enable them to work in wet weather. This seems to have been severe as members playing friendly games were asked to place the ball in wet weather. Ernie Page, aged fourteen, had joined the greenstaff in 1904, when the abnormal growing conditions necessitated employing extra greenstaff, and remained a faithful employee. While the provision of the capes may be seen as a practical rather than benevolent gesture, the club arranged an annual concert party for the greenstaff.

Concern about the course apparently went further than the wet conditions because at the committee meeting held in November 1929, a scheme for reconstruction of the course prepared by Hawtree and Taylor was referred to the green committee and a special committee set up to consider the implications and report to the next meeting. The Captain, R.W. Needham, and the green committee met on 29th November to consider the recommendations and what action should be taken. They decided that not all the suggestions were necessary but the secretary was instructed to implement the following alterations to the course.

A "slice bunker" on the first was to be moved nearer the green and a second one put in halfway between that one and the green. A bunker on the left of the fairway was to be modified. This work was completed by 30th December. On the second the green was to be reshaped to face the centre of the second fairway and the bunker on the left of the green was to be extended and remodelled to catch shots from the fifth fairway, while a bunker was to be added on the right of the green to catch slices and "overreaching" shots from the wrong fairway. The course must have been rather tight, for on the third a bunker was built on the left corner of the green to catch direct shots from the fourth fairway. All this work was carried out by the end of January 1930. A similar scheme was suggested for the fourth hole with reference to shots from the third fairway. The fifth hole escaped major change, only the semi-rough being cut. Hawtree and Taylor made no recommendation for the sixth apart from completing the original idea of reducing a bank on the right of the green. This was done by November.

Suggestions for the seventh were not adopted and no alterations were made to holes eight and nine. A new green was built for the tenth, designed by the secretary, and was in place by 9th February 1931. The eleventh seems to have suffered most change, being shortened by fifty yards and turned into a dogleg with a series of bunkers in a diagonal line from the tee. This was one of the first tasks to be completed. The bunkers on the twelfth were modified, the first being removed and the second lowered. A bunker at the back of the thirteenth was filled in and the fourteenth was to have a long, narrow and raised island green, the slope at the back being reduced as far as possible and the bunkers at the back being filled in. Again the secretary provided the shape for this new green.

All that was required on the next hole was the filling in of a hollow behind the green "as far as can be done, as opportunity offers". This was done by March 1930. A plan to clear ground in the wood to provide a new sixteenth green was postponed and for that reason no changes were made to the seventeenth. The final hole was rebunkered, the diagonal bunkers being replaced by a bunker at 180 yards on the right and a central bunker at 160 yards. A bunker on the left was filled in to give a shot into the green.

In February 1930, the secretary was instructed to purchase trees "to be planted behind the second green as a screen from the fifth tee and also to provide a hazard on the twelfth". A subscription list was opened in October to fund the purchase of more trees to improve the course and a screen of laurels round the first medal tee was authorised. It was also agreed to install bunkers in front of the brook on the fifth, similar to those on the second.

In October 1933 the green committee produced a plasticine model of a green designed to replace the ninth green. The committee approved of the intention. It was a common practice of the early golf architects to model their courses in this substance when presenting their plans to a club, the obvious advantage being that any desired alterations could be easily made. Further developments included the construction of a practice ground behind the eighth green for the use of the professional and beginners when the course was occupied and a new sixteenth green, for which it was agreed to employ extra labour. All this indicates a healthy, thriving club, which was also able to purchase a new tractor and mowing machine.

One disadvantage of the number of mature trees on the course was the number of rooks, which are quite capable of flying off with golf balls. In 1937 the secretary was instructed to have them shot and the carcasses hung on sticks about the course. This was also the time when the committee decided to dispose of the horses. At least a new dog had been donated to replace the old "club dog" which had died the previous year!

The outbreak of the Second World War led to the "garden ground" of the club being cultivated once again, as was the paddock. H. Thresher was transferred from greenstaff to garden staff to implement this and the sheep were moved back onto the course from the garden. It is unlikely that they were the cause of an epidemic of pearlwort but the greens had to be treated urgently with lawn sand. Middlesex County Council claimed part of the course for grazing in April 1942 and later that year decided to cultivate ground between the eighth and eleventh holes and

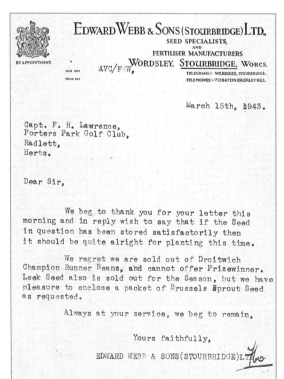

The war time vegetable garden was on the left of the 8th before the brook

in the paddock. In the first instance the club's rent was reduced and a further reduction was claimed when the plans to cultivate were announced.

The condition of the course continued to be of concern and in July 1943 it was decided that the eighth green would have to be forked up and a temporary green provided, and that Suttons should be called in to advise on the greens generally. It was also considered desirable to approach the County Council with a view to creating a turf nursery in the old paddock.

Suttons recommended treating three of the greens and this was duly done.

The war had left other scars on the course, some of which remain today, as concrete anti-tank obstacles were erected, the brook widened and deepened, and the soil spills deposited at the sides.

The short term of office as the club's secretary held by C.K. Cotton does not concern us here but it had other benefits for the club as he was retained as adviser on the course, reporting every two weeks on its condition. Charles Kenneth Cotton, 1887-1974, formed his golf architecture firm in 1946, the year after he left Porters Park. His partners were Charles Lawrie and Frank Pennink and their associates included John Harris and Donald Steel, an impressive roster of post-war practitioners. Among their courses in this country and abroad are Ross-on-Wye, Frilford Heath, The Berkshire, and Olgiata (Rome), while those remodelled include Blackwell, Ganton, Royal Lytham and St Annes, Saunton, West Lancs., Downfield, Ashburnham and Royal Porthcawl – a very elite portfolio!

Post-war activity included re-instatement of the sixteenth hole, construction of concrete bridges on the tenth and fourteenth holes and restoration work on the eighth, all made possible by a claim for war damage. The wartime agricultural committee had not finished its work in 1946, for they confirmed that it would be no longer necessary to graze sheep on the course provided that a hay crop was produced. This was grown between the eighth and eleventh holes.

Cotton supervised the installation of the culvert in the stream at the sixteenth, which was undertaken by Suttons. He may also have been responsible for the bulldozing of the "pimples" on the fifteenth green. Such features were fairly common on older courses but as the game became more sophisticated they were considered unnecessary and unfair. A feature which has become a part of modern courses was introduced in 1948 when distance markers for the longer holes were purchased.

War spoil on the fifth hole led to a new local rule permitting a free drop from the condition. The War Damage claim was not settled until October 1949, when it was agreed to accept £1,650. The bunkering of the sixteenth green was postponed for a year and a proposal to cut down the dead oak tree on the eighth hole caused quite a stir.

Porters Park, 1950s

The Clubhouse 1950

5th Green with 6th Green in the background

9th Green in its third and present location. Remains of previous green's bunkering can be seen to the right and beyond the row of pines

11th Hole

In 1950 the EGU recommended a new standard scratch score calculation of courses and it fixed Porters Park at 72 instead of 75. Up to this time the cards bore the legend bogey rather than par. As a result the third, eighth and eighteenth became par 4s. Handicaps were increased, scratch to 21 players being given back 3 strokes, 22 handicappers 2, those of 23 received 1 and the 24 handicappers remained as they were.

Despite the club's rather delicate financial situation in 1951 the committee voted an increase in the greenstaff's wages, arranged their Christmas supper and then informed them that if they could not keep down the number of rabbits on the course "other arrangements would have to be made". Finances were most certainly the reason that no new projects were undertaken on the course until 1953, when a scheme to lay wire over the ditch was drastically reduced on the grounds of cost.

The matter of purchasing the course from the council had been raised several times and deferred because of the financial situation but in 1954 the committee finally grasped the nettle and entered into negotiations with Middlesex County Council. A recruiting campaign to attract new members was already in progress and further schemes for raising the necessary money were discussed. Block and family memberships were offered and several taken up. To complicate matters further a clubhouse fire had caused considerable damage but the insurance money, augmented by members' contributions, enabled the club to make good the damage and buy new greens machinery, though the former was a long drawn out affair. So, too, were the deliberations of the County Council. Various offers of extended leases were made but the council seemed very loath to sell the land. The club was not happy with this situation and appointed a sub-committee to negotiate with the council. Valuations had been made at regular intervals, £12,000 being the sum quoted in October 1954, when a meeting was arranged with the County Treasurer. It was something of a shock, then, when it was reported to the general committee in December that the Middlesex County Council had offered the course to the Hertfordshire County Council "no doubt for any possible public use". However Middlesex felt it necessary to consult their own legal department the following January and in April Mr. M.G. Orchard-Lisle, the club Captain, who was negotiating with the council, reported that it had applied for planning permission on the Shenley Hill frontage and that it had received no decision from the Hertfordshire County Council, who wanted a further month to consider the matter. The Captain was empowered to continue negotiations and to make an offer for the freehold of the course. He offered the council £10,000 and requested the extension of the existing lease for 21 years.

Golf continued as normal while all this was taking place, new stroke indices being allocated and an equipment sharing scheme with Hadley

Wood Golf Club agreed when Messrs. Cumming and Hesketh visited that club to discuss course maintenance. New piping taking water to the fifth, eleventh and twelfth greens was installed at a cost of £270.

The new lease was granted in 1956, the rent remaining at £750. A sub-committee was formed to consider the implications of offering to purchase the course and produced its report in July 1957. The Middlesex County Council wanted to get rid of their holdings in Hertfordshire but as the course lay in a green belt area its options were limited. A value for the 132 acres had been agreed with the Central Land Board in 1947: the unrestricted value being £19,225 and the restricted value £12,000. Knight, Frank and Rutley had produced a valuation of £13,600 for the freehold of the club. Middlesex asked £20,000 for the freehold or £15,000 plus a further £5,000 if the club ever received planning permission for its land.

The sub-committee was in agreement that the ideal way to raise the money was to issue debentures, though these would not come near to covering the required amount. Both the club and the County Council realised that Porters Park Golf Club was most valuable an asset as a golf club, because if planning permission were granted it could only be for a limited number of houses and the remainder of the land would have to be used for agriculture.

The council continued to stall and in January 1958 proposed to grant a 999 years lease, as any future developments on the course would be to their advantage. However, Orchard-Lisle and his committee stuck to their guns and finally in March 1958 the council agreed to sell the course to the club. Orchard-Lisle at subsequent committee meetings expressed disquiet at the progress of the exchanging of contracts and in June the council rescinded the sale, offering a 21 years lease at £750 per year until 1962, thereafter £800. Conditions were attached pertaining to the upkeep of the steward's house. The new lease was eventually signed and the matter of purchasing the course did not arise again until 1962.

In the interim, trees were planted and removed, as poplars on the seventh were damaging a neighbour's property. New local rules protected the newly planted trees and permitted the removal of stones from bunkers. The membership shortfall had been eased by permitting members of Starveacres Golf Club to join when their club closed in 1957, although their committee tried to stave off closure by recourse to legal action.

C.K. Cotton was asked to advise on proposed alterations to the course with a view to reducing maintenance costs. He recommended removing or reducing the size of bunkers and also pointed out that the ladies were being "treated in a very ungallant manner" as their view of the sixth green was completely obscured by trees and bushes. He also recommended removal of more pimples, describing them as "a relic of the past and out of place in modern time". He further advised the club to obtain an aerial photograph of the course, which duly appeared, thanks to Fighter Command. Malcolm Reid, as Chairman of the Green, soon commenced the implementation of Cotton's report, assisted by donations from some of the members. He also reported to the committee that the architect was satisfied with the standard of work with which his suggestions were being implemented. Cotton continued to pay regular visits to the club until 1969, submitting another report in 1967, in which he pointed out that Porters was rather short by modern standards and was unbalanced in that the outer half was much shorter than the homeward nine. He recommended that any lengthening of holes should not be done piecemeal by adding ten yards here and there, but by adding as much as 100 yards to a hole requiring stretching. He also recommended that greens be relaid at regular intervals and later that year a greens expert, Mr. R. Stafford-Smith, was invited by Paul Orchard-Lisle, now Chairman of the Green, to make an inspection and he requested that Stafford-Smith be invited to make four visits per year at a cost of seven guineas per visit. Malcolm Reid insisted, however, that refinements to the course only be made with Cotton's approval.

Cotton recommended tightening the entrance to the first green by running the bunkers further round the front, although this work was not done until 1980. The two bunkers on the left of the second green should be made into one, the centre part well into the edge of the green, a task for the greenstaff which would ultimately reduce maintenance costs. He suggested two bunkers on the left of the third hole be removed and trees planted in their place and the bush on the bank of the stream on the fifth be removed to improve visibility. Trees on the sixth required trimming and thinning out and on the next hole the bunker on the right of the green was to be extended to tighten the approach to the green.

To obtain the extra length he suggested, Cotton enclosed a plan of new eighth and ninth holes, running parallel to each other, but this scheme was deferred on the grounds of cost, though it would effect a return to the tenth tee, where he recommended the use of the new back tee, the felling of an oak tree and the filling in of fairway bunkers. The entrance to the seventeenth green he considered too wide and recommended bringing in the right hand bunker. The committee thought that this was a dull hole and while welcoming Cotton's suggestion was concerned at the expense involved when added to current course expenses. His final thoughts were that bushes on the left of the hollow on the eighteenth should be removed to give the player driving down the right a view of the green. As it was, the fairway bunker on the right at 260 yards made the shot dangerous even if trees were lopped and Cotton stated that it was in the wrong place. His alternatives were to fill it in and make a new bunker 230 yards from the tee on the right to catch the sliced drive or, preferably, a central fairway bunker to lessen the danger to a tee shot down the left and still give room for a shot down the right. The President issued a cautionary word, though, feeling that too much construction was being considered and insufficient maintenance was being carried out.

Cotton died in 1974, by which time the club were consulting the STRI (Sports Turf Research Institute) at Bingley on matters of agronomy, and Donald Steel, the distinguished amateur golfer, *Daily Telegraph* golf correspondent and course architect.

A three-lane driving range was made available to members on 14th January 1961, and the professional was allowed to charge a small sum for the use of practice balls.

The head greenkeeper, Hesketh, demon-strated to the committee how he was attempting to eliminate the coarser grasses from the greens. Malcolm Reid had much faith in Hesketh and with the reduction of Ernie Page's hours after fifty years service attempted to recruit younger men as his staff. The committee even considered providing accommodation for the right person, should he apply. In the event a caravan was pro-vided, which became the residence of Williamson, his wife and child, from Ayrshire. No sooner had he settled in, though, than two other greenstaff resigned. To tide the club over patients from the County Hospital were employed two days a week. Mr. Reid made it clear that suitable greenstaff would only be recruited if accommodation were provided. This was obtained in 1963 when Mr. Baucher acquired 94, Villiers Road, Oxhey, for the club.

Greenkeeper Ernie Page in 1961 aged seventy-one

Then in 1962 another series of negotiations for the purchase of the course was opened with Middlesex County Council. Debentures were issued which by June 1964 totalled £20,150. The council was asking for £21,000 on a 999 years lease. In December 1962, after a meeting with the County Valuer, Mervyn Orchard-Lisle informed the committee that the sale would be on the basis of a 999 years lease, with the council retaining the rights to 50% development rights. While the Valuer expressed the opinion that £17,000 might be sufficient to effect the purchase the club was prepared to go up to £19,000. Mr. Baucher was also responsible for the club's offer of £17,000 to the council who responded with new proposals, causing yet more delay. In June 1963 the County Valuer offered the club a 99 years lease, subject to certain provisos, for a premium of £16,500. A provisional agreement with the council was signed by the President, Mr. Baucher and Mr. C.R. Glover in March 1964 and the lease was completed on 31st July. The ownership of the lease was now incorporated as Porters Park Golf Club Properties Ltd.

Chapter Three

Ours at Last

AT THE end of 1964 the English Golf Union decided that the standard scratch scores of golf courses should be reviewed, those of over 6,600 yards being rated at 72. So Porters, with a par of 72 and length of 6,283 yards would be SSS 70. It was felt that re-measurement of the course was necessary and when the Chairman of the Green, Mr. E.A. Judge, asked in January if the new tee markers should bear par or bogey figures, it was agreed to continue to give a bogey figure, as this appeared on the club's score cards. Par was first used in place of bogey four years later.

Ten years later the course was measured again using the "projection method", the total length coming to 6,216 yards, giving an SSS of 70, equalling par. However the tenth and thirteenth holes both fell below the minimum limit for par 5 holes, so they would have to be lengthened. It was suggested this be done on the tenth by reshaping the fairway to create a double dogleg, adding four yards to the centre line for measurement purposes (and making the hole more interesting to play) and extending the green at the back by four yards and increasing the depth of the apron at the front. This would give a length of 481 yards.

The thirteenth was more controversial, Mr. Wehner, chairman of the sub-committee, suggesting in his report that a new medal tee be built in the far corner of the course north-east of the twelfth green, extending the hole by twenty-eight yards to 502 yards. Fir trees behind the twelfth green would have to be removed, though. An advantage of this scheme would be to bring the pond fully into play for the low handicap player. The sub-committee drafted a new card, using par, not bogey, recommending its introduction the following Easter, by which time the tee markers would have been repainted.

The Variety Club of Great Britain, thanks in great part to Bernard Coral, brought a challenge match between Gary Player and Peter Thomson to Porters in 1967 on the day following the conclusion of the Open Championship, which had been won by Roberto de Vicenzo at Hoylake.

Aerial photograph of the course taken in 1968 (clubhouse is at top middle)

The committee in anticipation constructed two new tees at the tenth and eighteenth.

The tenth was set back left in the trees behind the current shelter. It necessitated a drive over the oak tree and a carry of 260 yards to the plateau. Anything less and the ball would follow the camber across into one of the three fairway bunkers on the right hand slope. It did not meet with the approval of either player, both of whom have subsequently engaged in course design.

The eighteenth, set back into the left hand corner by Shenley Road and lengthening the hole to 460 yards, was also roundly condemned as the drive was away from the out of bounds. At that time the only bunkers were at 180 yards on the left and 260 yards on the right, neither therefore being in play from the tee. The experiment was therefore rejected and the tees taken out of use.

Stafford-Smith had presented a report and recommendations in 1968, when Paul Orchard-Lisle had obtained a quotation for the irrigation system using pop-up sprinklers. He felt the best way to improve the greens would be the installation of such a system, which would cost £7,039.12s.0d. One advantage would be that the greenstaff would not have to water the course at night. The system itself would not cure the problem of meadow grass; £27,000 was the figure Orchard-Lisle quoted if the members desired perfect greens, which would necessitate relaying all of them. The system was installed in June, with the minimum disruption to the course.

Meadow grass was a major problem noted by the STRI's report in 1970, along with an excess of fibre in the root system and compaction above it. Four pages of foolscap contained their detailed scheme for treating these problems. The new Chairman of the Green, Mr. E.D. Broom, told the committee that the report would form the basis for work on the course and that the irrigation system was beginning to pay dividends. It was proposed to relay the greens and outside contractors would be brought in if the greenstaff were unable to do more than one a year. It was also intended to enlarge the tees, incorporating the ladies' tees, using soil removed from the banks of the streams. The thirteenth was the first green to be relaid, but the process was not continued.

Trees became an important issue in the 1970s, under the guidance of Douglas Cumming, Chief Accountant of I.C.I. by profession, but secretly a frustrated nurseryman. His vision encompassed planting feature trees to replace bunkers, and copses to include a wide variety of specimens, mixing deciduous with evergreen to give different shades throughout the seasons. In particular he was responsible for the area between the fifteenth and sixteenth, hand-watering throughout the drought years of 1975-77 to ensure their survival. Official felling occurred in 1976 when the G.L.C.'s Estates

43

1960s Christmas card

department visited the course, condemning several elms and an oak tree.

By 1977 the time had come to re-open negotiations for the purchase of the freehold of the course and Paul Orchard-Lisle continued his father's work in this matter. Two years later his efforts were rewarded by the unconditional purchase of the freehold for £18,000. Debentures were issued to cover this, two units of accommodation for the greenstaff and a new central heating system.

In the intervening year Donald Steel had submitted his report on the course and the first cuts of ground between the eighth and eleventh holes were completed, with the intention of making a par 3 course for beginners and juniors. This became a practice ground which was ready for use in August 1979. Steel recommended the removal of the two fairway bunkers at the eighteenth, replacing them with two new bunkers at 220 and 240 yards on the edge of the right hand rough.

Nigel Notley's first tour of duty as Chairman of the Green saw the introduction of a five-year plan to improve the course further. A major step in implementing this to the best advantage was an invitation to Jim Arthur, the R & A's agronomist, to visit the club. His first visit was made

44

on 13th February 1980 when he walked the course with Nigel, the secretary, members of the green committee, the head greenkeeper and the professional.

His detailed report pointed out that it would be rash to expect all the problems to be identified and diagnosed on the basis of a single visit in winter. Nevertheless he was able to make many constructive suggestions.

The grass type on the greens, but not the fairways, was dominated by annual meadow grass, which had very poor root development but was not suffering from thatch, and apart from agrostis in some areas, few other "alien" grass types. Although earth-worms had not been active on the

Mervyn Orchard-Lisle, Captain in 1955/56 congratulates his son Paul on becoming the youngest ever Captain in 1971

greens, some fairways were badly affected, due to the liming recommended earlier by the STRI, of whom he was rather critical. He was concerned about wear on the walk-offs round greens, due more to feet than trolleys, in his opinion, and around the tees, but praised the policy of enlarging the teeing areas.

Mr. Arthur condemned the original irrigation system and made detailed suggestions for its upgrading and positioning, reminding the club that it should not be over-used. He praised the club's compost but sympathised with the painstaking way in which the greenstaff were obliged to produce it. This encouraged further recommendations regarding machinery but he also pointed out that while machines do not save men on the course, they enabled previously impossible tasks to be carried out. Because of the players' demands on the course work had to begin early for maximum efficiency and so speedier machines would be required.

He even examined the sheds, which while not the worst he had seen, needed upgrading as did the greenkeepers' quarters, bearing in mind the soon-to-be implemented provisions of the Health and Safety at Work Act. Such upgrading would need to include workshops for servicing the machinery.

The report then outlined Jim Arthur's Basic Principles of Greenkeeping, emphasising the need for fast, firm and true putting surfaces all the year round, as good in winter as in summer, temporary greens being used no longer. Wiry, fast-running parkland fairways rather than lush meadows were what he wanted to encourage. This meant meadow grass had to be eliminated and fescue and agrostis re-introduced and allowed to dominate. He bemoaned the fact that chemists rather than botanists had held sway for too long and the study of soil chemistry had little to do with producing a good golf course!

He returned in May and expressed pleasure at the progress that had already been made, for the meadow grass/agrostis ratio was now 50/50. The greens were improving and were being carefully nurtured and the irrigation system completely replaced. The tees still presented a problem which he felt could be attended to "once we have won the battle on the greens".

The fairways were beginning to recover from the earlier mistreatment and worms were being expelled satisfactorily. Mr. Arthur went into some detail about the quality of the grass and recommended aeration to cure the problem of the weak turf caused by the liming.

The club had followed his recommendations regarding the purchase of machinery and also hired items when more economical to do so. Six pages of further recommendations followed, covering aeration, cutting six days a week at $\frac{3}{16}$ths to help the agrostis, verticutting to improve the texture of the grass, the use of root stimulants and fertilisers with appropriate recipes, irrigation to be done sparingly, and top dressing to eliminate disease, and thinning of the turf.

Weed control and a more intensive programme on the tees were next on his agenda, followed by a comprehensive regime for the fairways. Finally he recommended the clearing of scrub, the elimination of sycamore trees, still causing problems in 1998, and a ruthless approach to surplus trees – conservation not being preservation. Sensible culling was needed. This then was the inspiration behind the five-year plan.

In 1981 a second opinion was sought and Donald Steel of Cotton, Pennink, Lawrie and Partners returned to Porters Park. He was given a specific brief with regard to certain bunkers, tree planting and a number of new tees and was asked for his impression of how the best use could be made of the land. Perhaps the major item was the idea to dogleg the sixteenth left from the ridge at about 250 yards, pushing it through the trees along the natural ridge to the corner of the recently purchased wood. This would make the seventeenth also a dogleg, requiring a drive over the old sixteenth green. Mr. Steel's reaction to that suggestion was favourable, though he considered it a long-term project, maintaining that too much of a dogleg would be unnatural but that a fine par 4 would be the result and that the seventeenth would only be improved by a different angle of drive.

His other comments concerned trees, larger samples of which should be planted to avoid damage by players and greenstaff. Steel was concerned that modern equipment had made some bunkers obsolete and in any case they were useless if they did not influence the thinking of good players. He added, "It is quite wrong to build bunkers to catch poorer players. They have enough to think about. As Tom Simpson used to say, 'they carry their own bunkers'."

So, his aim was to ease the burden on the poorer players and build bunkers where they would embarrass the good golfers if they went slightly off line and thus reward good driving. He left detailed suggestions for the first and second holes, with a clear eye for the tactical demands of the latter. He welcomed the easing of the sixth hole for the benefit of the ladies and agreed with new bunkers on the eighth and tenth holes, suggesting the tenth green be set at more of an angle at the back right. He also recommended a "wiggle or two" in the line of the fairway. New tees on the twelfth, back right, and fifteenth, across the brook in the newly purchased wood, also met with his approval, but the question of mole and catchment drains round the eleventh green he thought best left to Jim Arthur.

It was therefore a happy Nigel Notley who could present a report to the general committee in October 1981, informing them that temporary greens would *not* be in use during the coming winter and detailing the huge amount of work planned for the ensuing months. The revised sixteenth/seventeenth project now encompassed doglegging the sixteenth right to a figure of eight, two-tiered green, utilising the site of the seventeenth tees. The committee had once again rejected opening the brook, but the extended green would now border the brook and give a very challenging second shot whilst giving members easy access as at present to the left side of the green.

The seventeenth tees were all to be resited at the bottom of the practice ground creating a genuine left hand dogleg.

The project was approved in total and a five-year detailed plan prepared for its implementation. As with a number of major plans approved by the committee over the years, the sixteenth/seventeenth project was never fully completed. Only the yellow tee was resited and an initial reluctance to give the dogleg sufficient space by felling trees contributed to the members' general dissatisfaction with the seventeenth hole.

A quieter period followed initially with Charles Capstick as Chairman of the Green and new head greenkeeper, Martin Smith, succeeding Paul Fitzjohns, who had moved to Thetford. Douglas Cumming's good work on the trees was continued by Charles and Humphrey Harlow, unsightly copses tidied up and feature trees given space to develop in an effort to maintain the parkland character of the course.

A fairway bunker on the fourth in the left rough at 260 yards was removed and replaced by trees in 1985. On the fifth a fairway bunker on the right was resited at 240 yards to make it visible from the tee and within range of modern equipment. The need to squeeze a few extra yards out of the course led to the creation of new tees at the eighth, fifteenth and eighteenth and extensions at the twelfth and sixteenth in the early 1990s. The course at 6378 yards still measures just below the 6400 required for an SSS of 71.

After a gap of twenty-six years, and twenty-eight years since Stafford-Smith's original recommendation, the club finally relaid another green, the fifth, which had persistently suffered from drainage problems. The existing turf was stripped off and the base relaid. The surface in only two or three years is already firmer, truer and quicker than other greens, proving the merit of the relaying policy and perhaps highlighting the error of not following through major projects to a conclusion. An opportunity was also taken to install two bunkers on the left side of the green, instead of just one, mirroring the green surrounds from before the First World War.

As the first century ends, the planning continues apace. A new architect has been brought in, Stan Ebey of European Tour Design, an American with a wonderful understanding of British tradition, his company upholding the philosophy of Cotton, Lawrie and Pennink. The latest five-year rolling plan includes restoration of disused tees which would be properly prepared and maintained for use as junior tees; various humps and bumps are to be eased either to improve the playing characteristics of the hole or to improve its appearance. The Artisans have agreed to renovate the bridges. The eleventh green may be relaid, preserving the original contours. The soil spills in front of the stream at the fourteenth have been removed to present a more aesthetically appealing vista, making the hazard visible. Further improvements include the doglegging of the second hole, taking play further left by running the semi-rough down from behind the fairway bunker on the right to the left side bridge. The ridge on the side of the green has been chamfered to bring the brook into play. The bunkering on the right of the fourth has been improved, bringing the hazard closer to the green. The defensive measure of planting copses, with trees donated by a member, will protect houses beside the seventh from erratic shots.

So the members can look forward to enjoying a challenging and attractive course not only in centenary year but for years to come under the sure control of the head greenkeeper, Martin Smith, who approaches twenty years in control, maintaining the long tradition of Smiths at Porters Park dating from the turn of the century.

Porters Park, the 1990s

Second

Third

Fifth

Eighth

Ninth

Eleventh

51

Fourteenth

Sixteenth

Chapter Four

The Evolution of the Management of the Club

WHEN THE club opened for membership, with a course ready for play, the first committee had already been formed. Mr. Grace, the landlord, was President, Mr. C.T. Part, Captain and they were joined by Messrs. H.J. Lubbock, C.G. Kekewich, H. McCorquodale and E.W. Thomas. The first honorary secretary was one of very few residents of Radlett to join the new club, Mr. Barre Goldie, who resigned after six months and was replaced by Dr. Smyth. Mr. Part looked after the club's accounts, a duty taken over subsequently by Mr.Thomas.

These gentlemen drew up the first rules of the club and local rules for the course but by November 1899, it was decided that a green and handicapping committee was necessary. Messrs. Part, Thomas and the honorary secretary agreed to undertake the task. The professional, Long, and his assistant were asked to look after the course. The first A.G.M. was held in May 1900 when Mr. Kekewich resigned and his place taken by Mr. Colebrook. The re-election of Mr. Kekewich was then proposed and carried. He resigned from the committee again in November owing to the pressure of professional work. His resignation was accepted with regret and he was asked to remain an ex-officio member of the committee. Mr. J.H. Robson was asked to take Mr. Kekewich's place. He was duly elected at the next A.G.M. and Mr. Lubbock was re-elected. Later in the year Mr. A.G. Josling was elected to the vacant seat on the committee and joined the green and handicapping committee. Mr. McCorquodale resigned from the committee in January 1902 and Mr. E.A. Haws took his place. He proved a great asset, particularly in his dealings with the Midland Railway Company and in forming a catering sub-committee.

The steady turnover of committee members continued with the resignation of Mr. Robson, and Major Creagh was elected in his place. He immediately took on the duty of house chairman and invited Revd. Gotto and Mr. H.J. Skelton to join him, taking over the problem of the catering from Mr. Haws.

This sub-committee recommended the appointment of a steward and Mr. J.J. Churchill and his wife were engaged at a salary of £50 per year, with free house, coal, light and food, subject to Mr. Haws' satisfaction with their characters. Their duties were to clean the clubhouse, wash all the linen and supply lunches, teas and general refreshments.

The A.G.M. of 1902 empowered the committee to draw up new rules and these were formally accepted at an Extraordinary General Meeting in July.

The professional, having had catering removed from his responsibilities, was left to find his own house and was awarded a pay increase to assist him in this. He was also appointed caddie master, for which he retained a percentage of the caddie fees. A shop was provided for him to conduct his business. It also seems that he had been relieved of responsibility for care of the course, Messrs. G. and A. Smith appearing in the list of Christmas gratuities in January 1903.

A more momentous event during that year was the election of Cecil Raphael as President. He clearly intended to be a "hands-on" President as well as landlord and began to exert an immediate influence. At the 1903 A.G.M. Mr. Part was elected a Vice-President and Mr. Thomas became Captain. Despite the questioning of the committee's method of obtaining the members' votes, ballot papers were handed out and Messrs Colebrook, Rumsey, Lohr, Kent and Revd. Gotto were elected to the committee. A new rule was passed allowing the captain to hold office for only one year, after which he became eligible for a seat on the committee.

A.E. Colebrook Captain 1904

Immediately after the A.G.M. Mr. Haws resigned from the committee and Mr. C.M. Humble was asked to take his place. In view of the frequency of the committee meetings, and that the committee members were busy professional men who came to Porters for relaxation, the regular resignations from the committee are understandable. Mr. Haws had worked particularly hard on the club's behalf.

Mr. Raphael then began to exert his influence, seeking to choose the committee himself in return for extending the lease. This was not acceptable and he eventually agreed that he could nominate only four of the eight committee members. However, he did extend the lease by 14 years.

PORTERS GOLF CLUB.

BALANCE SHEET, 1901=1902.

CAPITAL ACCOUNT.

Receipts:	£	s.	d.
By issue of Debentures, 1900 and 1901..£700 0 0			
,, Balance paid out of Revenue Account, 1900 .. .. 15 10 10	715	10	10
	£715	10	10

Expenditure:	£	s.	d.
To Implements and Labour laying out Links, 1899 ..	75	0	0
,, Building and Furnishing New Club House, 1900..	590	10	10
,, Building Ladies' Club House, 1901..........	50	0	0
	£715	10	10

REVENUE ACCOUNT.

	£	s.	d.
By Entrance Fees and Subscriptions up to 31st MARCH, 1902	691	12	0
,, Temporary Members' Subscription	2	11	0
,, Locker Rents	13	10	0
,, Green Fees	39	18	6
,, Entries for Competitions	19	17	0
,, Balance from last year	29	2	7
	£796	11	1

	£	s.	d.
To Rent of Club House and Links...........	124	5	0
,, Additions and Repairs to Club House and Links	124	7	0
,, Wages to Professional and Groundsmen	210	7	11
,, Fodder for Horses and Shoeing, etc......	45	5	11
,, Coal, Coke and Oil........	15	2	5
,, Printing and Stationery	13	16	6
,, Prize Money	14	0	0
,, New Tools, Sand Boxes, etc., for Links	20	16	3
,, Rates and Insurance	7	10	2
,, Interest on Debentures and Redemption	31	16	5
,, Solicitor's Charges	6	11	3
,, Sundry Expenses.....	9	10	3
	£623	9	1
Balance in hand........	173	2	0
	£796	11	1

(Signed) R. V. B. SMYTH, Hon. Secretary.

Audited and found correct,

(Signed) HAROLD McCORQUODALE, *April 18th*, 1902.

Balance sheet 1901-2

The next major step in the constitution of the club was the request that Messrs. Lubbock, Thomas and Kent act as trustees for the club and be empowered to sign the new lease on the club's behalf. The lease had been negotiated by Mr. Kekewich and with this security the planned extensions to the clubhouse could go ahead. That these were necessary became clear when it was voted to limit the number of gentlemen members to 250 and ladies to 50. No wonder, then, that it was felt necessary to provide the Churchills with a maid and man servant to assist them towards the end of the year.

Arthur Long had been professional since the foundation of the club. It is not clear how good a golfer or teaching professional he was but it was decided to dismiss him, for an unstated reason, in February 1905. No immediate applicant seeking the post, the dismissal was suspended. Long had not been asked to make the alterations to the course and his work on it was being done by the Smiths. He tendered his resignation in April, which was accepted. There is a gap in his story until 1908 when he became professional at Verulam.

Another resignation less welcome was that of Dr. Smyth as honorary secretary and it was felt the time had come to appoint a paid secretary and also an honorary treasurer. W.O.J. Sergeant was appointed secretary at £100 per annum and Dr. Smyth was elected Captain. The professional was replaced almost as quickly, James Bradbeer beginning his long association with the club in May. His service to Porters Park was broken only by the First World War.

Recognition of the ladies was an equally important matter at the 1905 A.G.M., for a Ladies' committee was formed, consisting of a captain and four members. Their power was restricted to arranging competitions, inter-club matches and handicapping.

Presumably the new secretary had been taking advantage of the proximity of the first tee to his office to neglect his duties, for in September the committee forbade him to play golf on Saturdays before 11.00 a.m., nor was he allowed to arrange matches in advance on competition days.

A more distressing incident occurred in October 1906 when a member, Mr. R.H. Moores, reported a sovereign missing from his locker. The minute book records:

> "suspicion fell on the house boy. It was decided to have the boy brought up. He denied all knowledge of it, but on his pockets being turned out a sovereign was found on him. It was decided that he should be handed over to the police."

The boy having been replaced, the house staff at the end of the year numbered five. There were nine greenstaff at this time.

Mr. Sergeant resigned as secretary the following May and Mr. F.G. Callow was appointed as his successor, on the following terms:

1. To receive salary of £100 per annum, paid quarterly.
2. That he should sign a Fidelity Bond for £500, the club to pay the expenses and premium.
3. That he should have lunch and tea at the club's expense during the appointment.
4. That he should reside in Radlett.
5. That he should be an Hon. Member of the club but not compete in club competitions.
6. Three months notice on either side to terminate agreement.
7. That the appointment shall be on and from June 15th 1908, on which day he should start his work.

As the treasurer had also resigned prior to the A.G.M. and Dr. Smyth had finished his year as Captain, it seemed only proper that he should fill the vacancy and he was duly elected.

The new Captain, Mr. Humble, proposed that a further member be added to the committee; as he had been an ex-officio committee member and was now captain, a vacancy had been created. This was carried once it had been verified that the proposition was in order.

Mr. Callow took up his duties and seemed to perform efficiently. However in February 1909 he requested permission to live in St Albans as he was unable to find a house with an affordable rent in Radlett. This permission was granted for one year, at the end of which, if the committee still felt it desirable for the secretary to be a resident of Radlett, he would have to comply. At this stage there was no hint of what Mr. Callow's shortage of funds might lead to.

At the same time the Churchills resigned and the quest for a new steward began, a sub-committee being appointed to deal with the matter, which it did speedily. They reported to the committee meeting on 3rd April that, after interviewing several likely candidates, they had appointed Mr. and Mrs. Frank Challis, at a rate of £60 per year plus house, coal and light. Their daughter would take the maid's position, at £18 per year, while their youngest child would be boarded out at the steward's expense. It would appear that the Churchills

C.M. Humble Captain 1908 & 1909, President 1925-1941

resigned due to ill health as the club refused to assist the defrayal of a medical bill but did re-imburse them for items retained by the club.

The Challises did not stay long, for as the result of a disturbance between the caddie master and the steward on 27th March 1910, the latter was asked by the captain to tender his resignation, or he would be given notice. The caddie master was the next to go, being deemed unfit for work in September. Nor was this the only setback the club faced for one month later Callow, the secretary, resigned. The club's auditors brought certain banking irregularities to light and Callow was suspended from duty during the period of his notice while investigations were set in motion. He was unable to furnish satisfactory answers to any of the committee's questions regarding sums which had not been banked. Mr. E.W. Whitehead volunteered his services as honorary secretary until the appointment of a successor to Callow.

This was duly resolved at a meeting on 20th October, when Major Walton of the West Cornwall Club was interviewed and engaged at a salary of £120 per year and on the same terms as those originally offered Mr. Callow. Major Walton accepted the terms, being quite happy not to play golf on a Sunday. In the meantime Mr. Whitehead spent practically all his time at the club trying to sort out the mess left by Mr. Callow as the club's papers were "in a state of very great confusion", as indeed, it appeared, was the perpetrator of the confusion:

E.W. Whitehead Captain 1912

"The Captain further reported that he had Mr. Callow before him again, cross-examining him further on the state of affairs and had invited him … to make a clean breast of his defalcations, but had not succeeded in getting any assistance as Mr. Callow did not appear to know exactly what he had done and what he had not done."

A hearty vote of thanks was extended to the captain and honorary secretary for "the resolute way in which they had tackled this business".

On top of all this the stock book for wines had gone missing and water was pouring through the committee room veranda and the ceiling of the smoking room!

Despite being presented to the membership at the A.G.M. as an experienced and businesslike man, Major Walton only stayed for one year and was succeeded in December 1911 by Mr. D.L. Cottam, a man of thirty-five years, temperate habits and private means, who had served as secretary at Hanger Hill and Ealing Golf Clubs. He was prepared to live in Radlett and give his "whole time and daily attendance at the club" despite the restrictions on his playing golf on Saturdays and Sundays. His salary was to be £175 per year and in January 1913 he was given a bonus of £25.

Donald Cottam remained as secretary until September 1916. He gave his notice in July as he was due to begin his military service. The committee appointed C.L. Richmond as honorary secretary in his place and expressed appreciation of Mr. Cottam's hard work on the club's behalf. Mr. Richmond also took over the treasurer's duties in January 1917.

Challis's successor as steward, Mr. Peasgood, and his wife, did not perform as efficiently as expected and received criticism with ill grace, as did their daughter – Mrs. Bradbeer, the professional's wife – who assisted the Peasgoods. They were dismissed for continued insubordination in 1917 and their replacements, Mr. and Mrs. Busby, lasted for an even shorter period, two months. The Peasgoods may have had some grounds for grievance, for in December 1917 the committee agreed to buy such "articles of furniture as were absolutely necessary to make the servants' quarters habitable".

The Vowles, from London, were the next incumbents. The new steward, having given and then rescinded his notice, was reported as becoming insolent and was duly dismissed anyway. One begins to wonder at the committee's methods of dealing with these servants, although there had been a complaint about the quality of fish served at lunch earlier in the year. However, Vowles' dismissal is referred to in the minutes for May 1918 but no replacement is recorded before the meeting in October, referred to in Chapter One, at which the steward was suspected of selling whisky to the members for use off the premises and also of having purchased his own sheep to graze alongside those of the President. The upshot was that Mr. and Mrs. Cook were appointed and took up their duties in November. They do not appear to have stayed for long, as in October 1919, the question of raising the salary of the steward, Mr. Bowden, was raised.

Bowden seems to have fitted in at Porters Park better than some of his predecessors and the *Evening News* of 19th August 1920 describes his pleasure in receiving a trophy in a competition for the club staff, even though it was for the highest score ever recorded on the course: 161 – 50 = 111! Bowden was described as a "doleful humorist" who had been the head waiter in the Smoking Room of the Devonshire Club for thirty-two years.

In the meantime, Mr. Whitehead, who had so ably filled the breach between secretaries, became a victim of the war, in that he was obliged to file for bankruptcy, which would lead automatically to his resignation from the club. However, a friend wrote on his behalf, apprising the committee of the circumstances, none of which could be said to be Mr. Whitehead's fault, and he remained a valued member, only to blot his copy-book in 1920, when he was reprimanded and asked to resign from the committee for discussing committee business in the public rooms of the club, thus breaking the confidentiality of the committee. Furthermore, he had been disagreeing with the committee's policy!

Mr. Whitehead duly wrote an abject letter of apology, which was accepted by the committee. It is sad to note his death recorded in the minutes of the meeting of 18th December 1920. His friends quickly subscribed to a trophy to be played for in his memory, which the committee accepted the following April.

Another loyal and hard-working member C. Lennox Richmond, the honorary secretary and treasurer, attempted to resign but was prevailed upon to continue. He was still in office at the A.G.M. of 1921, when he was elected a Full Life Member of the club and presented with "a very handsome filled dressing case" which was a gift from the members of the club. Richmond had taken over from Mr. Cottam mid-way through the war and had steered the club through the remainder of the hostilities and the difficult post-war years, in the process seeing off four stewards. In February 1922 it was unanimously decided to pay him £350 per annum with effect from 1st January 1922, Mr. Richmond to enjoy all the privileges to which the previous paid officers had been entitled. He finally resigned through ill-health in 1927 and was voted a pension of £175 a year by the club.

At this meeting it was also decided to accept the offer of an organisation called "The Golf Club Publicity Association" to produce a booklet about the club, which was gaining a reputation as a fine course. Many clubs took advantage of similar offers and a number of the best known golf writers, such as Bernard Darwin and Robert Browning, were employed to supply the words, with the result that these booklets are now collectors items.

Two interesting developments in the make-up of the club's membership occurred in March and April, 1924. At the March meeting a new rule allowed members taking up permanent residence outside a fifty mile radius of the club to be placed on a list of country members, at a subscription of three guineas for gentlemen and two guineas for ladies. This was strictly enforced as can be seen the following month when Mr. Henderson Neal informed the club he had taken a small service flat in London and enquired if this disqualified him from country membership. It did and Mr. Neal was asked to return the refunded full subscription of £7.7s.

Groundstaff competition 3rd August 1922. Back: David Smith, Herb Thresher, F. Lynn, T. Marshall, S. Chalkley (Captain), C.L. Richmond (Sec.), George Smith, Fred Smith, Fred Phillips, A. Bignell. Front: E.G. Shadbolt, F. Shears, J. Bradbeer (Pro), E. Page, J. Freeborn, Bill Phillips

Ground Staff Compétition
18 Hole Handicap Medal

August 3rd 1922

1st Prize	5 0 0	F. Smith	101 - 26 = 75	won Tie
2" .	3 0 0	Fred Phillips	93 - 18 = 75	
3 .	2 0 0	J Freeborn	82 - 4 = 78	
4 .	1 10 0	E Shadbolt	84 - 6 = 78	Decide
5 "	1 0 0	T Marshall	104 - 26 = 78	
6 "	1 0 0	A Bignell	81 - 2 = 79	
7 "	10 0	David Smith	106 - 24 = 82	
8 "	10 0	George Smith	98 - 16 = 82	
9 "	10 0	W Phillips	106 - 24 = 82	
		H Thresher	114 - 24 - 90	
		E Page.	99 - 8 = 91	
		F Shears	95 - 10 = 85	
Worst Score.	1 0 0	F Lynn	135 - 30 - 105	

Scratch Prize 2 0 0   A Bignell   81
Best 9 holes out. F Smith   A Club by J Bradbeer
            home T Marshall A Club by The Captain
            Clock. 12. hole.
   J Freeborn 1st £1
   E Shadbolt 2nd 10/-
   G Smith - E Page - T Marshall. tie 5/- Each

61

Mr. Raphael then raised the question of the number of local residents holding membership, feeling that an increase in these was not in the best interests of the club. The committee agreed with him and the number of Radlett parishioners was limited to fifty gentlemen and twenty-five ladies. When a Mr. R.W. Thomas wished to join the club in 1925, being "desirable as a member", he had to be given provisional membership and placed on a waiting list because the local residents, of which he was one, were in excess of the quota. However, because the course was apparently not used as fully as the committee thought viable on weekdays, the provisional members subscription was reduced from seven to five guineas. It would seem Mr. Raphael's feelings about local members were perhaps not in the club's best interests, after all.

The irascible Mr. Raphael had been the club's President since 1903 and had been both benefactor and dictator. Following a dispute with other stately home owners in the district he sold Porters and the estate to the Middlesex County Council. The club's response, forced upon them, was to draw up new rules, deleting "The Landlord" from those clauses which entitled him to assert his authority, and to introduce a rule whereby the President would henceforth be elected annually. Raphael was re-elected in 1925 but resigned from the club in January the following year when his sons were asked to pay green fees when playing on the course. Raphael maintained that they were entitled to the courtesy of the course. The committee disagreed. Earlier, one of Mr. Raphael's sons had been involved in an incident in which he had driven into the players ahead of him, causing a dispute which occupied a considerable amount of time to settle, so perhaps the resignation created a certain amount of relief in the committee room.

A gathering of Members at the 1927 Annual Dinner Dance (Captain Mr. H. J. Lane)
tickets: one guinea, exclusive of wine

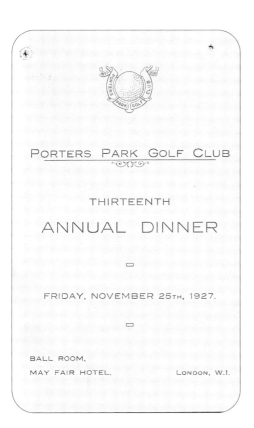

PORTERS PARK GOLF CLUB

THIRTEENTH

ANNUAL DINNER

FRIDAY, NOVEMBER 25TH, 1927.

BALL ROOM,
MAY FAIR HOTEL, LONDON, W.1.

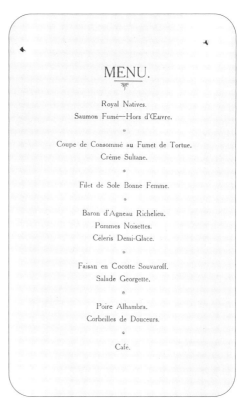

MENU.

Royal Natives.
Saumon Fumé—Hors d'Œuvre.

Coupe de Consommé au Fumet de Tortue.
Crème Sultane.

Filet de Sole Bonne Femme.

Baron d'Agneau Richelieu.
Pommes Noisettes.
Céleris Demi-Glace.

Faisan en Cocotte Souvaroff.
Salade Georgette.

Poire Alhambra.
Corbeilles de Douceurs.

Café.

Chapter Five

Post Raphael Years

AT THE 1926 A.G.M. Mr. C.M. Humble, a Past Captain and founder member, took office as President, which position he held for a number of years, a fitting reward for many years of hard work on the club's behalf. Two other founder members, Mr. A.E. Colebrook and Mr. E.W. Thomas, had already been accorded Honorary Membership in 1924.

This was the year when the Porters Park Benevolent Fund was set up, administered by trustees who were the captain of the year, the secretary and the president. This fund was set up to assist needy members of staff or their dependents at the discretion of the trustees. It could be used, for example, to supplement their old age pensions. Initially the scheme was funded by voluntary subscriptions but at the A.G.M. of 1929 a grant of £100 was made to fund the scheme. These finances were called upon later in the year, when the steward, Bowden, had to undergo an operation for rupture. As this had more than likely been incurred in the service of the club, the committee's acceptance of the responsibility for any expenses incurred was very commendable.

Mr. Richmond continued to run things smoothly until his resignation in 1927 when Captain Lawrence took over and in July Mr. Richmond handed over the keys of the club to the Captain, Mr. H.J. Lane, in what must have been a poignant ceremony. Captain Lawrence clearly operated as efficiently as Mr. Richmond: after two years in office he was awarded a £25 bonus in addition to his salary of £300 per annum, because of the satisfactory state of the accounts for the previous year's business. One of Mr. Richmond's last actions in keeping the membership in line had been to turf the nine years old Malcolm Reid off the course, in spite of his playing with the express permission of the Captain, "Bo" Roberts. A number of members had been disciplined already about allowing their offspring access to the course and no doubt this was one incident that inspired Malcolm in his future efforts on behalf of young golfers. His father, L.J.

64

No. 1763, April 10, 1935]

THE TATLER

GOLF CLUBS AND GOLFERS

PORTERS PARK GOLF CLUB—By "MEL"

The Porters Park Golf Club is considered one of the best around London, with the finest park course in the neighbourhood. The ground is well adapted to the purpose of golf, consisting as it does of beautiful old park turf on light loam over gravel, and sand. Yet it is not more than fifteen miles by road from Marble Arch, and within half a mile of Radlett village and station. The professional, Jimmy Bradbeer, is the eldest of that wonderful golfing family which hails from the West Country. There are six brothers, all professionals. Mr. M. J. Clayton, one of "Mel's" victims in this cartoon, is a past captain of Rochford Hundred Golf Club, and the first captain of Thorpe, Essex. Mr. Percy C. Burton is Vice-President of the Hertfordshire Union and a member of the English Golf Union Council. The Club has an energetic and popular secretary in Captain F. H. Lawrence, who is famous for his knowledge of grasses and their treatment

Reid, had been elected in September 1922 and joined the committee in 1925, becoming Captain in 1931, while Mrs. Reid became Ladies' Captain in 1925, having been elevated to full membership only as recently as December 1923. Malcolm was elected a juvenile member in June 1929 and his brother Colin the following year.

L.J. Reid worked for *The Daily Telegraph*, of which he was city editor for a time in the 1930s. He died in 1938 in America, where he had been sent by the paper to interview President Roosevelt.

The slump of the 1930s caused a spate of resignations and the committee struggled to find ways and means of maintaining the membership. Eventually it was decided to waive the entrance fee for new members and this created sufficient stability, assisted by the disposal of War Loans, to see the club through the worst of the crisis. Forty-six new members were elected, with the result that the entrance fee was reinstated. In all, £2,000 worth of War Loans were sold and the proceeds used to support the current and deposit accounts at the bank. Then in February 1932, the secretary was instructed to repurchase £1,500 worth of War Loans, and then told to sell £1,000 worth in September.

The entrance fee was suspended again in 1933 when there was another shortage of members. However, work continued on the development of

Porters Park beat Redhill and Reigate in the final of the 1932 "Star" Foursomes at Stoke Poges by 2 games to 1. Left: Major P.C. Burton, G.M. Turner, A.G. Snelling. Right: R.E.A. Bott (Team Capt.), J.M. Darroch, R.O. Burlison (Capt.), J. Grimditch

the course, and in 1935 a sub-committee was formed to consider the rebuilding of the club's lavatories. On receipt of the sub-committee's report, £500 was allocated for improving these facilities, including those used by the staff. In addition to this the condition of the steward's accommodation, Lodge Cottage, was giving cause for concern. It was considered barely habitable and plans were made for the temporary rehousing of the steward. This was complicated further by the steward's illness and the club sustained a sad loss in December when Mr. Mills died in a nursing home. He was described as "an honourable and able servant" and the committee authorised the secretary to issue his widow with a voucher so that she could "purchase something tangible and acceptable to herself". It should be noted that she had already received a gift of £5 for her excellent work during her husband's illness.

A more serious loss occurred two months later when the Captain, Captain T.C. Gilson, was killed in a motor accident. He had already been honoured by the club for redrafting and rewriting the club's rules and his demise was deeply regretted. The death of the Past President, C.F. Raphael, twelve months later was recorded more simply in the minutes book in an item in which "the secretary was asked to prepare a letter of sympathy to be forwarded to the widow of the late President of the club, Mr. C.F. Raphael, by Mr. C.M. Humble".

Middlesex County Council agreed to demolish Lodge Cottage and rebuild it, reducing the rent in the process, although the club had to find five per cent of the outlay. Progress was slow and the club wrote to the Council requesting permission to approach the Ministry of Health to discuss the delay. More urgently, in September 1936, the secretary was instructed to make inquiries in the immediate vicinity of the club to see if anyone was prepared to house the club's servants until the cottage had been replaced.

It was during this year that the Golf Clubs' Protection Association (now the National Golf Clubs' Advisory Association) urged all golf clubs to write to their M.P. to support a new Parliamentary Bill permitting clubs to extend their licensing hours, as this was meeting opposition from the licensed trade, who suggested that golf clubs should be liable to police inspection if operating within the same time limits as public houses, including Sunday opening, and from the Temperance Party. Porters Park's club solicitor drafted an appropriate letter. Eventually the Bill was passed allowing private clubs the right to open their bars for the agreed length of time without harassment. As well as a service to the members, the bar was a vital source of income, which was duly recognised by Parliament. Another matter addressed by the Association at the same time was the right of golf club professionals to open their shops on Sundays, which had previously infringed the Sunday Trading Act.

TABLE OF ENTRANCE FEES AND SUBSCRIPTIONS

(As from 1st January, 1938).

	Entrance Fee.	Subscription.
FULL MEMBERS :—		
*Men (Local)	—	12 Gns.
Men (other than Local) ...	—	11½ ,,
*Ladies (Local)	9 Gns.	9 ,,
Ladies (other than Local)	9 ,,	8½ ,,
PROVISIONAL 5-DAY (not Saturdays, Sundays, or Bank Holidays) :—		
*Ladies or Men (Local) ...	—	5 ,,
Ladies or Men (other than Local)	—	5 ,,
TEMPORARY MEMBERS (Limited to 12 months) 7 days per week :—		
1 month	—	1½ ,,
3 ,, ...	—	3 ,,
6 ,, ...	—	6 ,,
12 ,, ...	—	10 ,,
5 days per week (not Saturdays, Sundays or Bank Holidays) :—		
1 month	—	1 ,,
3 ,, ...	—	2 ,,
6 ,, ...	—	3 ,,
12 ,, ...	—	4 ,,
JUVENILE (sons, daughters, or wards of Members, 12 to 18 years of age) :—		
5 days per week ...	—	2 ,,
COUNTRY MEMBERS (radius 50 miles)	—	3 ,,
NON-PLAYING MEMBERS (Relatives of Members only)	—	2 ,,

At the Annual General Meeting of the Club held on 23rd February, 1935—It was proposed, and unanimously carried that the annual subscription of all members should be increased by 5/-, to support the Benevolent Fund of the Club.

*Local=resident within 4 miles.

The Council's dilatoriness in this matter may have been the cause of the club's appeal against their rating in October and in the same month the Inland Revenue offered to reduce the assessment against the club by £221. The offer was provisionally accepted. Such matters as these finally persuaded the committee that it was desirable to prepare an annual budget to determine the spending power of the club, particularly as the club was over-drawn at the bank. Mr. W.A. Henderson produced this in June 1937, one month after it had been suggested and was thanked unanimously for his efforts. However, "In connection with the accounts the question of supplying sandwiches at week-ends was raised and the matter left in the hands of the house committee."

More seriously, it was realised that subscriptions had to be increased by two guineas. This was put to an Extraordinary General Meeting and defeated by seventy votes to forty-four. An amendment was defeated but a new proposal calling for an increase of £1.11s.6d. was passed. A further E.G.M. had to be called, though, so that the motion could be put properly to the members. This proved counter-productive as more than fifty resignations were recorded in the minutes of the first meeting of 1938 and a further forty in December and in January the following year. However a new lease of £51 per annum for Lodge Cottage, on which work was about to start, was signed.

By this time the Benevolent Fund had been established for thirteen years and was well funded. Since 1935, five shillings of every member's subscription was added to the fund and ten per cent of all sweepstakes were included, giving an annual income of around £200. C.K. Cotton, now at Oxhey Golf Club, was the editor of *Course and Clubhouse* at the time and upheld Porters Park's scheme as a model to other clubs, concluding the article with the information: "At the present time there are three pensioners, who between them are drawing £135 per annum". Although the Benevolent Fund no longer exists, Mrs. Shadbolt, aged 101, widow of the former locker room attendant, still drew a pension from the club in 1998.

It was finally decided to invest in a burglar alarm and quotations were obtained in January 1939. An alarm could be fitted for nine guineas plus a further five for maintenance. It was decided to approach the insurance company to see if they would consider reducing the club's premium before proceeding. As they had not replied by March, the matter was raised again and it was decided to do nothing for the present. In the early hours of 11th April there was another burglary. The committee decided to wait for the insurance company's reaction before taking any action of their own and in June they decided to leave the installation of a burglar alarm to the captain and secretary.

Some economies were made as the war began to exacerbate matters: the greenstaff were reduced from eight to six; an application was made for a reduction in the rent; roller towels were installed instead of hand towels, paper serviettes purchased and the number of weekly periodicals was reduced by "at least a half".

An Extraordinary General Meeting was called in October to ask the members to vote in favour of vesting full powers in the committee "to deal with the management of the club as may become necessary, irrespective of anything that may be contained in the present rules of the club, and that on the occasion of any urgent business arising requiring an immediate decision, and a quorum of the committee not being obtainable, any officer of the club together with a member of the committee and the secretary shall have power to act in the place of the committee."

After some members had questioned the resolution a vote was taken, and when it was established that the correct majority had voted in favour, the committee was given the plenary powers as defined in the motion.

Service members and their wives were granted special subscriptions during the war. They were required to pay a minimum of one guinea plus two shillings per day green fee. Despite a large number of resignations at the end of the year, golf and social life at the club continued and in December a sweep was arranged to finance the blackout curtains required for the lounge. Half a crown purchased a ticket and any surplus when the costs had been defrayed would be spent on prizes to be bought in the professional's shop.

Economies had to be made, though, and five members of the club's staff were laid off, with the promise of re-employment after the war. A successful rent appeal led to the Middlesex County Council reducing the annual rent to £425 for 1940. Later in the year the rateable value was reduced from £625 to £520.

Fortunately there were a number of elections to membership and the greenstaff worked hard enough to be awarded a week's wages as a bonus, despite the club's financial state. Wounded soldiers at Shenley Hospital were given the courtesy of the course provided that they wore hospital blue while playing.

Several War Appeals were supported by the club's holding afternoon and evening bridge parties, Stableford competitions and combined golf and bridge parties. These raised useful sums and combined with the agricultural use of the land for crops and grazing the members could be seen to be "doing their bit" for the war effort.

Mr. Humble had been re-elected as President at the 1940 A.G.M. but sadly did not complete his term of office, dying in December. Mr. R.O. Burlison took his place as President and trustee of the club, while his trusteeship of the Benevolent Fund was taken over by Mr. A. Sherriff. Mrs. Humble was made an Honorary Life Member the following year.

By this time Mr. Watson was the steward and as a reward for his good work during the previous year, in January 1941 the committee voted to restore the salary cut they had imposed and to consider doing the same for the ensuing year. It was realised in 1942 that insurance against war damage would be advisable, the most expensive item on the premium being the wines and spirits.

As the war dragged on the club became further involved, the committee discussing such matters as the Home Guard's being allowed to use the club as a food centre, the purchase of chickens to provide eggs for consumption at the club and the feasibility of an Artisans' section. Further fundraising bridge parties and dances, including a "waste paper dance", were held in aid of war charities. Later it was decided that the eggs could not be sold to members but preserved in waterglass only for use at the club, at a charge of sixpence each, rationed at one for tea or two for supper.

Other indications of the general tightening of belts were the decisions to sell sherry and port only in club measures, to purchase vintage port only if it cost under £1 per bottle and to restrict the sale of gin to the weekends. This would be sold in the same measure as whisky and no "club" or double whiskies were permitted.

A more permanent and significant step in the management of the club came with the invitation to members to propose members for election to the committee. However at the A.G.M the two newly elected committee members were nominated by the committee. The new President was Mr.

Markham, an indefatigable worker on the club's behalf. He resigned from the office in November 1943 and was succeeded by Mr. J.P. Hall. Markham and Mr. Burlison were proposed as VicePresidents.

The attitude to the staff continued somewhat ambivalent; the steward's salary was reduced and then made up to the full amount yet again and the greenstaff continued to be well treated. Mr. Watson was congratulated for his work on the club's behalf.

The R.A.F. Old Comrades were given permission to hold a dance provided that they supplied their own glassware and a dance was arranged for the "Wings for Victory" appeal, several members offering prizes for the raffle. Wounded soldiers were entertained and members of the armed services from overseas were granted the same playing privileges as British soldiers.

Porters Park joined the number of clubs permitting artisan membership in August 1944, after deferring the decision for some time, a decision that was approved by the membership the following year. Twenty-five men applied for membership, six being rejected on the grounds that they ran businesses.

The secretary of the club, Captain Lawrence, having guided the club through the war years announced that he would be retiring from his position on reaching his seventieth birthday and Mr. C. K. Cotton was appointed in his place. Captain Lawrence was made an Honorary Life Member of the club and was granted a pension of £2 per week. Cotton was also the secretary of the County Golf Union at this time and was setting up his own business as a golf course architect. He tendered his resignation in September 1945, having been in office less than six months, explaining that he only considered the post a temporary one, that the club required a man aged between forty and forty-five to fill the position and that he was receiving many inquiries from clubs requesting his services. However, he remained in close contact with Porters Park, acting as advisor on the course and making frequent visits. Major David Keith was proposed as his successor and that gentleman took over in October, the Association of Golf Club Secretaries having been unable to suggest anyone in the desired age range. Only four months after his appointment the major had the privilege of a £100 salary increase. He was given Honorary Membership of the club in May 1947. Major Keith also acted for the Radlett Bowling club in an advisory capacity, "using the club's time for this purpose, as reasonably as possible". How much time he spent on the affairs of the bowling club is not certain but an entry in the suggestions book implies that perhaps either the major or his predecessors may have been a trifle lax in administering some of the members' requirements: "It is now eight years since I joined the club and I am still without a key to my locker. I have never had one. Will the committee please see that keys are obtained?" Major Keith's reply promised that the matter would be "enquired into and an endeavour made for keys to be provided for all lockers."

The special powers invoked by the committee for the duration of the war were rescinded in 1946. The only use made of them had been to increase the number of lady members from seventy to ninety. War damage to the course was repaired by the council after a successful claim to the appropriate authority. It was also decided that memorials to those members and staff who fell in both wars be placed in the clubhouse. This was designed by the club Captain, Mr. G. Brown, and took the form of an oak panel in the lounge, which was consecrated on 12th March 1949 by the Revd. Kenneth Blackburn.

The Watsons, who had done their best to provide bar and catering services during the war years, were given notice in January 1949 and granted a pension. It would appear, in addition to Mr. Watson's becoming too slow, that their attitude to the members left something to be desired, as in November 1946 the committee had agreed to increase their salary "subject to an increase in courtesy and geniality from steward and stewardess to members". The Watsons no doubt had to fend off requests for extra eggs for tea and to serve whisky on days other than the specified Saturdays, Sundays and Bank Holidays. The purchase of whisky in the years of austerity following the war was not the simple matter it is today, a quota system being in force, and occupied a considerable amount of the committee's time in determining the amounts to be ordered. For example in April, 1947, two tranches of twenty-five cases were obtained and the secretary was instructed to see if he could negotiate for a further fifty cases. In July it was decided that "at the present rate of consumption" stocks would be sufficient for a further two years. It was agreed in November, however, to purchase twenty-five cases of gin. The following May, though, it was realised that with only a year's supply of whisky left, fifty cases of "Brae Dew" should be purchased at the rate of ten cases per month.

The importance of minuting such items becomes clearer when the financial state of a golf club becomes insecure: an Extraordinary General Meeting was called on Sunday 29th November 1948. Few members attended because of heavy fog but the Captain's proposal to postpone the meeting was over-ruled. He explained that if the members wished to maintain course and house standards at the present level an increase in subscriptions would be necessary. The cost of house staff had risen because of the Catering Wages Act, extra greenstaff had been employed and the costs of all commodities necessary to run the club efficiently had increased. The House account had shown a decrease in its gross profit because of the increase in catering standards, the decrease in the whisky supply quota and loss of bar profits because sale prices had not been increased even though the purchase prices had. After a lively debate the members present agreed unanimously to the proposed new subscription rates:

Full men: £13 2s. 6d. Full ladies: £8 18s. 6d.

Provisional men: £7 17s. 6d. Provisional ladies £6 16s. 6d.

Twelve resignations were recorded in the minutes of the next committee meeting.

Another sign of the times was the negotiation of the club's lease in 1947, which was secured at a rental of £750 on condition that the club agreed to public play on the course at restricted times on Mondays, the Middlesex County Council to provide accommodation for those golfers wishing to take advantage of the scheme. This was a common occurrence at many London based clubs, some of which still have "public days".

In January 1949, Mr. and Mrs. Willis accepted the post of steward and stewardess in place of the Watsons, for whom it was proposed to set up a fund. However, the committee felt the arrangements they had already made were satisfactory. The Willises were given some guidance, too, for it was decided that soup would not be served between April and October and salmon, lobster and potted shrimps would not be provided "except in an emergency".

A Porters Park team at Deal in 1950. Back: Malcolm Reid, Gladys Quinn, Keith Nordon, Nesta Nordon, Dick Bott, Pat Bott, Barbara Balch, Morris Balch, Jean Nordon, Brian Nordon. Front: Jacko Hall, Pearl Reid, "Bill" Scott-Miller, Jane Hall, Stuart Scott-Miller

That the club's finances had not improved by mid-1950 is demonstrated by the increase in some bar prices (although it was suggested that a whisky measure be reduced rather than the price increased), by the committee's decision that the cost of building a shed for the storage of caddie-carts was prohibitive and by complaints in the suggestions book concerning the poor decorative state of the clubhouse. By November it was felt necessary to circulate the membership regarding another proposed increase in subscriptions as the treasurer's budget showed a considerable gap between revenue and expenditure. It was proposed to suspend entrance fees, and collect subscriptions on a half-yearly basis, supplying members with the appropriate figures showing the deficit. Committee members were asked to consider further ways of saving money and creating funds. Of slight assistance was the granting of a form of corporate membership to the Charing Cross Hospital to enable the staff to play the course on an annual basis, for a fee of one guinea per head. The Captain's circular also showed reductions in green and house staff.

Nevertheless a loss over the year of £1075. 12s. 10d. was reported which by skilful accounting, transferring the cost of a new motor mower and various repairs to the Capital account, was reduced to £519. 18s. 0d. It was noted later that this system of accounting might require some adjustment. The Artisans rallied round and their offer of a donation of £50 was gratefully accepted. This gratitude was expressed in more concrete terms when they were granted permission to hold second team matches against other artisan clubs, within their specified times.

Having been asked to address the problem of increasing the membership, the committee made several suggestions. Members of certain London clubs could be offered a reduced subscription and play on payment of a green fee; publication of competition results would be resumed in the *Herts Advertiser* in order to publicise the club's activities and hopefully generate more local interest; reduced green fees for societies and members' guests, to a maximum of three, including weekends; the larger London hospitals could be offered similar terms to those offered to Charing Cross Hospital; the qualifying limit for country membership should be reduced to twenty-five miles, reduced subscriptions but a green fee payable on playing. Finally Mr. E.C. Beck volunteered to contact Mr. Goodfellow of the *Evening Standard* with a view to obtaining a publicity article on the club's behalf.

An advertisement was duly placed in the *Herts Advertiser.*

GOLF: – the antidote to business or domestic anxiety – can still be had at reasonable cost. Porters Park Golf Club, Radlett, with a course in first-rate condition and second to none in Hertfordshire, has some vacancies for suitable members at fees of £7. 7s. 0d. for men and £5. 5s 6d. for women for six months. No entrance fee.

The advertisement also included details of non-playing membership at £1. 11s. 6d. per six months. Prospective members were to be proposed and seconded by existing members in the usual manner.

Despite the financial constraints the club continued to offer a full service to the members. A deep-freeze was purchased with a view to offering more choice of catering, as detailed by the house committee's report of May 1951, which also recorded that sales of whisky were outstripping supplies, still on the quota, and suggested increasing the cost of drinks.

The decoration of the clubhouse was another important item and Mr. E.C. Dix volunteered the services of two of the crew of his yacht to do the job. As this had already attracted comments in the suggestion book, it would appear the work was long overdue. However, at least one member had reservations:

"While admiring the spirit of those members who have volunteered to assist in decorating the clubhouse and in no way doubting their skill, I cannot help feeling that this task would be beyond them.

"I suggest an estimate from a firm of builders to have the entire clubhouse thoroughly decorated both inside and out. And I suggest the cost be met by way of a "special contribution" or capital levy of say £1 per member – or whatever sum be required."

At least one other member was in agreement with this suggestion, but the committee's reply was guarded but positive, as they were awaiting the availability of Mr. Dix's crew. It is worth noting here that many golf clubs throughout the country were in a similar plight: elderly members of Droitwich Golf Club in Worcestershire have, apparently, happy memories of "mucking in" with paint brushes to restore their club house to respectability. Material assistance had been received from the President, Mr. J.P. Hall, who had supplied a new boiler, and Mr. R.W. Armstrong had provided a new water tank. Despite all these difficulties the course and house staff continued to give sterling service, which was duly noted in the minutes.

It was not surprising then that it was felt impossible to go ahead with plans to purchase the course; indeed it was felt necessary to approach Middlesex County Council to request a reduction in the rent and a sympathetic reply was received on submission of the half yearly balance sheet. The loss for the period in question amounted to £585. The committee still did not neglect its duty to its employees, increasing the greenstaff's wages by generous amounts in September.

The Captain decided it was necessary to apprise the membership of the situation and a long letter was drafted, in which the seriousness of the club's financial state was left in no doubt. Subscriptions would have to be increased as economies made to retain them at the present level would have a drastic effect on the course, leading to loss of society revenue, which would be reduced anyway if economies were made on the catering side. It was also pointed out that a large influx of new members would lead to congestion on the course and loss of the atmosphere prevalent at that time. A questionnaire was provided for the members to give a limited view of their possible reaction.

At the Extraordinary General Meeting following the issue of the Captain's circular, it was decided that a levy would be imposed on all members, instead of the substantial increase in subscriptions, although some categories did attract an increase. An alternative subscription requiring the payment of green fees was also passed.

Sir Handley Page helped alleviate the situation by requesting facilities for his employees to play the course, which was granted at a fee of two guineas per head per annum.

Despite all these efforts to ensure favourable conditions for club members, twenty-six resignations were reluctantly accepted in December and six more members were struck off for failing to honour their subscriptions. Affiliated membership was offered to full members of selected clubs in the neighbourhood, without election but without voting rights or the opportunity to play in competitions. It is hardly surprising that J.P. Hall stood down after nine years as President after all his efforts to hold the club together.

It was proposed for 1952 that the tradition of the retiring captain to act as vice-captain be abolished. There was also a new secretary, Mr. D.E. Albany taking over from Major Keith at a salary of £100 plus an entertainment allowance of £150. A further fifteen resignations, including that of D.R. Jardine, the England cricketer and author of the infamous "bodyline theory", suggested that their tasks would not be easy ones. Nor was the steward, Willis, in a happy position; called before the house committee, it was put to him that his attitude to members left much to be desired. His efforts in the bar were not matched by his control elsewhere and serious catering losses had to be halted. New menus for lunch were drawn up, based on Ministry of Supply recommendations, for this was still a time of rationing, and the frozen foods stored in the freezer were discontinued.

By the end of May 1952, the club had a total of just 378 members, 151 men, 61 ladies, 33 provisional, 54 non-playing, 27 country, 17 juniors, 29 juveniles and 6 "specials". Clearly, something had to be done to increase membership. It was decided to keep subscription levels at the current rate to encourage new members and retain existing ones. Eleven applications were recorded in the May minutes, against four further resignations, and a similar number of potential members the following month.

Peter Lynn recalls the influx of new members, not all of whom impressed "the old guard", for on one wet day one new member played in flannel trousers and *bicycle clips*. After a quiet word from secretary Albany the new member made his next appearance decorously clad in plus fours. Peter also claims that his memories of the club characters are not suitable for family reading!

A change of caterers, involving an outside agency, the sale of hay, a further donation from the Artisans and the suggestion of a scheme that the club cultivate its own vegetables led to a much healthier balance sheet for the half-year in July and it was decided not to increase subscriptions or take up a further levy for the following year. To further encourage the new members a supper was arranged for them on 7th October.

Malcolm Reid driving into his year of Captaincy in 1953

Less favourable was the County Council's decision not to reduce the rent, a matter the Captain was resolved to take up further with the landlord.

Despite the committee's determination to offer the members satisfactory service, they were not helped by Willis's failure to improve his control over the staff and he was finally given notice in September; he requested to be released by November. There were 140 applicants for his job. At the same time it was decided to abandon the idea of outside caterers. His replacement, Brown and his wife, did not last long, not being sufficiently capable of coping with the job and in March 1953 the Collinges were appointed.

By the end of 1952 two distinguished members had completed fifty years of membership, Mr. E.S. Markham and Mr. R.O. Burlison. The former had served the club in several capacities and Mr. Burlison had also been both Captain and President. Honorary Life Membership was conferred on both gentlemen.

The redecoration fund closed at £224 from subscribers and it was felt possible to obtain estimates, that of Messrs. Wiggs, of £97.10s., being accepted. Further funds were made possible by the request of Aldenham Lodge Hotel to enable guests to play on the course. This was granted at an annual fee of £50. A shilling-in-the-slot "golf ball machine", that is, a gaming machine, produced £7 in its first week of use. The sale of hay realised a further £20 and the Artisans donated another £40 towards the upkeep of the course. Despite this, an Extraordinary General Meeting was called to explain to the members why subscriptions had to be increased by two guineas for all categories except juveniles, their fees increasing by one guinea. Second club membership was also to be offered to full members of other clubs and advertisements placed in *Golf Illustrated* in an attempt to attract new members. The recruiting drive's success was undermined by the number of resignations exceeding the applications, once again. However, the campaign had attracted a number of inquiries and Fighter Command took a block membership at forty guineas per year. Middlesex Hospital had also shown interest but had not reached a decision.

The New Year's Eve dance had caused the committee some problems: originally it had been decided to use a radiogram to provide the music, on the grounds that it would be cheaper than a band and funds for its purchase were raised at a bridge drive. The treasurer objected to this expenditure but in the meantime, following grumbles from members, the captain had taken it upon himself to book a trio of musicians. That the event proved popular and successful may be judged from the steward Collinge's letter thanking the club for his generous gratuity for catering the event and expressing the hope that he and his wife would cater for many more functions in years to come.

A less happy occurrence was the resignation of the secretary, Mr. Albany, for personal reasons. The committee expressed their gratitude to him for the "efficient and self-denying manner in which he had carried out his services". Mr. H.P. Hinde was offered the position.

Despite the financial plight of the club it was felt that unsponsored applicants for membership should not be admitted without the approval of the A.G.M. The treasurer stressed the need for an extra £1,000 of income and the strictest economies, from major items like printing costs down to the cost of clock-winding.

Prior to the Annual General Meeting, the President, Mr. J. Everington, proposed a "hearty and special vote of thanks" to Malcolm Reid as retiring captain: "he had of course worked for the club in other capacities for years before, but the amount of time and trouble he had given in the past year was really extraordinary. It was doubtful whether this or any other club had ever been so well and loyally served". Malcolm Reid did not sit back on his laurels, however, remaining an ex-officio member of the committee and subsequently expanding his influence on the game to national level.

It was discovered in March that the clubhouse needed rewiring – an item the club could ill afford at the time – and quotations were sought.

It was also considered a good idea to reconstruct the bar to afford more circulation space for a mixed bar. Before this could be done, however, the opportunity to alter the clubhouse presented itself on 17th May 1954 when the clubhouse was seriously damaged by fire.

Exhibition Match after Ryder Cup 1949. David Keith (Sec.), Dutch Harrison, Charles Whitcombe, Jacky Hall, Arthur Baucher (Captain), Eddie Whitcombe and Ed Dudley

Chapter Six

Rebuilding and Re-organising

MALCOLM REID'S dramatic photographs show the extent of the conflagration. Immediately following the fire, in which the men's locker room and the dining room were destroyed, the committee met to review the damage and praise the staff for their work during the emergency. Talks had already been held with the insurers and it appeared there were no problems which would prevent payment of the club's claim and work commenced very quickly. The costs of temporary accommodation would not be covered and the members were invited to contribute to a reconstruction fund, which they did in sufficient numbers to ease the situation. The sale of salvaged scrap also boosted the fund. In August the Captain was able to present a plan for the suggested rebuilding, based on using the site of the locker rooms as a dining room and moving the locker rooms to the staff area. That the business was being well managed is apparent from the following month's meeting when a revised scheme allowed for a larger mixed bar and a self-service dining room, a move forced on the club by economies in the catering, though the finances were within the budget for the year.

An appeal for the reduction of the club's rent was rejected and a sub-committee was formed to discuss subscription rates in the light of this, particularly those paid by non-playing members. The discussions Mr. Mervyn Orchard-Lisle held with Middlesex County Council regarding the purchase of the course and extension of the lease are described in Chapter Two.

In the meantime, reconstruction had progressed sufficiently to permit a New Year's Eve dance at the club, though unfortunately the band had proved unsatisfactory and the club refused them full payment. Although some of the tenders had been higher than expected, with the members' donations, the costs would fall within the budget.

Another important step forward was the formation of a sub-committee, consisting of Mr. J.Everington, the President of the club, Mr. E.W. Parkes

The Clubhouse fire in 1954

and Malcolm Reid, co-opted to this sub-committee, as he had been to the one which had determined new stroke indexes on the score-card. They recommended that the number of full members be limited to 250 men and 90 ladies and that the committee be empowered to elect provisional, country, junior, non-playing, honorary and temporary members as they deemed desirable, subject to the playing restrictions. Provisional members could not compete for club prizes nor play on Saturdays, Sundays or Bank Holidays. They could play on those days, however, on payment of a green fee and would be given priority over other applicants for full membership, paying the full subscription and entry fee on election. Provisional ladies could play in competitions which were held during the week.

Junior members between the ages of ten and eighteen were to be elected annually and had to be proposed by a parent or guardian, who was responsible for their conduct. Annual re-election was not as harsh an idea as it may seem, as it enabled the club to weed out those who did not take advantage of membership, thereby creating a place for another junior. Many clubs have been in the frustrating position of having junior members who had been proposed by keen parents, but who did not share their parents' enthusiasm. At the age of eighteen juniors became full members liable to pay the entrance fee, so non-active members would not take up a place which could be filled by a playing member.

Country members had to reside further than thirty miles from the club and if they moved within that radius they became eligible for a full subscription. Only full members were entitled to vote at general meetings. Special provision was made for student subscriptions and for cases of hardship. Payment could also be made in instalments.

Another proposal was the forbidding of members bringing their own food and drink for consumption at the club – previously corkage had been charged if members brought their own wine.

It was decided that some form of memorial to Mr. J.P. Hall, who served as President for the nine difficult years leading up to 1952, and had died not long after resigning from office, should be placed in the clubhouse. Mrs. Hall had commissioned an oil painting of her late husband, which she wished to be placed in the mixed bar. The memorial fund, donated by members, defrayed part of the cost, the remainder going towards refurnishing the mixed bar, Mrs. Hall bearing £100 of the £150 charged for the portrait, which was completed in February the following year. Once she had received the portrait, though, Mrs. Hall changed her mind and decided that she would prefer to keep it but would bequeath it to the club in her will. It now hangs in the secretary's office. In the interim a photograph of the painting was hung in the mixed bar. The surplus from the fund was divided between the Artisans, towards the cost of a new hut, and the Benevolent Fund.

The financial situation was improving, the treasurer hoping that the club would break even in 1956 but it was still necessary to review catering costs. The solution was to ask Collinge to increase the cost of lunches by one shilling, and to offer him one quarter of the profits as an incentive. Further economies were to be made on heating and printing costs, even though a surplus was reported at the end of the year, when a new subscription scheme was devised by the Captain, Mr. Orchard-Lisle, who had been elected in recognition of all his efforts on the club's behalf in the vexing matter of the purchase of the course. Unfortunately the members were less enthusiastic than the committee, for twenty-nine resignations were received at the beginning of the new year.

Negotiations were still continuing with the County Council for the purchase of the course. Orchard-Lisle informed the committee in January 1958 that he had made an offer to them, subject to contract, of a purchase price of £14,500 for the freehold, including the steward's house, with a commitment to pay the council half of any profits the club might make from development should future development occur. Mr. Renshell then outlined the proposed financing of the scheme, which entailed the setting up of Porters Park Golf Club Properties. It would be a company with capital of £100, for which only two shares would be issued and subscribed for by trustees of the club. This company would be set up to buy the course, raising the money required by the issue of debentures, and lease it to the club for, say, fifty years, the club paying an annual rent to reimburse the Property Company for its annual outgoings. Two forms of debentures were to be offered, each in units of £50. Subscribers to series A would have their annual subscriptions reduced by two guineas, while those subscribing to series B would receive interest at five per cent per annum. On winding up debentures would be repayable at par, holders wishing to sell would be obliged to offer them to the club first, then other debenture holders, before they could be offered to an outsider. However, the Council rescinded their offer, renewed the lease, and the club had to wait a further twenty years before owning its course.

While Mr. J.A.Randall had undertaken to revise the club handbook and had taken it from draft revision through to its printed form in very quick time, the issue of the club tie was only decided after two years' discussion, agreement finally being reached in January 1957. Negotiations with the manufacturers who required a minimum order of six dozen protracted the matter even longer.

Another local club, Starveacres, a nine hole course on the other side of Radlett, was reported as having run into difficulties with the new owner of their land who intended closing the course in September. The members were offered special membership of Porters at six guineas a head, with an opportunity to join the club if properly proposed and seconded. Twenty men and six ladies expressed an interest in joining. Although a letter was received from the captain of Starveacres informing Porters that the club had taken legal proceedings to prevent disturbance of their club, it would seem that this had a short-term effect as no doubt the Starveacres members would have felt somewhat insecure. This resulted in a healthy increase in membership and led to a waiting list being instituted in July 1958 and the scrapping of second club membership shortly afterwards.

In the meantime Mr. Hinde had resigned as secretary and Mr. Albany had been re-appointed to the office. The honorary treasurer, Mr. H.T. Nicholson, also announced his resignation as he was due to leave the area, but would continue to serve until a replacement came forward. Before he left he presented a full statement of the club's financial situation, which showed, among other items, a healthy profit on the bar of £2,464. His resignation was accepted "most unwillingly" but "it was unanimously agreed to record in the minutes a hearty vote of thanks to Mr. Nicholson for his sterling work during his term of office and an appreciation of his keenness and ability which had laid the foundation of the club's financial rehabilitation." Mr. L.A. Renshell was appointed in Mr. Nicholson's place and proved equally industrious. He formed a sub-committee in October 1958 and produced what was, in effect, a three-year plan for the club's finances.

Pointing out that the club's profit was produced solely by "indoor activities", the report anticipated further increases in expenditure and members having less spendable income than in the past. Plant, machinery and equipment had to be replaced to maintain the course to the desired standard, and these items would be subject to depreciation over the years. The ground staff's wages also had to be increased. It was demonstrated that certain sections of the membership were getting cheap golf. It is hardly surprising, then, that an increase in subscriptions was the recommendation of the sub-committee.

This was reinforced by Mr. Renshell's report and accounts for the year and the committee decided to seek the authority to raise subscriptions without recourse to a vote at an A.G.M., which was duly granted at that meeting. Nevertheless, when it became clear later in the year that subscriptions would have to be increased, the Captain, Mr. J. P. Graham, still sent a letter explaining the situation to the members, the main burden being the increased cost of the new lease.

At the end of 1959 a number of retirements and resignations were recorded. Shadbolt, the long-serving locker room attendant, finally retired from his post. He had already received a clock for his services and was now voted a pension of one guinea a week. Frank Scales, the professional, was suffering serious ill-health and was replaced by Bill Large. Shortly afterwards he died and a fund set up for his widow raised £940. Another even less welcome retirement was that of the President. Mr. Everington had held the office for eight years, most of which had had their crises,

Jack Everington Captain 1946

and he was warmly thanked for all he had done on the club's behalf. Before electing Mr. R.E.A. Bott as his successor the committee agreed that in future the President should only serve for three or four years.

A solicitor, Jack Everington apparently spent a lot of time at the club but did not play much golf during his presidency. Tony Brock remembers him as "a quiet man". Tony joined in 1959, having recently moved to Radlett. A member of Hadley Wood, he found himself within walking distance of Porters Park so decided to see if he could join. He strolled into the clubhouse one Saturday morning,

84

met the secretary and two other members, one of whom was Jack Everington and the other Jack Edwards, who was to take over the captaincy a year or two later. Brock realised that both were business acquaintances. Tony's enquiry about membership received a nod from the President, the secretary left the bar and returned with a form which Tony was asked to fill in. He recalls that the amount he was asked to pay as his first subscription was the equivalent of a round of drinks and a sandwich at today's prices and could be paid "at his convenience". When asked if that meant he was a member, he was told he was and could play that same afternoon, if he so wished.

The annual report for 1959 showed a deficit of £633, attributable to repairs and improvements to house and course. There were 426 members, an increase of 17 on the previous year, of which 235 were full members – 186 men and 67 ladies. Other categories of membership increased the number to 442 in 1960 and this along with the increase in subscriptions prompted the treasurer to forecast recovery of the loss during the year. He was indeed able to confirm this in his half-yearly report, the improvement in the club's accounts being assisted by a further increase in membership.

The steward's pay also came under review and it was noted that because of the Catering Wages Act, his salary was no longer in excess of the recommended level. As it was felt that the club had a "first class steward and wife", Collinge merited an increase, which was to take his salary to £950 plus a car allowance of £50, but he would no longer be entitled to a quarter of the profits. The steward was to be informed of this by the captain, "who would take the opportunity to speak to the steward on the matter of his undesirable conduct". Collinge had been in hospital earlier in the year, which may have accounted for the behaviour of this otherwise "first class" steward. His attitude must have improved, because in March 1961 the club allowed him to hold his daughter's wedding reception in the dining room and gave her a wedding present to the value of £25. Collinge was also granted £20 towards his expenses in attending a meeting in Scotland of the Golf Club Stewards' Association of which he was a past chairman.

Returning to the matter of acquiring the freehold of the club in 1960, Morris Balch re-opened negotiations with the County Council. This eventually led, in 1964, to a renewal of the lease for 99 years at £1 a year, subject to a payment of £17,500. The property company became owners of the land and the four shareholders became the club's trustees, each holding a single share. The current shareholders are Paul Orchard-Lisle, Dennis Johnson, who became Captain in 1979, Humphrey Harlow and Reg Radcliffe. The original debentures were redeemed over a period.

PORTERS PARK GOLF CLUB

Four and a half years after a design had been approved for the club tie, specimens were produced by Mr. H.A. Chapman for the committee's inspection. Mr. Chapman felt that the design was still not quite what was wanted and stated that he would be asking for further samples.

Accommodation in a caravan and a maisonette was provided for members of the greenstaff and Ernie Page was granted thirty shillings a week from the Benevolent Fund on reaching the age of seventy. It seems that despite the occasional grumbles about the attitudes of various employees over the years, Porters Park was very conscientious in safe-guarding the welfare of the club's staff. Accordingly, when Freeborn, Shadbolt's successor as the locker room attendant, announced his retirement after thirty-six years with the club, he was given £20 and a weekly sum of thirty shillings from the Benevolent Fund, which had recently been re-invested to produce more interest.

Malcolm Reid, still very active on the club's behalf, was put in charge of the Hertfordshire Golf Union Colts section and was given permission to use the club's committee room at any time. Reference to his achievements on behalf of younger golfers will be found elsewhere in this account, but he might have been slightly disappointed in July when it was noted that there had been such an increase in junior membership that in future entry might have to be restricted to the children of existing members. Mr. Overton accepted the invitation to look after this important section of the club. One of his protégés was Campbell Boal, who joined the club at the age of twelve in January 1963.

Another dedicated worker who had devoted himself to the club's finances, Mr. Renshell, announced his wish to stand down at the 1963 A.G.M. after six years in office and Mr. A.L.M. Collins agreed to take over as treasurer but only for one year. Honorary Membership was duly conferred upon Mr. Renshell in appreciation for his efforts. Mr. Collins, having managed the affairs well enough to report a profit of £725 in 1963, agreed to be re-elected in 1964.

The ladies were provided with a new lounge and the lower terrace was paved, with financial assistance from Mr. Baucher. This feature was further enhanced when Mr. E.S. Markham, wishing to mark his diamond jubilee as a member of the club, presented a cheque to provide four teak seats bearing name plates.

Tony Brock knew Reggie Baucher through their work as chartered surveyors, Baucher having been a pupil at his old firm before Tony joined. "By all accounts he never actually did any real work when he was with my firm and he made no concessions in this respect when he moved on to become a partner in the firm of Cluttons ... (where) ... he was known as the "sleeping partner" although he would awake, fully alert, at any mention of the Chartered Surveyors' Golfing Society, of which he was a great stalwart. His rather delightful laid-back personality made him a great companion on the golf course."

A further pleasant presentation was the return of four sets of blazer buttons by an ex-member and it was suggested that these be given to present and future captains of the club.

R.A.F. Fighter Command requested that service membership be available to its officers, rather than the block membership it enjoyed, which the club felt should either be terminated or restricted to weekdays only. The latter suggestion was implemented and it became clear that a number of officers would take advantage of the new arrangements for membership.

1964 began with new honours conferred upon the club as Mr. A. Forbes Ilsley was elected President of the English Golf Union. Porters Park accordingly made him an Honorary Life Member, although Porters was in fact his second club, Mr. Ilsley being a member of Old Fold Manor. He had already served as the Hertfordshire County President from 1956 to 1962 and in 1971 became Chairman of CONGU, having been made a Vice-President of the EGU on completing his year of office.

Mrs. Albany, the secretary's wife, had received an ex gratia payment of £50 for assisting her husband with clerical duties and she continued to do so for the first months of 1964, after Mr. Albany had died suddenly. In March advertisements were placed in *The Daily Telegraph* and the *Herts Advertiser* inviting applications, several of which were soon forthcoming. Lieutenant-Colonel O.S. Steel was appointed and commenced work at the end of August.

There were 235 full male members and 72 full lady members at the start of the year and new members were elected regularly to ensure financial stability. This had the effect, brought to the committee's attention by Mr. R.G. Wilson in November, of slowing up play, as many new members were high-handicappers. It was therefore necessary to consider limiting membership and the question of a waiting list, which was deemed unnecessary. A preliminary step towards this was the proposal by the treasurer, Mr. C.W. Greaves, that subscriptions be increased by 60%, but an amendment that they only be increased by 20% was carried, but members over sixty-five years of age, having been members for fifteen years would be granted a reduction.

This meant that full and service members in January 1966, would be asked to pay £30; members between the ages of twenty-five and thirty, £16; those between eighteen and twenty-five, £10. Full lady members would be charged £20.10s., with a reduction of £3 if their husbands were members. Other categories were also increased. This enabled a three-year plan to be devised, taking into account capital expenses. Fourteen resignations were noted in January and six more in February, but these were more than offset by elections and regradings. Having drawn up this scheme, Mr. Greaves left the club to live abroad and Mr. E.A. Judge took over as treasurer.

Mr. Paul Orchard-Lisle was elected to the committee, preserving family continuity in running the affairs of the club. He had taken on the responsibility for the junior section the previous December. As well as becoming the youngest Captain of the club in 1971, he was instrumental in acquiring the freehold of the club, thus completing a task his father had set out to achieve. This is described in the chapter on the course. He also raised £12,500 towards the cost of a new professional's shop.

Jimmy Tarbuck was elected to five-day membership in March but more importantly for the future of the club, Nigel Notley joined as a junior member in June and Mr. and Mrs. W.A. de Podesta were elected full members in November, with effect from the following March. Wilf de Podesta became secretary and then President of the County Golf Union, a position he relinquished in 1996 after long and dedicated service to Hertfordshire golf. He then became Chairman of the South-East Group of the EGU, finally retiring from administration at the end of 1997.

Membership continued to increase, rising to 577 in February 1967, of which 331 were full members (247 men and 84 ladies) and it was decided that future applications would have to be considered "more stringently". This had created a more healthy financial situation and a surplus was reported for 1966 in line with the treasurer's forecast. The ceiling on full male membership was reached in April, with 253 full men and no further applications for that category were to be considered. However, a figure of 254 was reported later that month, when junior membership totalled 56 including 6 girls. It was agreed that the future intake of juniors would have to be monitored very carefully.

A threat to the financial health of the club was perceived in November when the introduction of the breathalyser was looming. As there were a number of projects pending in the clubhouse and on the course, the captain wrote to the members, outlining these and the possible effect on bar profits once the breathalyser came into operation. Full subscriptions for men were raised to £40, £25 for ladies, and the entry fee became £25. This naturally caused a number of resignations but there were sufficient applications and re-grades to maintain a viable level of membership, 244 full men and 73 full lady members being the figure in February 1968. Unforeseen additional expenses occurred when the cost of repainting the assistant secretary's office was over its budget due to an outbreak of woodworm and when the committee responded to the following item in the suggestions book:

Of one fact I am now quite certain,
The smoke-room badly needs a curtain.
I cannot drink while ladies watch;
It makes me coy and I slop my scotch.
Then sometimes, when I take a nap,
Upon the window they will tap,
Crying "cooee, cooee", or some broader jest,
So ruining my hard-earned rest.
One Tuesday, while taking tea,
Above the din of bacchanalian spree,
I heard the words that froze my bone,
"He's here again – this time alone!"
And fearing what they'd do to me,
I scampered home to sanctuary.
This I have set out, the committee to convince,
Whatever else is wanted, the priority is chintz!

As at least twenty-three members appended signatures to this ditty it is impossible to credit the poet with his work, but Colonel Steel proved worthy of the challenge in responding:

The committee wept o'er your sad plight,
For they feel sure that you are right.
One thing is absolutely certain
It's essential that you have a curtain,
And we will do our level best
To ensure that you enjoy your rest.
We trust that, in sleep, you do not snore,
For that would really be a bore.
We wish you sweet and pleasant dreams,
Undisturbed by female screams.

On a more prosaic note, another member added a footnote to the suggestion "If approved, curtains available at trade prices." The house committee agreed to attend to the matter but it is not minuted whether it accepted the offer quoted above. Their approval of the secretary's reply was duly noted, however.

The club's continued interest in the welfare of the staff was exemplified further when a non-contributory pension fund was set up. Employees who had already retired would continue to receive pensions from the club's funds, but the professional was excluded as his association could make arrangements for him.

The treasurer in 1969 was Mr. D.J. Cumming, who caused some concern when he presented his report, as he and the auditor had discovered errors in the two preceding years' accounts. Commitments in respect of the Property Company had been understated which meant the accounts should have shown losses rather than profits for the years in question. Had this been known previously the deficit could have been made up by an increase in subscriptions. As it was, the members had gained by the error. Fortunately the breathalyser had not caused a decline in bar profits, although catering profits were down, and other expenses had increased, including insurance premiums, as several other clubs had also been seriously damaged by fire. He therefore deemed an increase in subscriptions to be necessary in 1970. At the time of Mr. Cumming's report the club had 241 full men members and 76 full ladies.

A few months later, the situation was not quite so healthy – bar receipts had fallen during the early part of the year, as had catering profits and green fees. Even the fruit machine takings were £250 less than normal, a situation exacerbated by the fact that with the introduction of decimalisation, as well as a gaming machine tax, the following year the club's machines would no longer be legal, which meant that there would be no point in purchasing them. Selective Employment Tax also increased the club's bills. By this time Mr. Cumming had become Captain of the club and Mr. J.F. Tweddle was the new treasurer. He forecast a deficit for the year.

Although the Trust Deed between the Property Company and the Debenture Holders had been altered the previous year, because all entry fees were paid to the property company and a number of debentures were due for redemption, it was suggested that these be re-issued. A sub-committee was set up to investigate all possibilities and eventualities and they reported back to the committee some months later, in October 1970, with their recommendations, which were to increase the number of debentures and to permit the Property Company to re-issue them, making any necessary amendments and changes to the Trust Deed between the club and the company.

Mr. Tweddle also proposed an increase in the number of members and in the entry fee, which would obviate the need for an increase in subscriptions. However, the committee did not wish to increase the membership by the recommended twenty-five, though they would consider admitting extra members if they were considered suitable.

The treasurer's report the following February blamed the gaming and selective employment taxes for the deficit on the year's accounts which would otherwise have been avoided. This was the month in which Mr. and Mrs. Collinge retired after sixteen years' loyal service, having been granted redundancy and other payments. Mr. and Mrs. D. Stewart were appointed in their place.

Paul Orchard-Lisle produced a detailed feasibility study with a view to forming a squash club at Porters, which was favourably received and it was decided to apply for a grant of £6,750 from public funds. Radlett Squash Club willingly supplied advice as to the correct procedure. Eventually it was reported that the grant for this project would not be forthcoming.

Under the terms of the club's lease with the Greater London Council, the public were permitted to play before 8.00 a.m. on Mondays and Wednesdays and also after 3.00 p.m. on Wednesdays. The G.L.C. intended publicising this, but the club decided to take no action. It would seem that it was not until 1974 that public usage of the course became noticeable, when the club disagreed with the Council over the term "curtilage" with regard to the members car park, as the club claimed the public had no right to use this facility. This was not a petty decision, as the car park had been deemed inadequate in 1970 and plans had been made to enlarge it, which would involve moving the Artisans' hut.

That was part of a much larger scheme of works, including altering and redecorating the mixed bar, hopefully with the support of the brewery, upgrading the central heating system, building a new professional's shop, either as part of the building housing the squash courts, if they were approved, or enlarging the existing one, and remodelling the kitchen. As

Ken Richardson at his driving-in ceremony, 1973 watched by left to right: Adrian Frost, Bar Harding, Paul Orchard-Lisle, Morris Balch, Douglas Cumming, Jack Ramsden (Pro.)

Geoff Platt, Eric Cheadle and Don Langrish-Smith at a Porters Park Prize Plan evening

there had been fewer complaints about locker room facilities in the past year, Mr. Hewitt, chairman of the sub-committee, did not consider enlargement necessary, provided the number of full men members remained at 250. This scheme was assisted by the proposed changes in the relationship between the club and the Property Company outlined above.

The club's finances, not helped much by the gaming machines, were given a boost by The Porters Park Prize Plan, which had quickly attracted over 120 subscribers. This short-lived scheme terminated in May 1971 by which time it had contributed significantly to club funds.

Colonel Steel intimated to the committee that he wished to retire at the end of March 1971 and the appropriate advertisements, placed in the national and golfing press, met with a good response, resulting in the appointment of Past Captain, Tony Randall. Owen Steel received a testimonial of £550, from which he was authorised to buy himself a commemorative carriage clock.

Problems arose again in 1977 when the local authority investigated the implementation of the two public days agreed in the original Middlesex County Council lease. The club had chosen to ignore this because it was felt the Artisans section met the requirements. Evidently it didn't and the club was told that it must offer two days for public play. This stimulated renewed interest in the purchase of the freehold, and Paul Orchard-Lisle headed the team which negotiated with the new Greater London Council. As 84 years of the lease at £1 per year were still to run, the club was offered the freehold for £17,500, a sum which would have purchased three attractive houses in the area at that time, although it may seem little in modern terms. There was a condition – if the club sold any of its land, for whatever reason, half of the proceeds would be payable to the London Residual Body (the authority dealing with former County Council properties since the dissolution of the G.L.C.). The purchase went ahead, using all available cash reserves, causing a complete restructuring of finances in 1981.

All debentures issued since 1964 were brought together, raising £65,000. They are due to be completely repaid by 2009 and so, effectively, fund the purchase of the freehold over thirty years.

With the captain as chief executive the club continued to be run by the committee, who decided that now the freehold had been acquired, the clubhouse should be suitably enhanced. After discussions with members it was decided that nothing less than a major rebuild was necessary. During the late 1980s subscriptions were increased to unprecedented levels, something previous committees had feared, and thus failed, to do; had they done so many of the club's past financial difficulties would certainly have been eased. In 1988 men's subscriptions were increased to £305 and ladies' to £255, followed by equally large increases in each subsequent year: 1989: £355/300; 1990: £435/365; 1991: £533/427 until by 1996 men were paying £798, and the ladies £639, representing increases respectively of 162% and 150% since 1988.

Half the cost of the new clubhouse was raised, partly by members' loans, by the time the work was completed in 1991 at a total cost of £1M. The club was committed to repay the loans by the end of March 1997.

As the chief executive the captain only held office for one year and a further year as vice-captain, creating a certain lack of continuity in running the club's affairs. It was decided to set up a Board of Management to look after long-term interests, finance, staff relations and the course. The committee would be responsible for golf and social arrangements. Things did not go according to plan, however, and with the club's finances in disarray the captain and committee took over the responsibility for running the club at the end of 1996. The Board of Management had been created to achieve continuity of financial and planning decisions. Reverting to control by committee would run the risk of short-termism creeping back in. A new role of chairman was created to counter this problem. Under the chairmanship of Ted Hurcomb, the finances were restabilised by 1997. Members' loans were restructured, becoming repayable on request after 2002, or on resignation, and in any case only after outstanding debentures had been repaid. No further debentures are to be issued but the four trustees retain their individual shares in the property company. Ted Hurcomb resigned as Chairman in January 1998, and was replaced by committee member Keith Hughes.

Helping to implement these changes, Peter Phillips has been associated with the club since 1986, when he was assistant secretary to Mike Stamford, John Roberts and then Bob Springall, whom he succeeded as secretary in 1997. Prior to that he had been a long-standing member of the Artisans.

Another means of saving money over these difficult years had been the experiment with franchised catering. Since the Collinges' departure, the Stewarts, then Tom Williams, had looked after the bar and catering. When Williams left, Mrs. Fallon took the first franchise in 1980, her husband being employed by the club as barman. By 1983 and after Mrs. Fallon had been succeeded by two more franchised caterers, the club realised it would be better off with an employed chef and Brian Overington moved into the club's kitchen, his wife becoming steward. They remained with the club for fourteen years before they had their contracts terminated.

Ice House on 3rd

Captains Prize.
June 8 & 15th 1912
Presented by E.W. Whitehead Esq
36 Holes Medal, the first 8 to qualify
for Match Play

H. L. Stephens	169 - 12 = 157	
C H Watson	195 - 36 = 159.	
A A Barron	173 - 12 = 161	
L. J. Clayton	161 - Scr = 161	Qualify.
D Von Braun	173 - 12 = 161	
A Blake	185 - 24 = 161	
A W Hymelay	168 - 6 = 162	
Maj Creagh	186 - 24 = 162	
I E. Negretti	169 - 6 = 163	
E N. Kent	175 - 12 = 163	
E S Markham	167 - Scr = 167	
A L Scott	181 - 14 = 167.	
J A Bates	191 - 22 = 169	

H Stephens ⎫ Stephens ⎫
A.W. Hymelay ⎬ ⎬ Creagh ⎫
A Blake ⎫ Creagh ⎬ ⎬ Both
Maj Creagh ⎬ ⎭ disqualified
C Watson ⎫ ⎫ Barron ⎬
A A Barron ⎬ Barron ⎬ ⎭
D Von Braun ⎫ ⎫
L J. Clayton ⎬ Clayton ⎭

What's the story behind this?

95

Chapter Seven

Club Competitions

N O SOONER had the club been formed than a competition was arranged. This was the first monthly medal, open to members who had paid their subscriptions, to be played on Saturday 15th April, for a sweepstake of 2s.6d. each to the winner; a substantial sum in those days, particularly as the committee which had set that entry fee proposed a similar sum for a guest's green fee. Unfortunately we have no record to tell us who pocketed the half-crowns. It was not until October that the committee got round to allocating handicaps for which members were required to complete two cards over eighteen holes.

Prizes were put up by the President, for a half-yearly competition on Boxing Day and Whit-Sunday, and by the Captain. The Part Cup was to observe the same conditions as the President's Prize (Grace Cup) and was to be played for on Easter Monday and the first Saturday in November. The Final Medal was to be played annually on the Saturday preceding Easter Sunday (creating a busy weekend of competition) "for a medal to be presented by the club *or otherwise*". It is evident that the golfers of Porters were already competitive and reasonably confident, because a challenge was accepted from the West Herts club for a match on 19th May 1900, at Porters for a team of eight men. Alas, there is no record of the result. This fixture was repeated the following year and Bushey Hall were challenged to a match.

That the competition bug was biting is illustrated by the presentation of two more cups in June 1901, one for a bogey competition from Mr. G.W. Jones and another from Mr. F.W. Kells for a 36 hole medal, with a handicap limit of 18.

Porters' golfers were now sufficiently confident to accept an away challenge and duly travelled to Bushey Hall in April 1902. We do not have a record of the result but *Golf Illustrated* of 11th April did record the result of the medal held on 31st March, which was won by Major Creagh with a nett 80 off his handicap of 22. D.C. Part and J.H. Robson tied for second place with nett 83 each, Part playing off 9 and Robson 14.

An offer of a small silver salver, to be competed for on the August Bank Holiday, was accepted from Mr. Grimwood, and in 1903 a major competition was initiated when Mr. A.A. Rumsey presented two goblets for a foursomes competition.

By now the ladies had begun arranging their own competitions and two Wednesdays a month were allocated for medal and bogey competitions.

Another fine tradition was inaugurated in June 1903 when it was unanimously agreed to award silver buttons to the winners of monthly medals. The indefatigable Dr. Smyth was asked to "procure" designs for approval. At the same meeting it was proposed that quarterly bogey competitions be held on the second Saturdays in March, June, September and December. The winners of these handicap competitions would receive a prize to the value of £2 for the entry fee of one shilling. The prizes for the Grace and Part cups were increased to £3 each. These events became the responsibility of Messrs. Thomas and Lohr.

In the event, it was Mr. Haws who presented the design that was accepted for the silver buttons and the same pattern was used for the brooches which the ladies awarded to the winners of their monthly medals. It was fortunate that the Past President's trophy was called the Grace Cup, because Mr. Raphael chose to mark his succession to the Presidency by presenting a challenge cup called The President's Prize, now known as the Raphael Trophy. This was an 18 hole matchplay knockout, which was to be played

for in April, although as it was already July 1903 that year's contest was started in October. Any player winning the trophy three times became the outright holder; in the meantime the winner would receive a memento worth £3 and the runner-up a prize valued at £1. The entrance fee was 2s.6d.

The Captain of the year, Mr. Thomas, also presented a prize, to be retained by the winner. From the conditions stipulated, he deserved to do so. The competition was to be held on the last three Saturdays in November, two rounds of 18 holes medal play, handicap limit 18, the two rounds to be played on any of the three Saturdays or one round on one Saturday and one on either of

E.W. Thomas Captain 1903

the others, provided that it was the first round of the day. Without the benefit of long-range weather forecasting the competitors must have had intriguing and frustrating decisions to make about their choice of days to play. The four competitors returning the lowest scores for the two rounds were to play in the finals by heats and holes under handicap. The first round to be played off by the 12th December and the final by the end of the year 1903. The entrance fee was the standard 2s.6d and the runner up received a prize to the value of £2.

On retiring as Captain, Mr. Thomas presented a Challenge Cup for the lowest two medal scores on aggregate in each year's medal competitions, with a handicap limit of 12 – further evidence of the improving standard of golf at Porters. This cup could be retained by anyone who succeeded in winning it three times, a fate that had already befallen the Grace Cup, for Mr. A.E. Colebrook, the Captain elect, had already laid claim to this trophy. He later presented it to the Past Captain's Circle where it is displayed at their annual dinner. His offer of a new trophy to replace it was therefore gratefully accepted. The Colebrook Cup would be played for under the same conditions as the Grace Cup.

A competition for groundsmen and caddies was arranged by Mr. G.W. Jones in 1903 and he was also instrumental in bringing a team of "Scotch" golfers to the club in 1905. They were given the courtesy of the course for the day on 28th April.

The first breaches of competition regulations were noted in a letter to the committee in April 1905 when Mr. Moores complained that four players had played their President's Prize matches after the closing date stipulated. There was no decision recorded as to what was done about this. Later in the year Mrs. Farmer protested her disqualification in the ladies medal, having forgotten that she had failed to pay her subscription.

The election of Dr. Smyth to the captaincy brought the offer of the Shenley Cup, 18 holes against bogey, to be played for on the August Bank Holiday and the last Saturday in February. The prize would be worth £3, the runner-up receiving £1. Dr. Smyth also agreed to present a Captain's Prize under similar conditions to previous competitions.

The next prize to be offered was for a mixed foursomes competition, Mr. A.C. Cory-Wright being thanked for his kindness. 11th November was the date set for the first encounter. The ladies were clearly making their mark, for in February 1906, Dr. Martin offered a challenge cup for them to play a 36 hole medal off handicap on the second Wednesdays in May and November. The lady winning it three times would retain it and the prizes were worth £1 to the winner, ten shillings to the runner-up.

A more contentious issue was raised in September of that year when Mr. Mudie complained that Mr. E.S. Markham had won the Shenley Cup playing in a threeball match which was against the rules. After a lengthy discussion he was disqualified.

Another moot point was raised in the suggestions book that 18 should be the maximum handicap for competitions. The committee felt it had no power to alter the conditions under which trophies had been presented and that this was a decision for a general meeting. This arose partly from the decision made in November to increase single figure handicaps by two and all other double figure handicaps by one. This action prompted an offer from Mr. Haws of a prize for members whose handicaps had been put up by one – roughly the equivalent of modern handicap categories 3 and 4. It was decided that a bogey competition be played on the third and fourth Saturdays in June over 36 holes, with the option of playing both rounds in one day. The entrance fee was one shilling and three prizes were offered. Mr. Haws' suggestion that a draw be made for partners was rejected owing to the difficulty of making draws for 36 hole competitions and a notice was posted drawing the competition to the members' attention. The rules for bogey competitions published by *Golf Illustrated* in 1905 were adopted, being recognised as official by the club.

One sad development was that there were no inter-club matches that year, no reason being given in the minutes, nor did the club enter the London Foursomes the following year.

The next matter to cause concern was the number of ladies' competitions. A letter was received from Mrs. Smyth, the Ladies' Captain, complaining that new holes had not been cut for their medal in February and that the tees were bad. Not only that, as the secretary explained in a letter to Mrs. Smyth, the greens had not been rolled either and in future new holes would be cut for ladies' competitions when necessary. This gave rise to an investigation into the number of competitions played by the ladies. When it was discovered that there were 27, for which entrance fees amounting to £1.5s.0d had been taken, against prizes to the value of £11.7s.0d. it was quickly resolved that the ladies be recommended not to hold competitions between October 1st and March 31st and that there should be six medals, three bogey competitions and two cup competitions in the summer months, with entrance fees of one shilling each for medals and bogeys. An interesting ramification of the matter was that Mrs. Smyth had been disqualified from the competition as her card had not been marked by a member of a recognised golf club. Dr. Smyth's views are not recorded.

The ladies also competed very successfully in their inter-club matches in 1906, beating Bushey Hall by 6¼ to 1¾, Highgate less convincingly 3¼ to 3 points and annihilating Muswell Hill ladies by 7 points to ¼. Mrs. Smyth played a prominent part in these victories.

The gentlemen also resumed inter-club matches in 1906, beating Bushey

Hall on 12th May by a quarter of a point. Dr. Smyth lost his game but C.L. Richmond won his to secure the victory in the final match.

A tie between Mr. J. Pope and Mr. R. Stephens for the Thomas Cup resulted in a 36 hole medal play-off.

Mr. Humble became Captain in 1908 and offered to present the Captain's Prize under what were becoming traditional conditions and Mr. A.A. Barron offered to present The Barron Cup to replace the Colebrook Cup which he had won outright. Unfortunately his initial conditions were unacceptable to the committee and he was asked to attend the next committee meeting when he agreed to the original terms of the Colebrook Cup. The same meeting also acknowledged the gift of two challenge cups for a foursomes competition from Mr. W.H. Lynch and Mr. E.W. Whitehead to be played for annually under conditions decided by the committee. This was a handicap matchplay knockout open only to club members who could select their own partners. The usual rules about triple winners obtained and the entry fee was 2s.6d.

Perhaps of more importance was a new table of stroke indexes following the changes to the order of play.

There was no doubt that the golf at Porters was improving and in July 1908 Mr. C.L. Richmond's handicap was reduced from 7 to 5. The following month his offer of a Scratch Cup was gratefully accepted by the club. Further evidence of the higher standard of play may be adduced from Mr. Humble's suggestion, to be put to the next A.G.M., that a maximum handicap of 18 be imposed on future club competitions. As this meeting was not due for another six months, in the interim, at a Special General Meeting in February 1909, the adoption of two divisions was recommended: Seniors 12 handicap and under, Juniors 13 handicap and over. A full list of competitions was drawn up, the Final Medal having to be played before Good Friday, the Church of England's request that no competitions be played on that day having been honoured by the club. They made up for it by having three days of competitions on Easter Saturday, Monday and Tuesday.

Matches with South Herts and Hendon were arranged on a home and away basis, although Porters were only prepared to play the latter at first team level despite the request for a second team match as well. The difficulty of raising teams was demonstrated in 1910 when no club matches were played.

In 1911 the ladies gained control of their own competitions and the men lost the ledger recording their medal results! In 1912 the ladies were given permission to hold an Open Meeting and the men entered the London Foursomes. One year later they decided to alternate the medal competitions with bogeys but this was short-lived, as all competitions were suspended for the duration of the war. However, when competitive golf resumed after the war this scheme continued until 1930, when a medal with an optional bogey sweep was re-instated on the final Saturday and first Wednesday of each month. The only match played during the hostilities was against the Royal Flying Association, who were entertained by the club on 3rd June 1917.

Competitions resumed on Boxing Day 1918 with a medal in aid of the British Red Cross Society and monthly medals recommenced in January 1919. It would appear that silver medal buttons were no longer awarded to the winners of these competitions, for in March it was decided that memento prizes would not be awarded, nor would there be an Open Meeting nor a Final Medal. Monthly medal winners were presented with silver spoons instead of buttons. Otherwise competitions would be as in 1914. The Captain, Mr. Thomas, offered a cup for 36 holes medal play off handicap to supplement the growing number of club trophies. The next such offer came in 1921 when the friends of the late Ernest Whitehead offered a perpetual challenge cup in his memory. The Whitehead Trophy was a magnificent silver inkstand (an exact replica of one in the Houses of Parliament) which unfortunately was stolen from a member's house a few years ago. It has been replaced by two salvers.

Some idea of the playing ability of our early members can be deduced from the result of a match with Old Fold Manor on 12th May, 1921. The Captain, E.S. Markham, and A.E. Phillips played off +2, J.H. Skelton, M.J. Clayton and C.L. Richmond, scratch, C.C. Arnell and Lt.-Col. Rolleston, 3 and J.H. Raphael, 4. Porters won, away, 7½ to 3½.

By 1925 the 36 hole events were declining in popularity with what may have been an ageing membership and the captain decided that the Dearbergh Cup be contested over 18 holes, with the opportunity to play a second round if desired. As this had proved successful the committee decided that the Barron Cup would be played under the same conditions.

In 1926 C.M. Humble presented the President's Challenge Salver in which the top 16 in a medal qualify for matchplay knockout. It was renamed the Humble Salver in 1946.

Mr. A.A. Nathan donated a challenge cup in 1927 for a mixed greensome competition. It was suggested that an 18 hole medal be played off half combined handicap, the first eight pairs qualifying for a matchplay knockout to be played under three-eighths difference in combined handicaps. This was the year of the first recorded match against Radlett Cricket Club on 24th April. Played off handicap, the match was halved.

The first veterans' competition was arranged and took place on 19th July 1930, when those members who had passed their fifty-fifth birthday competed in an 18 hole bogey. The Whitehead Challenge Trophy was

Match.

Porters Park v Radlett Cricket Club.
Sunday, April 24th, 1927.

Porters Park — Morning Foursomes — Cricket Club.

Porters Park			Cricket Club	
Major Burton (Ser.) A.G. Snelling (Ser.)	4/3	1. v	R.H. Baucher (2) Miles Brunton (4)	0.
E.S. Markham (Ser.) G.F. Roberts (1)		1. v	T.P. Norris (6) Major Raderick (7)	0.
J.P. Hall (2) J.D. Swinstead (2)	0. v	A.W.H. Baucher (8) R. Woodbridge (9)	6/5	1.
C.C. Arnell (2) C. McKenzie (4)	0. v	L.J. Reid (14) G. Goodyear (14)	3/2	1.
Major Chandler (6) T.J. Lane (8)	1 up	1. v	Jack Baucher (15) A.W. Knee (20)	0.
F.A.B. Farquharson (9) J. Hallam (18)	0. v	J.V. Upsdale (20) H.J. Knee (20)	3/2	1.
		3.		**3.**

under handicap

Porters Park v Cricket Club.
Singles — under handicap.

Porters Park			Cricket Club	
A.G. Snelling (9)	0. v	R.J. Baucher (2)	1 up	1.
E.S. Markham (Ser.)	1. v	Miles Brunton (4)	0.
G.F. Roberts (1)	0. v	T.P. Norris (6)	3/1. 1.
J.P. Hall (2)	6/5 1. v	Major Raderick (7)	0.
J.D. Swinstead (2)	0. v	A.W.H. Baucher (8)	2/1. 1.
C.C. Arnell (2)	4/3 1. v	R. Woodbridge (9)	0.
C. McKenzie (4)	0. v	L.J. Reid (14)	2/1. 1.
Major Chandler (6)	0. v	G. Goodyear (14)	1.
G.S.A. Wheatcroft (7)	1/2. v	Jack Baucher (15)	1/2.
H.J. Lane (8)	4/3 1. v	A.W. Knee (20)	0.
F.A.B. Farquharson (9)	1/2. v	J.V. Upsdale (20)	1/2.
J. Hallam (8)	4/4 1. v	H.J. Knee (20)	0.
	6.		**6.**

102

changed to a fourball bogey, the club retaining the trophy and the winners receiving mementoes.

Dick Bott was permitted to arrange a private match against the Cambridge University team on 8th March 1931, provided no cost was incurred by the club. [It is a pleasing conjecture that the inimitable Henry Longhurst might have played in this match. It is known that he took his team, when he was Captain, to Verulam to be coached by Abe Mitchell.] An earlier match against the University had been played in 1922, which was halved 6 – 6 and in which the famous amateur Eustace Storey played for Cambridge.

More matches were arranged in 1932, this time against West Herts, Oxhey, Old Fold Manor, The Metropolitan Police and the masters at Aldenham School. Mr. Thomas requested that the Thomas Cup be renamed the Ernest Thomas Cup and be played for to be won outright that year, to which the committee assented. This decision must have been reversed because it is still played for today.

The English Golf Union, founded in 1924, was beginning to assert its authority by this time and introduced a new standard scratch score system with effect from January 1933. As a result Porters Park had to raise the handicap limits for competitions. The Senior division limit was increased to 12 and the Junior division encompassed handicaps 13–24.

Ashridge and Harpenden joined the previous year's opponents for club matches, but a request from Moor Park seems to have been rejected. Another trophy was presented to the club when Mr. R.O. Burlison donated a cup in aid of the Benevolent Fund. This was to be contested in two periods, May, June and July and then October and November.

Highgate were unsuccessful in their bid for a fixture with the club in 1934 but Trinity College, Cambridge enjoyed better fortune. Mr. G.F. Roberts won the Shenley Cup outright and the customary offer to replace it was accepted. The troubles of the 1930s had considerable influence on midweek competitive golf, for in 1935 Ladies' Open meetings were abolished and the King George V became a competition for the previous year's Senior division medal winners, held concurrently with the June monthly medal. Fortunately this was only necessary for that year, as in 1936 it reverted to a 36 hole competition with scratch and handicap prizes.

Five trophies (Shenley Cup, Grace Cup, Part Challenge Cup, Paper Trade Challenge Cup and Colebrook Cup) are no longer played for because they were won outright under the three years in a row rule. Sometimes trophies were re-presented, as in the case of the Grace Cup to the Past Captains' Circle, and Mr. and Mrs. Bott re-presented the Mixed Foursomes Cup in 1931 after three consecutive wins. When C.L. Richmond presented the Richmond Trophy in 1908 he made it a condition that it was never to be won outright.

— Barron Challenge Cup —
- 1936 -

R.E.Q. Bott.	69 - 3 = 66 . Course Re-play 8/36
Q.C.McCarthy	86 - 20 = 66 .
R.H.Burdon Cooper.	85 - 18 = 67.
T.F.Mitchell	82 - 14 = 68
W.Q.Gray	78 - 7 = 71.
V.Grindtich,	75 - 3 = 72.
R.V.Henderson.	78 - 5 = 73.
E.Arnold	84 - 10 = 74
V.R.Grundy.	84 - 10 = 74.
V.H.Stelton	82 - 7 = 75.
M.H.Robinson	93 - 18 = 75.
L.G.Hutchinson	92 - 16 = 76.
H.S.Lane.	98 - 22 = 76.
M.Q.Holzapfel	96 - 20 = 76.
Q.Sumner.	93 - 17 = 76.

Ties for strokeplay trophies were played off over 18 or 36 holes until the late 1930s, when the card count-back came into use. Trophies played for under bogey conditions were changed to Stableford in 1970. (The Stableford scoring system devised by Dr. Stableford of Wallasey became generally accepted in 1931 after earlier prototypes were used at the Doctor's clubs in South Wales earlier this century.)

The two period format of the Benevolent Cup only lasted for the first year, 1933, a further change in format coming in 1938, when ladies were allowed to enter and multiple entries were permitted over the holiday weekend.

In 1935 Ivan Maltby presented the Maltby Challenge Cup, for the best performance in matchplay against the professional each year. It started out as a singles match, then in 1969 became a fourball against the Captain and the professional and is now a foursome against them.

Dick Bott set a new course record of 69 in June 1936 while playing in the Barron Cup. His score actually equalled the score of Mr. C.J. Anderson in the 1934 Open Meeting but as the course had been lengthened since then it was decided that Mr. Bott was now the record holder. This was soon equalled by A.G. Snelling in his second round of the K.G.V., to take the trophy. His record stood until 1951 when L.W.G. Perkins of Grim's Dyke reduced it by one stroke.

A review of club competition results in November 1937 demonstrated that the majority of matchplay and bogey competitions during recent years had been won by low handicapped players. In future the full handicap allowance would be given, to a maximum of one stroke per hole. However, this idea only lasted a year and in December 1938 the club returned to the previous allowances. It was during this period that the club's team enjoyed success in the Star Foursomes Tournament. A team consisting of Dick Bott partnered by J. Grimditch, A.G. Snelling and R. St. B. Emmott, and P.C. Burton with A.R.M. Harding beat Royal Wimbledon 2–1 at Moor Park in 1937 and the following year the same team and pairings beat Langley Park 3–0.

The James Bradbeer Cup was presented by Mr. G.F. Roberts in 1937 for a competition to be played the next spring in aid of the National Playing Fields Association, all the 2s.6d. entry fees going to the Association's funds.

The club's first victory in the Herts Club Championship came in 1939 on the home green, R.D Henderson (74+76=150), A.R.M. Harding (76+77=153) and J.M. Darroch (77+76=153) securing the trophy.

With the outbreak of war all competitions were cancelled until January 1940, but in December the committee reversed its decision and permitted medals and bogeys. Then it was decided to hold an Open Competition for men and ladies at Easter in aid of the Red Cross. In April further concessions were made to competitive golfers: the Raphael Prize, the Rumsey Goblets, Mixed Foursomes and the Barron and Roberts Challenge Cups would all take place. Later, the results of these competitions were expunged from the record. These competitions were resumed after the hostilities and continue to this day, although some variations in their respective formats have occurred from time to time.

A variety of matches against other clubs have been played since the war, including the first match against the Artisans in 1946. The Herts Constabulary and Metropolitan Police 'S' Division have been entertained, as have R.A.F. Fighter Command, London University and the second teams from Oxford and Cambridge, the 'Divots' and the 'Stymies'. Clubs from outside the county include Royal Cinque Ports and Penrith. The formation of the Herts Scratch League in 1986 led to a reduction in friendly matches with local clubs but brought success in the League, which Porters have won three times, twice under the leadership of Sandy McCallum and most recently in 1997 under Phil Tolley.

The First Team programme begins with a squad get-together when the over-35s play the under-35s, and friendly matches with Collingtree Park and the Herts Boys. As well as the Scratch League the club plays in the Evening Foursomes League and enters teams in the Knebworth Gold Bowl, the London Amateur Foursomes and the Hudson Trophy at South Herts, a club also celebrating its centenary in 1999. Porters have won this trophy four times, the most recent being 1988, when David Gleeson, Bruce Sandford, Paul Tolley and Richard Latham represented the club.

The post-war years have also seen a large addition to the number of trophies: in 1968 Bernard Coral presented the Coral Salver for a winter foursomes knockout competition; and the Hangover Stakes, a foursomes Stableford, was started in 1974. It is played the morning after the Men's Dinner and partners are drawn. A book is run, bets placed and any profits go into Douglas' Hospital Jar.

In 1976 it was decided that the Club Championship should be decided by matchplay. Previously the club champion was the winner of the 36 hole Richmond medal. The Past Captains' Circle presented a salver for the new competition. The first eight in the Richmond now qualify for the matchplay championship.

Jack Ramsden (Pro.) and Eric Cheadle,
Captain's Day 1974

The weekly Thursday Eclectic competition was started in 1977 by Alec Wilson and Ted Hurcomb to encourage full members to use the course during the week. The committee was somewhat reluctant to sanction this event but after a slow start (eleven played on the first night) and with the later introduction of five-day members the turn-out increased and it has become a very popular competition with its own dinner and prizegiving. A mixed eclectic, which was started unofficially in the late 1980s by Paul Harrington Brown, takes place every Friday evening, while the Winter Foursomes Stableford competition was initiated by Peter Phillips in 1993. This takes place once a month from November to March and has proved very popular at a time of year when there is little competitive golf.

Meanwhile in 1991 Paul Orchard-Lisle presented the President's Cup for a strokeplay competition for all the medal, matchplay and trophy winners throughout the year and also initiated the match between sides selected by invitation by the President and the Captain, the match being followed by supper.

A year later the Paul Harrington Brown Four Nations Charity Day was started in his memory. The money raised goes to various cancer charities. Teams of four are made up, by country, from all categories of membership. The trophy for the winning country was made by Brian Young and Henry Abercrombie.

Ronnie Samuels presented a salver for the Porters Park Mid-Amateur in 1993. This is a 36 hole event for men over thirty-five. In the same year an Order of Merit was instituted in response to the county starting the Herts Golf Union Members Cup, for which each club in Hertfordshire is invited to send a representative competitor. Ours is chosen by taking the best performance in eight nominated events.

Three matches played within the club are worthy of note, for while camaraderie is evident, the intense rivalry between the English and Scottish

Representing Club, County and Country in the European Champion Club Tournament at Aloha in 1985. Richard Latham, Paul Tolley, Andrew Cotton and Campbell Boal

teams, the Yorkists and Lancastrians and the Irish and the Welsh in their respective matches ensures keen, highly competitive golf.

Nearly every golf club in England includes amongst its members exiles from the true home of golf and Porters is no exception. It is inevitable that national rivalry rears its head from time to time and in 1968 this led to a challenge match at Porters. This first match was foursomes, played between teams of eight, selected on merit by the respective captains. For many years these were Tony Randall for England and Eric "Sinkey" Sinclair for Scotland, the latter abetted by Arthur Sanderson. Sadly, none of these are still with us. The result of the match is determined by the number of holes up over the full eighteen holes, the losing team paying for the port, the winning team receiving the Arthur Sanderson/Tony Randall trophy.

The current captains are Phil Marsh for England and John Liddle for Scotland and teams have been increased to twenty a side. Originally the dinner was held in a pub at Tyttenhanger but since the club's dining facilities have been improved, it is now held in the clubhouse.

Despite suggestions made by gentlemen such as Paul Harrington Brown, the Ireland v. Wales match was not inaugurated until 1982, when Ken Richardson, a Welshman, was club President. Jim Connell captained Wales and Paddy Watters, Ireland. They remained "in office" for three years, when Llewellyn Rees and Paul Harrington Brown took over. They did the

107

job for two years, since when it has been an annual appointment. Brian Young and Henry Abercrombie presented a trophy in 1986. The match is a fourball with all matches going to the eighteenth and the result based on holes up. Players have either to be born in their respective country or have parents from there.

When Eddie Foulkes, a devout Lancastrian, was Captain of the club in 1980, he challenged his friend Ron Hewitt (who became club Captain in 1985) to raise a team of eight players so that the Wars of the Roses might be continued.

The first match was played as foursomes to the eighteenth green and Yorkshire won. Thereafter at the request of both teams, the annual match was changed to fourball better ball but still played to the eighteenth. There was no match in 1983. One match has been halved; Yorkshire have won 3 and Lancashire 13.

A dinner is held in the evening following the match and all sixteen players invite another member of the club as their guest, the club Captain being the Guest of Honour. The losing team pays for the port. After dinner the two captains present their teams with the appropriately coloured roses.

In 1994 Eddie and Ron resigned as captains of their respective teams and invited Ronnie Samuels (Captain in 1993) to captain Lancashire and Mike Shields to lead Yorkshire.

Another important group of members which formed a section for the purposes of playing matches against other clubs is the Commandos, formed in 1970 when club secretary Tony Randall discussed the possibility of a friendly match with his old friend Charles Hofton of Hammonds End Golf Club. In 1966 this club had gathered together a group of retired members who played twelve holes and then adjourned to the clubhouse for a sociable hour.

A match was arranged for the following year, under the management of Freddie Taylor, and subsequent years saw a gradual increase in the number of matches, Harpenden Drones, East Herts, West Herts and Sandy Lodge being added to the fixture list, which now features fourteen clubs as well as the Porters' Ladies.

Around 100 members over the age of sixty are eligible for membership of the "Commandos", who now elect their own captain and secretary and appoint a manager for each match.

Throughout its history the club has mixed a high degree of competitiveness with sociability across the broad kirk of its membership and there is no sign of that impetus letting up as the club goes into its second century.

Andrew Tolley, John Warne, Campbell Boal, Russell Lewis, Ewen Wilson and Phil Tolley (Capt.) at Deauville for the Mail on Sunday *finals in 1997. The team came third out of an entry of 1400 clubs*

Chapter Eight

The King George V Coronation Amateur Challenge Cup

GOLF CLUBS being patriotic institutions, it is not surprising that many trophies exist commemorating national events, particularly those involving the Royal Family and the successful termination of military activity.

King George V succeeded to the throne of England in 1910 and was crowned the following year, when Mr. J.H. Riches presented a cup to Porters for open competition over 36 holes played off scratch, members of recognised golf clubs being eligible to enter. What was not understood at the time were the uses to which the Royal name may be put and this led to some interesting correspondence at a much later date.

The first event attracted a large and talented entry and was won by Mr. O.M. Kerr of Hendon. The tournament's establishment as a major amateur competition was temporarily thwarted by the outbreak of war in 1914, but not before Douglas Grant of Royal Mid-Surrey had become the second winner from that club, J. Livingston having won in 1912. No club is recorded for the 1913 champion, J.S. Worthington.

The K.G.V., as it is normally referred to, resumed in 1920 and was won by O.C. Bristowe of Stoke Poges, who retained the trophy the following year, a feat repeated in 1924 and 1925 by C.N. Flint of Bushey Hall. The first home winner was E.S. Markham in 1927, when a letter was received from the Home Secretary. His attention had been called to "a competition held by the club for which the scratch prize was The King George V Challenge Cup and by whose permission the club used His Majesty's name?" Secretary Richmond replied, giving the correct title of the trophy and explaining the circumstances under which it had been presented. The response from the Home Secretary came more quickly than the original complaint, stating that "no objection to the title of the cup would be raised provided the word "Coronation" was used in all reports and records of the competition".

In keeping with the prestige of the event it was decided in 1929 that ties would be decided by a 36 hole play-off. This was the second year when a club member won the cup, J. Grimditch being successful, and the club's next winner was Dick Bott two years later. The depression years of the early thirties are the most likely reason for declining interest in competitive golf and in 1933 the K.G.V. was held on a Saturday for the first time to encourage a better entry, when another home player, A.G. Snelling, recorded the first of his two victories, the second coming in 1938. In the following year a midweek date was chosen and proved no more popular, so in 1935 it was suggested that the trophy be contested by the winners of the previous year's senior division medals, but this was rejected and no competition was held that year.

The 1936 contest must have been a normal Open Meeting as it was won by R. Pattinson from Derbyshire but the following year it was decided to raise the handicap limit to 12. This did not prevent Grimditch recording his second victory and in 1939 S. Seddon completed a hat-trick for the home club, by which time the handicap limit had been increased to 18. Once again war intervened and put an end to competitive golf. Club competitions resumed in 1945 but the Open Meeting was not re-instated until the following year.

The first post-war K.G.V., held on 27th June 1946, was won by L. Perkins and was considered a tremendous success by the committee. £60 was allocated for the purchase of prizes in 1947 and Mr. Perkins became the third golfer to win the trophy in consecutive years. Dick Bott had his second victory in 1950, nineteen years after his first winning performance, although the committee had initially decided to suspend the tournament until further notice, then agreed to hold it in September. There was still a poor entry, however, and it was decided to revert to a Saturday in the future. This was agreed for 1951, with a handicap limit of 12, and the cup was won by E.J. Wiggs of Moor Park Artisans.

As a result of another disappointing entry it was even suggested that the 1952 event be a mixed competition and that it be held earlier in the year,

---

Entries close Saturday, September 23rd.

PORTERS PARK GOLF CLUB.

King George V. Coronation
AMATEUR CHALLENGE CUP,

Open to Members of recognised Golf Clubs,

On Saturday, 30th September, 1911.

36-Hole Scratch Medal Competition
For CHALLENGE CUP.

The Winner will be presented with a Silver Replica of the Cup, value 6 guineas, and the Runner-up will receive a prize value 4 guineas.

A 36-hole Medal Competition,
under Handicap (limited to 9),

The Winner of which will receive a prize value 6 guineas.

A further prize value 3 guineas will be given for the best 18-holes in either round, under handicap, in either of the above events.

Competitors in the handicap events will play on their lowest handicap at any Club.

Competitors will be accorded the free use of the Links and Club House from September 23rd to 30th inclusive.

Entries must be received not later than SATURDAY the 23rd SEPTEMBER. Entrance Fee, 2/6 for either 1 or 2 event.

Further particulars will be sent on application to the Secretary, Porters Park Golf Club, Radlett.

Particulars of the Draw and Times of starting will as far as possible be sent to all competitors. *Train Service:* Midland Railway, 15 miles from St. Pancras.

John Putt, John Cook, Michael King and Alec Holmes played off for the 1969 K.G.V., Putt winning with a 71

subject to other tournaments on the fixture list. A date in May was chosen, then altered to 28th June. The K.G.V. itself was not competed for, another factor being that His Majesty King George VI died in the spring of that year.

Normal service was resumed in 1953 when Eric Holt won; after a two year interim, when it was apparently decided, in 1955, to make it a members' invitational competition, with the Cup going to the best scratch score, Porters enjoyed a series of victories from 1956 until 1960, Eric Holt being successful again in this last year. As the country began to recover from post-war depression in the decade when we were told that "we had never had it so good", entries improved and many high quality players were attracted to Porters Park. Welsh international Hew Squirrell won in 1962 and then Peter Townsend revealed his potential by taking the trophy three times in four years.

The 1969 K.G.V. produced an exciting four-way tie between English Amateur Champion John Cook, now a leading teaching professional, Mike King, a Walker Cup player who became a successful tournament professional until a painful arthritic condition ended his career, A.W. Holmes, the County Champion and J.A. Putt of Oxford City. After a

112

Nick Faldo at the 1975 Men's Dinner with Bob Curwain (Pres. HGU), Ron Johnson,
Eric Walton (County Capt.) and Malcolm Reid

postponement due to the Clark/Townsend exhibition, it was Putt who won the play-off and to prove that it was no fluke he won again in 1971, this time playing out of Frilford Heath.

England Internationals Warren Humphreys and Bob Durrant added their names in 1970 and 1974 as the tournament's prestige grew. 1975 saw what may be the most extraordinary shot played in the competition. The unfancied Chris Phillips of Dulwich and Sydenham Hill played-off over sudden death against the all conquering Nick Faldo who had already won the County Championship and the Berkshire Trophy, and later would win the English Amateur. Having tied on 146 in parched, drought conditions, Phillips topped his tee shot at the first hole, but it still rolled onto the green to match Faldo's impeccable faded No. 3 wood to twelve feet.

At the second, Phillips' wedge flew right of the green and landed in the brook where it hit a flat stone and bounced out, hitting the flag and securing Phillips a half. Not surprisingly, the immaculate Faldo became overwhelmed by Phillips' good fortune and three-putted the fourth to lose the play-off.

Ten years after the previous home winner, Nigel Notley had his name engraved on the cup for the first time in 1976 and repeated the performance in 1983.

1982 was washed out, rearranged and washed out again and Porters' next home victor was Wayne Henry in 1987 and he was followed by Richard

Latham. Warren Bennett of Ruislip intervened in 1989 and in 1990 Campbell Boal, in his finest year, won the trophy. He was the last member of Porters to lift the trophy. Since then the growing number of "full-time" amateurs, including those with ambitions to play for a living, have featured prominently in the K.G.V., perhaps the best known of whom is Steve Webster who won the Amateur Medal in the Open at St Andrews and then earned his tour card by finishing in first place at the tour school. Steve won in 1994, S. Jarvis of Gog Magog in 1995, Neil Swaffield of Stourbridge, a long serving county player for Worcestershire now hoping to earn a living at the game, in 1996 and, in 1997, Hampshire's James Knight, whose opening 64 is the lowest round recorded, although it does not count as the amateur record because of the need for preferred lies at the March date. In 1998 the competition was reduced to 18 holes because of atrocious weather conditions, which did not prevent Matthew King from Lincolnshire shooting an inspired 65 on an unforgiving course.

The K.G.V. is held in the same esteem as a number of prestigious tournaments, many of which are of later origin, and as a result have had fewer fluctuations in their conditions and popularity. The competition was twinned briefly with the Moor Park Stag but most recently it has shared a weekend with the Berkhamsted Trophy, although it is not twinned with that tournament.

Past winners of the King George V Coronation Challenge Cup
P.E. Huddy, E. Holt, G.V. Keith, H.C. Squirrell, S.R. Warrin, D.St.J. Brew, J.A. Putt, R.A. Durrant,
N.J. Notley, J. Earl, M.T. Seaton, D.G. Lane, J. Ambridge

114

Chapter Nine

Notable Players

I T IS inevitable that a club with a course as good as that of Porters Park will produce good golfers. The best players have a full array of shots, the ability to play them at the right time and the nerve to complete each little exercise by being able to put the ball into the hole as economically as possible.

The first record of a plus handicap at Porters occurred in June 1914, when P.R. Harrap was reduced from +1 to +2. Perhaps more than any other member he had most cause to regret the events of the next four years, as we have no further record of his exploits.

An early stalwart of the club, from 1903, E.S. Markham attained a similar mark in 1920, as did A.E. Philips, but it was the former who became the first member of the host club to win the King George V Coronation Cup, which he did in 1927. Two years later J. Grimditch won it for the first of two victories, separated among visiting winners by R.E.A. Bott in 1931 and A.G. Snelling two years later.

Dick Bott was a successful player for the club and county over a long period, having joined in 1923, winning the trophy again in 1950 and was still active in 1968 when he was appointed first team captain. In 1973 he was elected an Honorary Life Member, his wife having been accorded that honour a year earlier. He was also instrumental in arranging private matches with the Cambridge University Golf Club, permission to do so having been granted in 1931. A major "club character", Dick Bott's fame extended beyond Porters, for he presented the Bott Cup for competition on the Cresta Run, the famed toboggan run on which he had damaged a knee, the severed piece of patella being attached to his watch chain. This event is still held annually, a tribute to a member of the English Bobsleigh team and Captain of our Winter Olympics team in 1951. Dick died in June 1980 and was sadly missed by the club.

Brian Nordon recalls partnering him in the London Foursomes when they beat a pair of Walker Cup players, only to lose in the next round.

The Hudson Trophy team at South Herts. in 1965. Robin Neill, W.A. Belshaw (Capt. South Herts. 1965), Bill Large (Pro.), Drury Dailey and Eric Holt

Brian remembers being able to beat Dick by using a little quiet gamesmanship.

Snelling had another win in 1938, followed by S. Seddon in 1939. Following Bott's first post-war victory club members dominated the competition in the 1950s, the most successful being Eric Holt who won twice, in 1953 and 1960. He recalls his early interest in the game, first as a caddy at Oxhey, and then playing there unofficially in the evenings with his brother. Eric only possessed one club at the time, a mashie, with which he became proficient in all types of shot. Shortly after becoming an official member at the age of eighteen, with the backing of a neighbour, Cyril Ostler, the club was reduced to nine holes by the G.L.C. who built on part of the course, which then became a public facility. From a first handicap of 8, Eric progressed to scratch without the benefit of lessons, having a natural swing. When Malcolm Reid invited him to join Porters he jumped at the chance, although he admits to sadness at leaving Oxhey, having won the Herts Championship while a member there and representing the Public Courses against England at Hillside when on holiday at Southport. He broke the course record there with a 68. Eric played regularly in the English Amateur and Peter Lynn recalls monitoring his progress with interest until,

116

following an accidental fall from a roof, Eric ceased competing in this event. A county player for thirty rewarding years, he misses his friend Cyril, who emigrated to Australia, otherwise he, too, would have had a long county career. Eric is now one of the "Commandos" and as recently as 1997 won the Sanford Seniors Cup, playing off 7, a handicap he still wishes to reduce.

However, the two most successful golfers on a wider front at this time were Brian Chapman and Peter Townsend. The son of Arnold Chapman, Captain in 1962, and Joan Chapman, he recalls starting to play golf at Starveacres with his mother at the age of eight. On joining Porters Park, Brian had the rare good fortune to be able to play all summer after his prep. school had burnt down. No less an authority than Raymond Oppenheimer was asked to take a look at Brian's game and he recommended lessons with Arthur Lees at Sunningdale.

Brian reached the quarter finals of the Boys' Championship at Formby in 1952 and the following year was one of four boys the R & A sent to Sweden to play in a championship. He lost in the final to Michael Bonallack. Two years National Service was followed by three at Cambridge, where there was then a high standard of golf. Youths in those days did not have the same incentive to become professionals as they do now because they had to wait five years before they could earn prize money.

After graduating from Cambridge, where he enjoyed his golf in the company of Ted Dexter with coaching from John Jacobs, he reached the last 8 of the English Amateur in 1958 and the last 16 of the Amateur Championship in 1960, losing to the eventual winner, Joe Carr. He had his revenge on Carr in 1962, in the fourth round. Two down after three holes Brian covered the next 11 holes in 35 shots – 7 under par, and won on the seventeenth. Carr admitted he felt powerless to stop the barrage. In an in-depth feature in *Golf World,* John Stobbs recalls "the particular toughness, calmness and guts with which Chapman fought him" on their first encounter. The "return" match he described as "beautiful; and those purists of the game who always haunt championships were left breathless, not just with the perfection of the match, in which neither gave an inch … but at the miraculous firmness of Chapman's golf under the heaviest combative pressure Carr could bring to bear on him". Unfortunately he lost his semi-final to J. Povall from Whitchurch, Stobbs citing his suppleness, which he considered less than "ideal for the strongest sort of golf", and a lack of stamina which he attributed to the little time Brian had for practice.

He was selected for the 1961 Walker Cup match, having beaten Martin Christmas in progressing to the last 8 in the English Amateur at Wentworth. The Walker Cup was held in Seattle and Brian was given only one game in the heavy defeat typical of the time. However, with partner Jimmy Walker, that

Brian Chapman with the Golf Illustrated
Gold Vase he won at Sunningdale in 1962

one game was against none other than Jack Nicklaus and Deane Beman in the top match in the foursomes. Five down after 8 holes, a containing operation led to a defeat by 6 and 5. His representative career continued that year in the Home Internationals.

The Stobbs article was illustrated by a sequence of photographs demonstrating Brian's swing, with its "Jacobean touches", a rare accolade for an amateur golfer. It also describes Porters as a "pleasantly tree-clump-dotted and by no means badly designed course"!

The winner of the *Golf Illustrated* Gold Vase and a losing semi-finalist in The President's Putter in 1962, Brian Chapman then represented his country for the last time. Mindful of his club affiliations, he agreed to look after the junior section during that year. He married in 1963 and ceased playing at International level to pursue family and business interests as an executive of an oil company, which he had joined on graduating. The company agreed to give him leave to play in International matches if he had qualified to play in them in his own time. He enjoyed some success in club competitions while still living in the south but returned to Lancashire in 1966 and played very little golf. However he joined Pleasington in 1971 and, later, Hoylake. He was elected to membership of the Royal and Ancient and was deputed by them to inspect the course when the qualifying rounds for the Open Championship were held at Porters from 1984-89.

While this international career was quietly coming to a close another was taking off most noticeably. Peter Michael Paul Townsend was born in Cambridge in 1946. He was elected a junior member of Porters Park in 1959 and by 1961 was good enough to be picked for the national boys' team, holding his place for the next four years, after which he graduated into the youths' team. To earn this distinction he had won the British Boys' Championship in 1962 and 1964, in which year he also won the stroke play championship for the Carris Trophy and the Hertfordshire Amateur. He became the second member of Porters to play in the Walker

Cup, in 1965, and the Home Internationals, 1965 and 1966 as well as in the Eisenhower Trophy matches and against the Continent of Europe. John Van Gelder recalls him driving the fifteenth green and challenged him to repeat the feat. He did.

Peter's tournament record was no less impressive: he won the Duncan Putter in 1965 along with the major Irish Amateur stroke play championship, the Mullingar Scratch Cup, which he retained the following year, a golden year, for as well as the English Open Amateur Stroke Play Championship he added the Lytham Trophy, the Golf Illustrated Gold Vase, the Prince of Wales Challenge

Peter Townsend in 1967

Cup and the Berkhamsted Trophy. This in addition to putting his name on the King George V Cup for a third time, having enjoyed back to back victories in 1963 and 1964. Peter Townsend and Brian Chapman were both made Honorary Members of the club in 1965, when a champagne reception was held for them in October. He had not neglected his club responsibilities, having been part of the team that won the Herts Golf Union Club Championship in that year. He also set a new course record of 65. Peter completed all four rounds of the Open Championship at Muirfield during this season, finishing equal twenty-second, but despite this high finish the amateur medal went to Ronnie Shade.

It was hardly surprising that Peter Townsend decided to play for a living at the end of 1966. He became attached to the club for playing purposes on a retainer of £200 until 1970. He was soon successful, winning the Dutch Open in his first year on the European Tour. A steady string of victories around the world followed and he became one of the few to play in both Walker and Ryder Cup teams when, in 1969 and 1971, he represented Great Britain and Ireland, winning 3 points in his 11 matches. He played in all four rounds of the Open on six occasions, his best performances coming in 1972 at Muirfield and 1974 at Royal Lytham finishing in joint thirteenth place on both occasions, the score of 288 at Muirfield being his lowest in all his appearances.

In 1983 Peter Townsend, already attached to Portmarnock as touring professional, became club professional at Ireland's premier club, in

119

20 Becketts Ave,
St. Albans,
Herts.
Dec 18th.

Dear Mr Ross,

Thank you very much for your letter of good wishes.

I consider it a great honour to be made an honorary member of Porters Park. I am so happy that I am going to be the playing professional at Porters Park. I shall look forward to seeing you all when I'm at home.

Yours sincerely,

Peter Townsend.

Peter Townsend's letter acknowledging his honorary membership succession to the legendary Harry Bradshaw. The following year brought a further accolade, captaincy of the PGA, an honour previously reserved for the previous year's Open Champion. As Tom Watson had scored his hat-trick victory in 1983, it was perhaps only right that the honour should go to a home player who had served the game so well. He left Portmarnock eight years later to take up duties with the PGA.

There is no doubt that Peter Townsend was an example and inspiration to two youngsters who joined Porters in the 1960s, school mates Campbell Boal and Nigel Notley. Both have achieved much for the club as players and committee men, particularly as Chairmen of the Green.

Campbell first represented the club in 1969, captaining the first team from 1989-92. In 1974 he and Nigel won the Herts Inter-club Foursomes, the club's seventy-fifth year. He finally attained a scratch handicap in 1990, at the age of thirty-nine, and this proved to be a vintage year for him. Because of alterations to the course his score of 65 in the Humble Salver qualifying medal replaced Peter Townsend's course record. Campbell, also reputed for his

Competition .... Player .... C. C. BOAL ....

.... HUMBLE SALVER .... Handicap. 1

Date .... 19 MAY 1990 .... Strokes received ....

Marker's Score	Hole	Yards	Par	Yards	Stroke Index	Player's Score	Points	Marker's Score	Hole	Yards	Par	Yards	Stroke Index	Player's Score	Points
	1	254	4	237	17	3			10	484	5	469	8	4	
	2	356	4	339	11	4			11	432	4	417	2	4	
	3	411	4	406	3	3			12	196	3	175	14	4	
	4	453	4	434	5	4			13	502	5	478	6	5	
	5	384	4	372	9	3			14	160	3	142	16	3	
	6	149	3	133	13	3			15	338	4	299	18	3	
	7	398	4	386	7	3			16	411	4	399	4	4	
	8	411	4	397	1	4			17	385	4	376	12	4	
	9	155	3	136	15	3			18	434	4	425	10	4	
	Out	2971	34	2840	Out	30			In	3342	36	3180	In	35	
									Out	2971	34	2840	Out	30	
									Total	6313	70	6020	Total	65	

Marker's Signature ... Nigel Notley,

Player's Signature ... C C Boal

HANDICAP	1
NET SCORE	64

AMATEUR COURSE RECORD

WHITE TEES S.S.S. 70
YELLOW TEES S.S.S. 69

Three County Captains – Peter Robinson (1990-1992),
Campbell Boal (1987-1989) and Nigel Notley (1984-1986)

matchplay ability, has won the club championship 9 times amongst 42 club trophies. He also won the K.G.V. during this year.

In 1994 he set a new course record at Coombe Hill in a Mid-Am and was runner-up in the County Championship of 1997. With Jack Ramsden, Nigel Notley and Paul Tolley he helped win the Hudson Trophy at South Herts in 1979.

Because of the demands of a highly responsible job which entails unsocial working hours, Campbell has not had many opportunities to play in the major national events but has not been prevented from serving his county, for which he first appeared in 1980. Seven years as a regular player was rewarded with the captaincy in 1987, a post he held in a non-playing capacity, by his own choice, for three years. In the first of these Hertfordshire won the League, the Eastern Counties Foursomes and qualified for the English County Finals. In 1986 Herts qualified again and Campbell Boal was a member of Nigel Notley's team which won the final. He was still holding a county place in 1997.

Nigel Notley made his county debut in 1974 in the Eastern Counties Foursomes at Hunstanton; this event is part of golfing history, as it was on this occasion that Bob Taylor of Leicestershire holed out in one at the sixteenth hole in the practice round and then again on both the next two days. He claims that the tee shot lipped out on the final day. No doubt the Porters Park representatives enjoyed his hospitality!

Nigel's first League appearance was at Chelmsford against Essex in 1976 and it was here that he also made his final League appearance in 1984, in the year he became county captain. Under his leadership that year Hertfordshire won the Eastern Counties Foursomes and the qualifying tournament at St Georges Hill for the English County Finals. These were held at Hollinwell and Hertfordshire came fourth. They improved the following year by finishing runners-up at Burnham and Berrow, having prevailed at Chigwell. In 1986 Herts qualified again, this time at Kings Lynn, under Nigel Notley's inspired captaincy, which was finally rewarded in his last year in charge, when Hertfordshire won all three matches in the finals at John O'Gaunt. This was the first time Hertfordshire had been champions of England.

Nigel has been losing finalist twice in the County Championship, in 1974 and 1977. He reached the semi-finals in 1983 and the quarter finals in 1976 and 1980. He has been a member of the teams which won the Hertfordshire Club Championship on six occasions, twice in the County Foursomes and in the 1979 Hudson Trophy winning team. He won the K.G.V. in 1976 and 1983 and reached the fourth round in the English Amateur in 1976.

Although very different in stature both Campbell and Nigel attack the golf ball with considerable aggression, in Nigel's case occasionally presenting him with the opportunity to exhibit his extremely deft short game. Getting down in two from a gorse bush seems to present him with few problems.

More recently, Nigel as Chairman of the Green has been heavily involved in the development of the course and his research, together with Campbell and Malcolm, has enabled us to trace its history for the purposes of this volume.

Another club member who earned county recognition during the reigns of Campbell Boal and Nigel Notley is Richard Latham, who joined Porters in 1983 and immediately represented the club. He made his county debut the following year and it is reckoned that he has now represented Hertfordshire on over 120 occasions. He was voted county player of the year in 1989 and was captain in 1996 and 1997.

Richard qualified for the Open Championship at Royal St Georges in 1985 and has reached the final qualifying stages on ten out of fourteen attempts. He has a consistent record in top amateur events and has won ten 36 hole events including the K.G.V. which he won in 1988. Richard holds two course records: 65 at Parkstone and 69 at the new Windmill course at Hawkstone Park. He has also equalled the Porters Park record. He was a finalist in the 1987 County Championship and reached the semi-finals on six other occasions. He won the Hertfordshire Cup, a 72 hole event, in 1991.

A team-mate of Richard's, Andrew Cotton joined the club as a junior and by 1984 was good enough to play for the county, for whom his record was excellent. From 19 foursomes he earned 9½ points and 14½ points from his 18 singles. Nigel Notley suggests that this makes Andrew the most successful Herts player from any club. He generally played number one, so met and beat such players as Peter McEvoy, Chris Mitchell and Paul Downes, all of whom he would have met in his two appearances in the English County Finals. It was Andrew's final stroke at Kings Lynn which took Herts into the final, holing a 7-iron for an eagle 2 on the thirty-sixth hole. He turned professional in 1986, prior, alas, to the county finals and was denied the Player of the Year award as the idea of it being presented to a professional could not be countenanced by officialdom. Earlier in the year he reached the sixth round of the English Amateur. Although not large in stature he had an elegant swing and generated immense power. Nigel recalls that his line on the eighth was straight over the bunkers and on the eighteenth over the left edge of the tree line on Shenley Road. Sadly he did not achieve the same success as a professional.

Another successful player who immigrated to Porters from Scotland was Robin Neill, whose recall of dates is rather hazy, but he came to the club with an impressive record. An old boy of Trinity College, Glenalmond, a school not only famous for producing many of Scotland's finest rugby footballers, but also possessing its own nine hole course designed by James Braid, Robin captained the golf team there. He twice reached the last 16 of both the Scottish and British Boys Championships and played county golf in Scotland for Renfrewshire. At Porters he recollects his finest achievement was winning the Dearbergh and Richmond Cups on the same day with scores of 69 and 66. His course record of 67 at South Herts (1964) still stands and another course record of 66 at East Renfrewshire lasted one weekend. However, he captained that club's team to victory in the West of Scotland Team Trophy and had a fine record in the Scottish Amateur Championship.

Before joining Porters, Robin played a round with assistant professional Tony Grubb, who earned a telling-off from steward Collinge for inviting a guest into the bar. Robin himself was on the carpet some years later for complaining that the greens were overfertilised. He was accused of slandering a member of the committee and his reminiscences conclude with the comment that as all the amusing incidents he can recall at Porters are slanderous he had better keep quiet, having learnt the hard way. However, he remembers that the club had little difficulty winning things in the early 1960s. He played for Hertfordshire about four times but was never a regular.

Other county players of a later era were Paul Tolley and Peter Robinson. Peter was a regular player with an excellent record which came to an end when he emigrated to Australia in 1993. He has an equally good record in the English Amateur Championship. A losing quarter-finalist in 1983, he was runner-up in 1985 to Roger Winchester and in 1988 and 1989 it was Russell Claydon and Steven Richardson respectively who eliminated him in the semi-finals. In all he has played 42 matches in this event, winning 30 of them. He followed his victory in the County Championship of 1985 by winning the EGU President's Bowl for the Champion of Champions and was a member of the national squad. County Captain from 1990 to 1992, he played in many winning teams in his 36 appearances for Hertfordshire and was a member of

the Porters Park team who finished runners-up in the 1990 EGU Champion Club
Tournament. He won the Club Championship in 1989.

Paul Tolley, who described himself quite
correctly as a "bloody nice bloke" played
for Herts from 1977 until 1995, being
Captain from 1993 to 1995. He played in
the County Finals in 1985 and 1993 and
in the teams that won the South East
League and League finals in the latter year.
He had a very sound record in his 80
county matches. As well as three team
championships he won the Herts Stag at
Moor Park in 1987.

He has twice been champion at Porters,
where he has also won the Rumsey Goblets
three years in succession and the
Richmond, Raphael and Dearbergh Cups.
Sadly he left Porters in 1992 to join
Berkhamsted but happily has now rejoined
his old club.

*Graham Maly with the County
Championship trophy he won in 1994 at
Sandy Lodge (the first Porters Park winner
since 1965)*

Wayne Henry achieved considerable
success as a junior, being selected to be Captain of England Boys at the
age of sixteen – normally a seventeen year old is given that honour. He
had already won the Peter McEvoy Trophy in 1984, an event he particularly
enjoyed, coming third in 1985, second the next year and winning again
in 1987. Wayne's early successes also included the Golf Foundation's Golfer
of the Year award in 1984, when he came first in the Under-16 International
Championships. Area success in the *Daily Express* Championship the next
year won him a trip to the final in Spain, where he finished third. He also
won the South-East England Championship during this season, a feat he
repeated a year later. His final year as a junior brought him the Herts
Boys Championship.

His record as a boy international won him promotion to the full England
side, having played in every England match from early summer 1984, to
1987. His 44 matches included 28 wins, 7 halves and 9 losses. He had
begun his county career in 1982 and two years later became the youngest
ever regional qualifier, in first place, for the Open Championship in a
field which included 135 professionals and several top amateurs. His record
as a senior amateur was not quite so scintillating, but he did win the Under-
21 championship in 1987.

All this may have persuaded Wayne that he would be able to earn his living at the game but unfortunately he is still restricted to satellite tour events.

When his studies at St Andrews University permitted, Graham Maly made a number of appearances for the county, after winning the County Championship at Sandy Lodge in 1994, at the age of eighteen. He also won the Richmond Trophy and the Club Championship in that year.

The most recent international representative from the club is Carl Duke, now taking his first steps as a professional. A protégé of Malcolm Reid, who, Carl writes: " helped me greatly and advised me on practice routines and the type of competitions that I should play in. He set me goals and was always available for advice and guidance. My main memory of him is that wherever I played, no matter the weather, he would always be out on the course checking on progress and taking stock of the ability and potential of all the young golfers."

Carl moved to Porters in 1989, at the age of twelve, after taking up the game at Fairways, then Batchwood and later, Verulam. He shot a 76 at Porters in the Boys' Championship and, recognising it as the top club in Hertfordshire, obtained membership along with his brother. By the age of eighteen he was playing off +1, for the county boys', youths' and men's teams. In 1992 he won the English Schoolboys Under-16 Championship and was selected to play against Scotland. He also won the EGU Under-16 tournament at Sunningdale. He won the Schoolboys Under-18 title the following year, for which part of the prize was a lesson from another Herts golfer, Nick Faldo, and was selected to play against Scotland, twice, Wales and Sweden, winning all five of his matches. He won the Under-16 section of the Carris Trophy and came fifth in the *Daily Express* Boys' final at La Manga, an event he won subsequently in 1994. During this year he reached the quarter-finals of the British Amateur at Nairn, defeating Padraig Harrington on the way. He played in the Boys' Home Internationals at Little Aston, winning three matches and halving one. On the strength of this he was picked to play against the European team.

By 1995 Carl was considered worthy of selection for the full international squad and attended training at Valderrama. He won the Peter McEvoy Trophy and numerous other events and visited Japan with the English Boys team. He remained in the England squad in 1996 and played several representative matches as well as enjoying more local success in the Herts Colts Championship, which he repeated in 1997, adding the Herts Men's Amateur Championship for good measure.

Omitted from selection for a training session at Valderrama, Carl was invited to play, as an amateur, in the Benson and Hedges International Open at the Oxfordshire in May. Conditions are usually difficult at this time of the year and on a wide open course in blustery weather Carl could only manage 77 in the first round. Nothing daunted, he started the second round brilliantly, making birdies at three of the first four holes; three more birdies, an unlucky double bogey and one other bogey saw him finish three under on 69 and missing the cut by just two shots. It was a tough introduction to a professional tournament but the way in which Porters' representative comported himself was a lesson to many of the professionals as Carl Duke revelled in the challenge. One shot in particular brought a standing ovation. The seventeenth hole at The Oxfordshire has a fairway split by a lake. By driving over water to the left it may be possible to reach the green in two, a hazardous prospect against the chill wind. Carl opted for the sensible right hand route, but overhit his third shot, finishing on top of the steep bank surrounding the green. With the hole twenty feet below him and cut close to the water's edge the next shot was one of the most challenging that could have been imagined. Opening the face of his wedge, Carl coolly flopped an exquisite pitch to within a yard and then equally calmly knocked the putt in. His professional partners could hardly believe it; the crowd rose to their feet and applauded.

Carl Duke has been particularly fortunate in that he had Malcolm Reid to set him on the right path and in the vastly increased number of opportunities for young golfers to compete at the highest level. It is to be hoped he will continue to succeed at the professional level; he will certainly have the good wishes of everyone at Porters Park to encourage him.

Ramsden Bell, 8th green by Tony Jennings

Chapter Ten

Support for the Golf Unions

THE MALE golfers of England lagged a long way behind their counterparts in Ireland, Wales and Scotland in forming a national golfing union. It also has to be said that they were a long way behind the ladies, too, as the Ladies' Golfing Union was formed in 1893, two years after the formation of the Golf Union of Ireland and two years before the Golf Union of Wales. Scotland's Golf Union was not formed until 1920 and it was another four years before the English Golf Union was formed.

Hertfordshire formed its own Union in the same year under the chairmanship of the Earl of Strafford, and so became one of twenty-six founder members of the EGU. Percy Burton, a member of Porters Park, became President of the EGU in 1936-7, President of the HGU from 1944-53, a member of the Joint Advisory Council of British Golf Unions (forerunner of CONGU) from 1936-48, helped found the European Golf Association and served on the board of the Greenkeeping Research Unit, which became the STRI, from 1936-47. Naturally, Porters Park was one of ten clubs affiliated to the County Union at that time. By the time the EGU published its first handbook in 1932, twenty-one Hertfordshire clubs were affiliated. Other Presidents of the HGU who were Porters' members were A. Forbes Ilsley, Mervyn Orchard-Lisle, Douglas Cumming, Malcolm Reid and Wilf de Podesta, who was also secretary from 1978-94. It was during Wilf's years of office that the county enjoyed the most successful period in its history.

However, there appears to have been some form of inter-club organisation within the county prior to this as the club was asked for "the usual subscription" to "the Herts Golf Club" in 1910. The ladies' attempts to join the LGU had twice been deferred by the committee until permission was granted in July 1908, and it may have been the ladies who staged the first county match to be played at Porters Park in 1912. They received permission to hold another one in 1922, by which time C. Lennox Richmond had been partly instrumental in forming the Hertfordshire

Alliance with the county's professionals. The highlights of the club's involvement in these are recorded in the chapter on the professionals.

The aims of the EGU were, and still are, to further the interests of amateur golf in England; to assist in the setting up of a uniform system of handicapping; to arrange the English Championship, Regional Championships and such other matches and competitions as they authorised; and to co-operate with the R & A, CONGU and the other national golfing unions. The initiative behind its formation seemed to come from the North, with Lancashire, Yorkshire and Cheshire prominent among the founders; indeed the inaugural meetings were held in Manchester. Nevertheless the first English county union had been formed in 1893 by Hampshire and the Isle of Wight.

An early major project was research into greenkeeping and Porters Park contributed their £2 to the fund along with the other clubs in 1929. The first sign of the Union as a disciplinary force came three years later in the form of a letter requesting the club to "discountenance the giving of prizes for holes in one". The secretary was instructed to relay the club's conformity with that request to the Union.

The donor of the Bradbeer Cup, Mr. G.F. Roberts, became the second member of the club to serve on the County Golf Union committee in 1939. As a long-serving and hardworking member, he must have found election at this particular time rather frustrating.

Porters Park has been invited to hold the County Championship regularly since staging the first event in 1924, and although a club member has never won the championship on his own course, Porters has provided a champion on ten occasions: Dick Bott in 1931, Eric Holt in 1953 and 1955, Cyril Ostler in 1954, Brian Chapman in 1956, 1962 and 1965, Peter Townsend in 1964, Graham Maly in 1994 and Carl Duke in 1997. In 1977 and 1987 respectively, Nigel Notley and Richard Latham were runner-up, on both occasions on their home green.

It was not until 1974 that Hertfordshire earned a place in the final of the English County Championship, when the county team finished third at Walton Heath. After a gap of ten years with strong representation from Porters Park – Nigel Notley as non-playing captain, Richard Latham, Andrew Cotton and Andrew Clark, whose second club was Porters – Hertfordshire qualified again, finishing fourth. This was the beginning of a golden era: the following year Hertfordshire were second, Paul Tolley joining the four from the previous year. Hertfordshire won the Championship in 1986, Notley again in charge and with just Latham and Campbell Boal from the club in the side. The county slipped back into third place in 1987, thus occupying all four positions in as many years. Campbell Boal had taken over as non-playing captain, Richard Latham retained his place and Wayne Henry earned selection. The most recent success in this event was fourth position in 1993, with Richard Latham representing the club.

Porters Park also figured as a club during this golden era by winning the English Club Championship at Pleasington in 1985, its second year of competition. They qualified for this by winning the Hertfordshire Club Championship, a feat accomplished by the club twenty-one times since presenting the trophy in 1924, on four of which occasions Porters was the venue. Having won the English title, the club then went on to the European Club Championship in Aloha, Spain. The team was Richard Latham, Andrew Cotton and Paul Tolley, with Campbell Boal as non-playing captain and finished in seventh place. The club has also hosted the County Inter-Club Foursomes Tournament, begun in 1925, and has won it twelve times. The Herts Boys Championship was won by Malcolm Darroch in 1952, Peter Townsend in 1963 and 1964, Wayne Henry in 1987 and Carl Duke in 1995. Carl then went on to be Colts Champion in 1996 and 1997. The County Seniors Trophy, a handicap event up to 1986, has been won on eight occasions by members of the club, R.E.A. Bott in 1958 and 1961, A Piggott (an artisan) in 1962, G. Cooper (also an artisan) in 1969 and 1976, F.T. Phillips in 1970, J. Schofield in 1983 and H. Harrison in 1985. The Herts Seniors Championship which started in 1987 was won by Don Lewis in 1992.

More recently, national success has been the responsibility of the boys who won the English Boys' County Championship in 1993 at Sherwood Forest with Carl Duke winning five points out of a possible six. This followed third place the previous year at Ross-on-Wye.

The ladies of Porters have also been prominent in their County Union and several ladies have held office in various capacities. These are detailed in the chapter devoted to them.

A Collage of County Successes

The Hertfordshire team that won the English County Championship at John O'Gaunt in 1986. Back: Richard Latham, P. Cherry, A. Clapp, J. Ambridge, A. Clark. Front: Campbell Boal, Nigel Notley (Capt.), Peter Robinson

Winners of the County Foursomes in 1985 Andy Cotton and Richard Latham

The seventh time in nine years that Porters Park won the Herts Club Championship, this time represented by Paul Tolley, Richard Latham and Peter Robinson in 1989

An all Porters Park County Championship final at West Herts in 1997. Campbell Boal, Richard Latham (County Captain and referee) and Carl Duke who won by 3/2

Hertfordshire Ladies champions Julie Smith 1977 and Pam Lane 1960

Ovaltine Cup Winners 1993, Sue Hawkey, Fionnuala Smith, Rosemary Watters, Caroline Robinson and Ena Drewery

Past Lady Captains Day, June 1996. Front (L to R): Gwennie Parkes, Poppy Harris, Berry Wilson, Phyll Bailey, Pam Lane, Pam Viner (Waterfield). Middle: Rena Connell, Sheila Palmer, Majorie Cumming, Mary Williams, Sheila Radcliffe, Jan Macfarlane, Myra Wilson, Peggy Rawlings. Back row: Brenda Tattersall, Jean Howell, Liz Copley, Moira Stanbury, Heather Wythe, Yvonne Frankland

The Hertfordshire Challenge Bowl 1995. Anita Healy, Fionnuala Smith, Yvonne Frankland (Lady Captain), Ena Drewery, Margaret Nelson

133

INTER COUNTY FINALS AT CHISLEHURST G.C. KENT

PORTERS PARK WON THE INTER COUNTY FINALS AT CHISLEHURST GOLF CLUB
KENT ON JULY 28th 1997. THE CLUB LAST WON THE PEARSON TROPHY IN 1950.
WE WERE THEREFORE ELATED TO WIN IT AGAIN FOR HERTFORDSHIRE,
AND FOR THE CLUB AFTER 47 YEARS.

RESULTS   AM – PORTERS PARK vs TENTERDEN, KENT. **WON 6/1**

TEAM – ANITA HEALY, DAGNY MOFFAT, JANET PERCIVAL, LINDA
LAMBERT, ANN DUNCAN, MOIRA STANBURY, JEAN BRYCE.

PM – PORTERS PARK vs BURHILL. **WON 5/2**

TEAM – ANITA HEALY, DAGNY MOFFAT, JANET PERCIVAL, LINDA LAMBERT, ANN
DUNCAN, MOIRA STANBURY, JEAN BRYCE.

TEAM CAPTAIN – ROWENA HEMMINGS

E.L.G.A.

PEARSON TROPHY MATCHES
on JULY 28TH 1997

PORTERS PARK L.G.C. v. TENTERDEN L.G.C.

4 COUNTIES FINAL.

Handicap	Winning Team	Won by	Pts.	Handicap	Losing Team	Won by	Pts.
13	ANITA HEALY			13	PRU DOBSON	2/1	1
14	DAGNY MOFFAT	4/3	1	15	SARAH BRISTOW		
16	JANET PERCIVAL	4/3	1	15	BETTY JEFFREY		
16	LINDA LAMBERT	5/4	1	17	JENNY BISHOP		
17	ANN DUNCAN	4/3	1	19	VAL BRENT		
19	MOIRA STANBURY	4/3	1	19	MARY STRONG		
21	JEAN BRYCE	3 up. AFTER 15 HOLES		23	MARGARET PARKER		
			6				1

MATCH WON BY PORTERS PARK

The Captain of the WINNING TEAM must within two days of the match being played, fill in and post this form to her Divisional Manager.

Both Captain's Signatures R. Henman J & _____ Played at CHISLEHURST G.C.

E.L.G.A.

PEARSON TROPHY MATCHES
on JULY 28TH 1997

PORTERS PARK L.G.C. v. BURHILL L.G.C.

4 COUNTIES FINAL.

Handicap	Winning Team	Won by	Pts.	Handicap	Losing Team	Won by	Pts.
13	ANITA HEALY	2/1	1	13	ANN FLEW		
14	DAGNY MOFFAT			14	PAT ROBERTS	3/2	1
16	JANET PERCIVAL			14	DAWN COLLINS	3/2	1
16	LINDA LAMBERT	6/5	1	14	ANNIKE WILLIAMS		
17	ANN DUNCAN	3/1	1	15	MARY GARRETT		
19	MOIRA STANBURY	5/3	1	18	LYN COX		
21	JEAN BRYCE	2 UP AFTER 15 HOLES	1				
			5				2

MATCH WON BY PORTERS PARK

The Captain of the WINNING TEAM must within two days of the match being played, fill in and post this form to her Divisional Manager.

Both Captain's Signatures R. Henman & _____ Played at CHISLEHURST G.C.

135

Chapter Eleven

The Ladies

I T HAS been noted already that from the very beginning Porters Park had a substantial proportion of lady members, who soon had their own course, red tee boxes being provided in 1901. They had to wait a little longer for their own clubhouse, however, Boff's estimate of £58 for a building measuring 10 feet x 10 feet being considered excessive. That there was need for such provision is evident from the notice the committee had put up in May of that year to the effect "that the saloon in the clubhouse is for the use of Gentlemen only and that Ladies are not allowed to have refreshments in that room". The segregation was made more complete by an accompanying notice: "The Ladies' clubroom is for the use of ladies only and gentlemen are not allowed to have refreshments in that room".

The ladies were made of sterner stuff and in July the committee authorised the sum of £60 on a small detached clubhouse for lady members, five further debentures being issued to defray the cost. One imagines that the driving force behind all this was Mrs. Emily Beatty Smyth, the wife of the good doctor to whom the club already owed so much. In October an oil stove was purchased to heat the room and Mrs. Smyth authorised to buy the furniture. To further aid their comfort the secretary was instructed to take steps to have a closet built out from the side of the ladies' clubhouse for the convenience of lady members, *limited to the sum of £10.* New lady members also became subject to a £3 entrance fee. Membership of the section was limited to fifty in October.

These early lady members were very competitive and in 1903 were given permission to hold two monthly medals and two bogey competitions. This was to have repercussions later.

Further progress was made in 1905 when the A.G.M. empowered the committee to form a ladies' committee, with the Captain, secretary, the Ladies' Captain and four members. Their powers were limited to suggestions for competitions, inter-club matches and the management of their clubhouse. Mrs. Smyth was elected Captain, her husband being club

Porters Park ladies in 1902

Captain at that time, and was joined on the committee by Mesdames Lohr, Martin, Pendle and Sudbury.

The ladies' subscription was increased in 1905 to £2, entry fees rising to £5 and their wish to join the Ladies Golf Union was deferred, as it was again the following year. It was not until 1908 that this permission was forthcoming. The fact that a similar union did not exist for men members until 1924 may have had some influence on this prevarication.

Intimations of inequality seem to have prompted the ladies' suggestion, adopted as a club bye-law, that "On Saturdays, Sundays and Bank Holidays ladies must allow men to pass them, and they must not arrive at the first tee until all men waiting to start have driven off." Presumably equality prevailed on weekdays.

Their first trophy was presented to the ladies in February 1906 by Dr. Martin, whose wife succeeded Mrs. Smyth as Ladies' Captain. This was for a 36 hole aggregate medal played off handicap and any lady winning it three times was entitled to keep the trophy. Entry fees were one shilling and a memento prize to the value of £1 would be given to the winner and ten shillings to second place. It was first played for as the West Grove Cup in 1908 and was won in 1911 by Miss Sewell with 82+75 = 157. Mrs. C.L. Richmond won this cup outright in 1925 but re-presented it for competition.

A concession was made at the same time, ladies now being permitted to use the dining room ONLY in the gentlemen's clubhouse.

It was found desirable to recruit new members in March 1907 and it was proposed to admit up to fifty provisional lady members, paying £3 entrance and £2 subscription, with a further £2 entry fee on becoming full members when vacancies arose. They were not allowed to play at weekends or bank holidays and had no voting rights, but they could play in medal and bogey competitions. A month later the committee decided to ask the ladies if they wanted these provisional members to play in competitions and received a very positive answer.

In 1908 Mrs. Smyth was the Ladies' Captain once again and wrote a strong protest about a lack of new holes for the ladies' monthly competition and the fact that the tees were in poor condition. Mrs. Smyth had, in fact, been disqualified from the competition as her card had been marked by a non-member and her protest led to an investigation into the number of ladies' competitions.

These proved to be excessive, the prizes amounting to more than ten times the entry fees. The number of competitions was reduced and in April 1908 the following format was proposed: Tuesday was to be Ladies' Day; there would be a monthly medal for which the entrance was 2s.0d. per year, a quarterly bogey for the same entrance fee, and a cup competition.

The new stove had finally been installed in the ladies' clubroom in 1907, initially with the wrong size flue pipe. Now a damper and fender were required and the men's committee generously sanctioned the cost of £2. 8s. 0d.

The gentlemen's committee had the final sanction over all matters and when Mr. Tatham wrote to them indicating that he would like to propose that ladies living within a four mile radius of the club might be proposed as provisional members, up to a number of twenty, this was turned down. Mrs. Tillyer Tatham was also unsuccessful in seeking election to the ladies' committee as Mrs. Meyer, one of the other candidates, was considered a better golfer. In the event Mrs. Tatham was duly elected on 9th May. She clearly became a much better golfer, because in 1910 she became the County Ladies' Captain, holding office until 1913, and was re-elected for a second term from 1920-23. She lived at Kendall Hall, Elstree, which later became a guide camp and is now a country club and leisure centre.

At the 1909 A.G.M. the number of full lady members was increased to seventy, but their playing time at weekends was limited to until after 3 p.m. They were allowed to order *The Field* for their clubhouse, though.

By 1911 the ladies were fully in control of their competitions and recording all details, the first being that there were no competitors in the January monthly medal. However, seven ladies entered that month's bogey, two tieing for first place on 8 down, the remainder being nil returns. The tie was settled by matchplay and Miss G. Kell, playing off 8, won a sweep of 2s. 6d. Another lady, Mrs. Biggs, held a handicap of 6.

During that year the ladies played 12 matches home and away against Bushey Hall, Stanmore, Berkhamsted, West Herts, Verulam and Highgate, the teams comprising 7 players.

The Tatham Cup was a half-yearly trophy, the three lowest scores under handicap over eighteen holes in each six months determining the winner. Extra cards could be taken out on Tuesdays and Thursdays only. The format for this trophy was changed in 1926, becoming the combined best nett scores in the Spring and Autumn Meetings, Mrs. de Paula winning with 76+77=153.

The first matchplay trophy was the Kell Challenge Cup, inaugurated in 1911. The following year this became subject to a rule stating the players' handicaps remain the same as at the time of the draw. Mrs. Nathan won it outright in 1922 and re-presented it in 1923 as the Nathan Challenge Cup. From the twenty-nine contestants Mrs. de Paula emerged as the winner.

The first Ladies' Open Meeting was held on 13th June 1912, with handicap prizes for first and second and for scratch. This was won by one of the most famous lady golfers of all time, Miss Cecil Leitch, with a score of 80. The best nett scores were 75 and 76. A mixed foursome bogey was

First Ladies Open 1912

played in the afternoon, won with 1 down. In the same month the ladies organised a mixed foursomes knockout with fifteen pairs, not all husband and wife, taking part, only one week being permitted per round.

An interesting new competition was held in 1913, when a Miss Pennington gave a prize called The Grave Diggers. Mr. and Mrs. Clayton responded the following year by presenting a Cemetery competition, which Miss Pennington won.

Few competitions were held during the war and the first recorded post-war contest was the April medal in 1919, the mixed foursomes tournament being resumed that same year.

The committee must have been concerned about poor entries for competitions in 1922, because the fixture card read "No prize will be presented in any competition unless there are eight or more competitors". It also demanded that cards be returned immediately on the completion of the rounds and no later than 6 p.m., nor could competitors start before 10 a.m.

The first Ladies' Spring Meeting was held on 8th May 1923 when the scratch prize was won with 84. The first division, up to 20 handicap, was tied with 76 nett and the second division, 21-36, with 78 nett. There were also prizes for the best 9 holes home in both divisions and a booby prize. Apparently 40 ladies competed in an afternoon foursomes bogey. The Autumn Meeting was held on 25th September with a similar format but with only 28 competitors.

On the 9th tee

On the 11th

That same year on Sunday 1st July, an all day Lady members versus Men members match was held. Of the 17 players per side the lowest man's handicap was +2, the lowest lady's, 6. The men won the morning singles 10½ – 6½ and the afternoon foursomes (8 pairs) 5 – 3.

In 1922 the Alliston Challenge Bowl was played as bogey foursomes, then as foursomes Stableford before the competition was changed in 1928 to the Ladies Foursomes Challenge Cups, which were presented by Mrs. Kathleen Farquharson, County Champion in 1925 and Ladies' Captain in 1927. The new format was 36 hole foursomes medal and was won by Mrs. R.G. Lane and Mrs. Matheson. These trophies are now known as the Farquharson Cups.

Cecil Leitch returned to Porters in 1924 as Captain of the Ladies Medical Golf Association, leading her team to a 6-3 victory.

The winners of the 1925 Spring Meeting afternoon foursomes, having finished all square, were absent from the prize-giving and forfeited their prizes, the next two pairs being 5 down. In April the ladies lost a match against Oxhey 4-1, which was played at West Herts in the Star London Ladies Inter-club Tournament.

Some interesting matches were played in 1926, Porters' Ladies beating the Ladies Parliamentary Association 4-3 but losing to a United Services Ladies Golfing Association at Moor Park and the Stage Golfing Society at Beaconsfield.

Another item of note in that year was the renaming of the handicap divisions, Senior (up to 20) becoming Silver and Junior (21 and over) becoming Bronze.

The club President, Mr. C.M. Humble, presented a salver during the year, the best 8 scores qualifying for matchplay. The number of qualifiers was increased to 16 in 1927 then varied from year to year until 1938, when the four best nett scores in a medal were used. In 1950 the trophy became known as The Humble Salver.

The fixture list for 1929 offered many opportunities for competitive golf and qualifying for the President's Salver was over 36 holes. A new venture was an invitation day.

Mr. Humble seems to have been more sympathetic than some of his colleagues to ladies' golf and suggested serious consideration be given to ladies playing at weekends. The ladies placed a notice in their clubroom requesting their members not to play between 9.30 and 11.30. a.m. on these days – not a rule but an understanding to be observed to prevent more drastic rulings being enforced.

The Swinstead Cup for a bogey competition was introduced in 1930 and the Marguerite Barnes Challenge Cups a year later, for foursomes (later greensomes) bogey. This was the year in which Porters' ladies won the Herts

Bowl for the first time in its revised format; records prior to 1930 had been lost, but Porters Park was one of the five clubs who subscribed to the bowl to commemorate the Coronation of King George V at the suggestion of Mrs. Alfred Wills, who was the handicap manager of these clubs. The other clubs were Berkhamsted, Bushey Hall, Sandy Lodge and West Herts. The successful team was: Mrs. Bott (5), Mrs. Farquharson (6), Mrs. Nathan (8) and Mrs. Martin-Smith (10). The club enjoyed further success in this event in 1935, 1937, 1938 and 1939, after which the tournament was not held again until 1947 when Porters carried on where they left off. Unfortunately the ladies had to wait another thirty years before setting hands on the trophy once more and eight more years before no less than six victories between 1985 and 1997. The ladies responsible for this latter-day run of success were Mesdames Hall, Horne, Arthur, Stanbury, Drewery, Harrington Brown, F. Smith, Robinson, Hawkey, Healy, M. Nelson, Dulieu, Beardwell and Prosser, all but Mrs. Horne, Mrs. Arthur and the three last-named ladies having played in more than one winning team.

In the meantime the ladies' committee had been busy framing and reframing their constitution. Two ladies had to retire from the committee

LADIES GOLF UNION TEES.

Player's Name: Mrs. Bott — Scratch Score 75. West. Grove G.C. Competition

Out	Length of hole Yards	Bogey	Holes where strokes are taken	Mark Won + Lost− H'ved 0	Score	Home	Length in yards	Bogey	Holes where Strokes are taken	Mark Won + Lost− H'ved 0	Score
1	245	4				10	385	5			4
2	302	4				11	400	5			4
3	360	5				12	146	3			3
4	410	5				13	405	5			4
5	345	4				14	140	3			3
6	123	3				15	288	4			
7	377	5				16	307	4			
8	361	5				17	340	5			5
9	145	3				18	376	5			4
	2668	38									

			Home	2787	39	Home	
Won +			Out	2668	38	Out	
Lost−		N.B.—In Bogey Competitions, Competitors must enter their actual scores for all holes won or halved.	Totals	5455	77	Total	
Halved 0			All cards must be returned immediately on completion of the round; penalty for breach thereof, disqualification.	Handicap	
Bogey result				Net Total	

Date: 23/6/31

Signature of Marker: K. Farquharson

Ladies' London Foursomes played at Sandy Lodge, March 1932. Finalists Miss Jean Forsyth,
Mrs. R.E.A. Bott, Miss E. Wilson, Miss G.E.C. Rudgard

each year and were ineligible for re-election. This was then changed to permit re-election. Mrs. G.F. Roberts was unanimously re-elected as Ladies' Captain for 1933 but was given a travelling case for her captaincy in 1932. The gift was not, apparently, intended as a hint! This second year of her captaincy was not without problems, for it was discovered that the prize for a foursomes event had been wrongly allocated. The ladies considered that a replay was necessary but on referring the matter to the men's committee were told that the result should be annulled and the entry fees go to the Benevolent Fund.

The seriousness of these ladies' approach to golf was exemplified by their committee's decision that ladies taking out extra medal cards when winter rules were in force should play the ball as it lay, subject to the approval of the men's committee.

In 1936 the ladies decided to introduce a prize fund for Spring, Autumn and Invitation Meetings. Each lady would be asked to subscribe the sum of five shillings and anyone refusing to pay would be ineligible for a prize. Fortunately, there appears to be no record of any such refusal.

Despite the success of the ladies' teams at this time, it would seem that not all the lady members were proficient golfers because in 1937 the secretary was asked to write to the LGU to enquire if it was the intention to have ladies playing off a handicap of 36 who had not returned cards within 46 shots of the scratch score of the course. The answer was in the affirmative and probably not a lot of help to Mrs. Clark on becoming the first handicap secretary of the section. (Previously ladies' handicaps were dealt with by an area manager responsible for a number of clubs.) It was decided to enter the *Morning Post, Daily Telegraph* and Royal Free Hospital competitions and early the following year, the London Ladies' Foursomes.

Some idea of the cheerful and confident approach of the ladies can be inferred from their proposal to host the Men v. Ladies match in 1938, with a cold supper and impromptu dance to follow the golf. The men's committee agreed "unconditionally" to this.

Miss Beryl Goddard, a member of the winning Herts Bowl teams in 1935, 1937, and 1938, won the Ladies County Championship in 1938 and was also a member of the team which, in that year, won the County Ladies' Inter-club Tournament for the third year in succession. Shortly after beating Mrs. Caird of Bushey Hall 4 & 2 in the final of the championship, Miss Goddard married Mr. Julian Rowntree, who was a Quaker, and on the outbreak of war in 1939 they moved to Ireland, where it is believed she continued her successful golfing career.

Although the war put an end to external competitions the ladies decided to continue to hold their medals and bogeys, although few are recorded as having been played. Handicaps were suspended during the hostilities so the ladies' committee decided to manage their own. A "war committee" of four was formed under Mrs. Clifford Turner in 1942 and raised over £2,000 for various war charities, such as War Weapons Week, for servicemen, some of whom were entertained once a week to tea in the clubhouse. Dances and bridge drives helped make this vital work more enjoyable.

Chapter Twelve

A Fresh Start

THE CESSATION of the war was the signal for a fresh start, not just for playing the game but in its administration. At the Ladies' A.G.M. of 1946 Mrs. R.E.A. Bott was elected the first ladies' honorary secretary and was introduced by the club Captain, Mr. Boggon, who said he "did not know of any better worker, no greater enthusiast and no better friend to the club than Mrs. Bott". The new Ladies' Captain was Mrs. Joan Chapman, mother of Brian and Frances, who were to make their own marks in the future. She summed up the situation by saying "Our 1939 handicaps have lapsed and we are all starting from scratch together."

More mundane matters were broached with the request for some form of heating in the ladies' changing room.

The LGU permitted handicaps to be assessed over nine holes at the beginning of the year to enable competitive golf to restart. Handicaps having been regained by a sufficient number of the 90 lady members, of whom 77 were full members, the first medal was held in April and a full programme was arranged, although cup competitions at Porters would not begin again until the following year. In any case, the Swinstead Cup and one of the Barnes cups had been lost and were written off by the men's committee.

The LGU were less helpful in that they did not accede to the request to raise the scratch score to match the bogey score, citing the situation regarding re-allocation of handicaps as a reason. A further request eventually elicited the response that two holes would have to be lengthened to par 5's to justify an increase in the scratch score. Mrs. Chapman responded by requesting that two golfers visit the course in the spring of 1947 to give their views.

Entry fees for competitions became 2s. 6d., the same sum being requested for a prize fund. As spoons were expensive and difficult to obtain, it was suggested that cocktail glasses be presented in their place. These also proved so hard to get that it was agreed to give a ball instead. Although

TEAM

MRS R.E.A.BOTT,   MRS V. DORIE,

MRS J.P. GRAHAM,   MRS J.B.HOPKINSON,

MRS H.L.LIDDIARD   MRS T. ROBSON,

MRS J.M.DARROCH, CAPTAIN.

RESERVES WHO PLAYED IN EARLIER ROUND MATCHES

MRS H.A.CHAPMAN,   MRS R.H.BURDON COOPER,

MRS L.M.COLLIS,   MISS J.INGRAM,

MRS E.PARKES.

It is not recorded when Porters Park ladies first competed for the Pearson Trophy, but they won 5 points out of a possible 10 in 1920, playing Berkhamsted, Bushey, Oxhey, Sandy Lodge and Verulam. The competition, initially for handicaps 1 to 24, was started in 1910 by Issette Pearson, co-founder and secretary of the Ladies Golf Union, for clubs in Hertfordshire, Kent, Surrey and Middlesex as rail access was easiest for members of clubs in these counties. From 12 original clubs the number had grown to 172 in 1997. Porters did not win it until 1947, repeated in 1948, 1950 and again in 1997 silver and bronze divisions were re-introduced, it was decided to have only one as there would be only nine ladies in the silver division.

That the handicapping was still not entirely satisfactory may be inferred from a note of an informal committee meeting in October, 1947: "Miss Ingram's handicap has been discussed and it was agreed, after careful consideration of competition cards returned by her this year, that she is playing below her handicap of 26. It was therefore decided as she had not put in any extra day scores this year to put her on half handicap for the rest of 1947. If in the meantime she reduced her handicap sufficiently to satisfy the committee she would be immediately be restored to full handicap."

Within a week Miss Ingram had reduced her handicap in the October medal sufficiently to satisfy the committee and her full handicap was reinstated.

Four ladies, one in the bronze division, having started a greensome before 4.30 p.m. one Saturday, caused the men's committee to write to the Ladies' Captain, bringing the incident to her attention and enclosing a notice withdrawing permission for ladies in the silver division to play three and fourball matches prior to 4.30 at weekends. This was later modified to allow silver division ladies to play in three and fourball matches *if there were two or three men in each match!* Cocktail glasses having become more readily available, eight dozen were ordered to be used as prizes for medal and bogey competitions.

Mrs. McKenzie resigned from the ladies' committee as she was unable to attend midweek meetings due to the abolition of the basic petrol ration. Her resignation was received with regret as was the decision of Mrs. Hopkinson who was unable to accept the captaincy for the following season because of ill-health. Mrs. Bott was proposed and elected in her place.

As Moor Park, Old Fold Manor, Verulam and Berkhamsted had all requested first team matches, the burden on the captain had become more onerous. A new fixture in 1947 had been a match with the Artisans.

In the event the fixtures arranged for 1948 were first team matches with Moor Park, Stanmore and Verulam and first and second team matches with Old Fold Manor. This doubtlessly reflected the less than ideal travelling arrangements which were in force at the time. Joan Chapman reached the semi-final of the County Championship in this year and Miss June Gubbins was the beaten finalist. Mrs. Chapman also addressed the question of providing towels for the ladies' room without having to use valuable coupons. She managed to obtain seven linen table cloths, each of which was cut into six towels.

The club committee asked the ladies to appoint a representative to attend the house committee meetings *if required* and Mrs. Bott was duly appointed.

The LGU asked for a donation to the International Match Fund and a competition to raise funds was held on 10th May. They also wrote to say they would permit scores to count for handicap purposes under winter rules if the ball were lifted and dropped, rather than placed with the club-head. At this time, as older readers will remember, a ball had to dropped behind the player from over the shoulder, thus affording no sight of the point where the ball would land. Equally, the practice of "nudging" was frowned on. A letter was sent to the men's committee asking that the ladies be allowed to follow the procedure requested by the LGU.

The possibility of holding a Ladies' Open after the lapse caused by the war was discussed in July and at the same meeting it was decided to make every other bogey competition a Stableford instead. Improvements were proposed for the ladies' room but a much more serious issue was raised by the club committee and passed on to the ladies for action. Accordingly Mrs. Bott agreed to speak to Mrs. Watson, the stewardess, about the complaint that cats and dogs had been sitting on club furniture causing dust and hair on chairs and settees. How valuable it was to have a lady attending house committee meetings!

This was exemplified by a rather more important contribution to the Herts Alliance in November when at the suggestion of Mrs. Bott the ladies alleviated the shortage of house staff by assisting with morning coffee, lunch and tea and by providing cakes.

In that same month the Ladies' A.G.M. was moved forward to November. Mrs. Hopkinson had now recovered and was able to accept the captaincy and Mrs. Chapman was congratulated on winning the Benevolent Challenge Cup which was open to men and ladies. As the Pearson Trophy had been retained, 1948 was a good year for the ladies of Porters.

A transport fund had been set up, enabling the ladies to play Ashridge in 1949, for the first time. Mrs. Hopkinson requested that sandwich lunches become available and later in the year improvements were sought, and promised, in the teas. The stock of cocktail glasses having been issued, EPNS spoons were purchased as prizes for monthly medals.

Miss Gubbins reached the County Championship final again and also the third round of the English Ladies Championship. This earned her selection by the LGU for special training.

Ladies winning the scratch prize at a meeting were given the opportunity to choose between that or the first handicap prize. If she chose the latter, the scratch prize became the first handicap prize, a practice that held for county events.

Partners were drawn for the White Elephant Foursomes competition in aid of the National Playing Fields Association, a body the Ladies' section still supports annually.

Joan Chapman and son Brian at the Burhill Family Foursomes in 1950 when they lost in the final to A. Forbes Ilsley and daughter

At the request of the ladies, light luncheons became available from Tuesdays to Fridays, provided the steward had been given notice prior to 9.30 a.m. Tea and biscuits became available on Mondays and to increase the ambience of the clubhouse ladies not on the committee were invited to assist with flower arrangements.

The LGU altered their ruling on lifting and placing for winter competitions, outlawing the practice, unless the men's committee had a rule permitting this for the preservation of the course, in which case scores would be accepted, provided such a rule was prominently displayed in the clubhouse.

Mrs. Chapman reached the fourth round of the English Ladies' Championship in 1950 and the final of the Burhill Family Foursomes with her son Brian.

It will be recalled that 1951 was a difficult year financially for the club and the ladies were invited to join the men on a social committee with the object of raising funds.

At this meeting a decision to support the newly formed English Ladies' Golf Association and to apply for affiliation was approved.

1953, Coronation Year, was a busy one for Porters' ladies. The LGU had organised a King George VI National Memorial Fund and the ladies contributed their 1s. 6d. each on Ladies' Captain's day. The same body also proposed to hold a Coronation Medal Foursome and Porters agreed to participate. The LGU also permitted an alternative starting point to be used in medal play and the club designated the tenth as this point, from which medal scores could be accepted for handicapping purposes.

In March, a further opportunity for the ladies to be involved in the running of the club presented itself when Mrs. Parkes was co-opted to the catering sub-committee and Mrs. Everington's name was put forward to fill a second place following a request from the men. A bridge drive raised £47.2s.6d. enabling the ladies to pay for the fitting of a gas fire, presented by Mrs. Shirley Copley, in their room, the surplus to be spent either on a new carpet or curtains. However the versatile Mrs. Chapman offered to make and present lace curtains and her offer was accepted. The purchase of the carpet was postponed because of cost but curtains for the general lounge were bought for £6.1s.6d. from the bridge drive funds.

A suggestion that the ladies run the club dance received a cool reply and their offer to provide lunches while the steward was on holiday was refused as it had been decided that lunches would not be available. The ladies were asked to arrange the Juniors' dance on the day of the Juniors' meeting, though. This must have been a success as they were also asked to run the Juniors' Christmas dance, at which a radiogram the club had recently purchased would be used.

ELGA announced the awarding of Rose Spoons for the best nett scores in each division in medals between April and September. £35 was sent to the International Match Fund.

The ladies were asked to volunteer to help with lunches while the steward was away the following year, when a ladder competition was agreed upon.

Miss Pam Lane presented a silver salver in 1955 for a 36 hole competition and it was agreed to call it the Lane Salver and play for it in conjunction with the May medal. Pam Lane won it herself this first year with a score of 151. She went on to be Ladies' Captain in 1957, during which year she was selected for England, being a reserve. Two years later she was County Champion, retained her title in 1960 and lost on the twenty-second hole of the semi-final a year later. Miss Lane was losing finalist in 1967, and in 1968 had a similar result in the Sunningdale Ladies' Foursomes, partnered by Jean Hetherington. She qualified for the British Ladies' Championship at Gullane in 1970. Pam played for the county first team from 1956 until 1975, being captain in 1961 and 1962, and was the first winner of the Mary Oliver Brooch in 1971, having won six out of her eight matches. She also won the Club Championship twelve times between 1953 and 1971. On retiring from competitive golf she served on ELGA's South-east committee and was scratch assessor for Kent, Surrey and Sussex for twenty-two years. One ladies' captain reported of her "I'm sure there were many other achievements, but she is far too modest to tell me."

Joan Chapman was county second team captain in 1956, when Vicki Baucher was the club's Ladies' Captain. Both served the county in several roles, Joan being junior organiser in 1962 and first team captain in 1965, while Vicki was second team captain in 1962 and 1963, "meetings organiser" in 1966, County Captain in 1968 and 1969, the first of these years coinciding with her second year as Ladies' Captain, her first term being in 1956. She lost to Pam Lane in the semi-finals of the 1967 county championship, played for the county in 1969 and 1970, losing only one out of five matches. She was Club Champion in 1956.

This was the year in which the LGU presented two brooches for silver and bronze divisions, in recognition for the club's support for the International Match Fund. It was decided that these should be played for at the Spring Meeting.

Petrol rationing was in force again in 1957 and it was agreed that if transport problems arose as a result of this, a large car would be hired and costs shared. That the ladies of Porters were determined believers in self-help showed itself again when Mrs. S. Copley was thanked for the supply of shoe cleaning materials. Much of what is taken for granted today was a very different proposition even as recently as forty years ago.

With more ladies employed in business, those unable to play in midweek competitions were to be allowed to play the monthly bogey on the Saturday before the usual date. However, in February 1958, this was changed to the monthly medal, the LGU having consented to the arrangement. Permission was also given for the ladies to play knockout competitions at the weekend, subject to club rules. On the other hand, the request for a shower was turned down!

Difficulties arose in raising a team for the Pearson Trophy in 1959 and it was feared it might not be possible to enter in 1960. However, when Miss Woods agreed to be captain of the team, it would appear that participation was possible. Mrs. Phyl Bailey took over as Ladies' Captain at the annual meeting when it was agreed that a golf ball would be awarded as a prize for future bogey competitions, for which the entrance fee would be sixpence. Further charitable works were undertaken by donating the proceeds of the eclectic competition held from December to March to the World Refugee Fund. The following year the Red Cross benefitted from this fund. At this time nine ladies had handicaps of 10 and under, while there were fourteen on 15 and under.

Mrs. Pearl Reid, Malcolm's step-mother, became Ladies' Captain at the end of the year. It was suggested that non-competition Tuesdays also be designated Ladies' Day to enable ladies to play golf and bridge together, the aim being to widen the circle of friends within the section. It was decided to try this on one Tuesday a month initially and Mrs. Reid promised to examine the idea and advise members accordingly. It may be deduced that the idea was a success as in April a bridge drive raised £107 for club funds.

Later that year, a request for a Towel Master Service having been turned down by the men, the ladies requested more towels, a shower and better heating facilities for their room. They also asked for a small sitting room, which could also serve as a committee room, suggesting either an extra room at the back of the clubhouse or a room at the front overlooking the course. The club captain indicated that while it would be impossible to extend the ground floor, it might be possible to build a sitting room over the existing locker room, thus eliminating the disadvantage of having a locker room on two levels. Mrs. Reid thought that the ladies would approve of this, provided that there was a downstairs lobby where notices could be posted, as the ladies might not read them in the sitting room. By March an architect's plan was available for the ladies' consideration. This incorporated half doors on lockers to create more seating space which impressed the ladies' committee but they suggested that the windows be higher in the front changing rooms to create further space and that the side entrance be put back as far as possible. Mrs. Berry Wilson, that year's Ladies' Captain, was also asked to stress the need for adequate heating arrangements and sufficient power points.

Changed plans for the new room to be on the ground floor were exhibited in September. These met with the committee's approval, apart from the proposals to have two power points in both sitting room and front locker room, the hatch cupboard being above ground level to allow for a fitted carpet and a double, instead of single, boot rack. These details were minor compared with the turbulent meeting called by the Ladies' Captain when Mrs. Chapman complained that three of the committee members had over-stepped their powers.

She felt that the three ladies responsible for the alterations were not keeping their colleagues in touch with plans and progress and that the section was being run by just three people. The secretary pointed out that it was minuted that the Ladies' Captain, Mrs. Sheffield and Mrs. Reid had the committee's authority to choose furniture, fabrics and wall-paper, but Mrs. Glover felt that samples should have been available for inspection. Mrs. Chapman disapproved of the vice-captain's involvement, asking if she had been willing to be nominated before the committee had been informed and proposed the committee revert to the rules of the club. Mrs. Reid pointed out that they had operated in the same way as the men's committee but Mrs. Chapman was adamant. A few days later, the captain and secretary having looked up the appropriate rules were able to inform the committee that they had acted in no way contrary to the rules of the club, and so did not feel justified in putting Mrs. Chapman's proposal to the A.G.M. Mrs. Chapman announced her intention to resign from the committee at that meeting and suitable replacements were sounded out to replace her. In a calmer frame of mind in November, she proposed the Ladies' record score should be displayed on the notice board and the following January presented a bowl of bulbs for the new lounge, which was gratefully accepted.

In the meantime Mrs. Jackie Sheffield had become the new Ladies' Captain. She thought it would a good thing if the ladies continued to support the professional, Bill Large, by continuing with the Maltby Cup which had been instituted for ladies as well as the men a year previously, provided this was in accordance with the club captain's wishes.

At the first meeting to be held in the new sitting room, finally situated on the ground floor overlooking the course, on 29th January 1963, it was suggested to invite the club captain, the committee and their wives, the immediate past and present ladies' captains and committee and their husbands to a cocktail party in the new room, on 10th March. It was later realised that this was too large a number and would also prove too costly, so the invitation was sent to the captain inviting the officers, committee and secretary of the club.

When Mrs. Glover announced her resignation from the committee and as ladies' secretary with effect from the next A.G.M., with nobody able to take her place, the ladies were in a slight quandary. Mrs. Broom, who was not on the committee, was asked to become vice-captain, which led, at a later meeting, to Mrs. Harris stating the office should not be filled at the invitation of one person, but that the vice-captain should be elected by the full committee. The Captain pointed out that the system, which had been in operation since 1951, had always worked well and it was agreed that the incoming captain would continue to nominate her vice-captain.

The standard scratch and bogey disparity arose again in late 1963, as it was felt the latest difference of two shots was too great. It appeared that most other clubs were about to adjust the bogey to be in line with the SSS at the start of 1964 and Mrs. Hopkinson, the new Ladies' Captain, suggested it would simplify things if the ladies' bogey were altered to coincide with that on the men's card. This would mean altering the eighth and eleventh to bogey 4, leaving the third as 5 but making stroke allowances identical to the men's, thus simplifying the handicap allowance and making it easier in mixed competitions.

The club Captain, Mr. Chapman, refused a second request for teas to be served in the ladies' lounge, "unless the temperature in the main lounge was so cold it was impossible to sit there". He was also of the opinion that a ladies' representative was unnecessary on the main committee, although Mrs. Harris expressed the view that there should be more liaison between the two committees, as she found it very embarrassing to confess ignorance when other members asked her about club matters. However, Mrs. Hopkinson was invited to sit on the house committee. The new lounge was now further embellished with a "very beautiful" picture painted by Mrs. Brendon and Mrs. Albany offered to present a clock. Thanks were recorded for this gift at the same meeting which expressed its condolences to Mrs. Albany on her husband's sudden death.

Mrs. Broom having become Ladies' Captain, she took upon herself to question the club Captain, Mr. Balch and the new secretary, Col. Steel, about the booking of societies on Tuesdays, some of which were competition days for the ladies. The reply was that the ladies were only entitled to two of these per month, although the provenance of this rule was not clear. Mrs. Broom requested that the societies should only be permitted to start from the first tee and after 2.30 p.m.

The 1965 Pearson Trophy team beat Brookmans Park and East Herts on the county finals day and lost to the eventual winners, Littlestone, in the Inter-county semi-finals, at Knole Park, Kent. The Vice-captain, who was now responsible for the Pearson team, Mrs. Jane Glover, received the committee's congratulations. The standard of ladies' golf at Porters was high, as we have seen, and this could only have been achieved with practice. In January 1966 some ladies were reported to the club captain for occupying the practice tee at weekends while men were waiting to use it. When Mrs. Glover raised the matter with him, he preferred not to make a ruling about the matter, but to leave it to the ladies to "be considerate about it".

Another matter that ran for a while was the question of the ladies wearing slacks. This had been raised before March 1966, when a notice was placed on the mirror in the Ladies' room reminding ladies that "slacks were not welcome in the lounge on weekends".

This prompted Mrs. J. Arthur to write in November suggesting slacks should be permitted. The Ladies' Captain, Mrs. Phyl Liddiard, replied that while it was not a club rule, the matter should be left to the ladies' good taste and discretion.

1967 began unhappily with the announcement of the death of Mrs. Glover. In paying tribute to her, Mrs. Liddiard spoke of her unceasing efforts on the club's behalf, saying that her quiet, efficient help and influence were irreplaceable and that she would be sadly missed.

The struggle to obtain teas continued. The house committee informed the ladies that the house staff were overworked and underpaid and the bar would remain closed between 3 and 4 p.m. A letter expressing the ladies' disappointment at this response brought the more encouraging reply that teas would be available on weekdays from November to February from 3.30 p.m.

Perhaps with Mrs. Harris's earlier complaint about lack of representation on the club committee in mind, the ladies were asked for suggestions for course alterations. These included cutting back bushes on the sixth, returfing bare patches in front and to the left of the pit on the eighth, lopping the bushes in the ditch on the tenth and enlarging the fifteenth tee. The seventeenth tee was also being rebuilt, and the Ladies' Captain felt that if it proved unsatisfactory it should be permanently back on the other side of the ditch, where they were using a temporary tee. Her successor, Mrs. Vicki Baucher, who was also County Captain elect for 1968,

Frances Chapman

reported that the club would like the ladies to use the new tee behind the ditch permanently. This would be enlarged and the fairway brought back fifteen yards, giving a hole of 355 yards. Mrs. Baucher was determined that this tee would be solely for the ladies' use. It would seem that this was short-lived as by 1970, the new tee was in use.

Further concessions to the ladies were offered at the beginning of 1968 when the men's committee agreed that inquiries from ladies about membership should be referred first to the Ladies' Captain. Equally any member wishing to sponsor a lady should first effect an introduction with the Ladies' Captain before making an application for membership.

Miss Frances Chapman, a junior member, had attained a handicap of 25 and became eligible to play in all the ladies' competitions but could not participate in sweeps. Later in the year she was recommended to the LGU for extra junior coaching in 1969. This paid off, for Frances became County Junior Champion in June.

Medal winners were offered a choice of a one guinea voucher or a spoon. Mrs. P. Harris and Mrs. M. Baynes, having had the club's best Australian Spoons result, came third in the south-east division and, because of a cancellation, were invited to Hillside to compete in the finals on 9th September.

The incoming Ladies' Captain, Mrs. Marjorie Cumming, announced that she was donating the "Does Platter" for a knockout competition for ladies with handicaps 30 to 36. Ladies with handicaps of 30 and above were enabled to reduce their handicaps on the strength of one card under a new LGU ruling. Ladies under 30 reduced their handicaps on the average of their two best scores. All ladies were required to return four cards for handicap each year.

1969 was also a vintage year for complaints: it seems that junior members were playing three and fourball matches at weekends when ladies were forbidden to do this; some ladies felt that the Spring Meeting should not be used as the club championship qualifier as players had been allowed to start from the tenth tee; it was also felt that the field for this meeting should have been divided into two equal divisions, not silver and bronze; three final complaints concerned the condition of the ladies' tees, that dogs were roaming the course and that small children were being brought on to the course by new members.

On a more positive note, the ladies were asked to consider any revision they might wish to make to their section in the club's rule book, which was about to be redrafted. The recent decision that prospective lady members should meet the Ladies' Captain was put forward and was clarified the following May. Any application received by the club secretary would be passed immediately to the Ladies' Captain, who would arrange for the candidate to be interviewed by two committee members before recommending the applicant to the secretary.

Mrs. Marjorie Baynes, the immediate past secretary of the section, died in July and was paid the customary tributes to her efficiency and devotion to her task.

The 1970 playing season ended with a great success when Porters won the Ovaltine Cup for the Herts Scratch League for the first time. The team of Pam Lane, Mrs. Bottomley, Mrs. Baucher, Mrs. Johnson, Mrs. Sheffield and Frances Chapman beat Moor Park in the final. They repeated the feat in 1971 by beating Berkhamsted. A former member of the club, Mrs. June Baucher, née Gubbins, now of Beaconsfield, set a new course record of 73 in the 1968 Ladies Open Meeting, but this was soon broken in September at the South Eastern ELGA championship, when Miss Carol Le Feuvre went round in 72.

An unpleasant letter from a member of Hendon Golf Club complaining that her car had been scratched by the steward's dog when she attended the Ladies' Open Meeting led to an agreement that that lady's entry would no longer be accepted for the event.

The Ladies' Captain wrote to the club Captain requesting that Mrs. Albany be made an Honorary Life Member. He replied that the ladies might like to look at the issue more broadly and pointed out that many ladies had made great contributions to the club and it would not be possible to confer the honour on all of them. However, the name of any lady deserving the honour should be put to the ladies' committee first for their consideration. The ladies reluctantly accepted the Captain's reply and asked that Mrs. Albany's name be placed first on the list of honorary members in the future.

One of the Barnes Cups was lost and a replacement, suitably engraved with the legend that it was a replacement, was purchased.

1972 began with a suggestion to hold a bridge drive to celebrate Mrs. Bott's fifty years of membership, on 22nd May, the same date as that when she first became a member. Mrs. Bott had other ideas, preferring a tea party and she submitted a list of her old friends whom she wished to invite.

A major tournament was arranged on 4th-6th July when the club was host to The Hovis Ladies International Tournament in aid of the National Association of Master Bakers and Confectioners' Pension Society. A field of 90 ladies limited to handicaps of 12 and below played 18 holes on each of the first two days, after which the best 14 scratch scores and the same number of nett scores qualified for 36 holes on the third day. A course of 6,060 yards with a par of 74 was laid out. The leading qualifier was the Scottish international Sandra Needham on 151, followed by another scratch player, Carol Le Feuvre on 152, the same score as Mickey Walker, off a handicap of 1. Ann Irvin of Royal Lytham, playing off +1, lay fourth on 153.

The twenty year old Mickey Walker won the tournament by 9 shots, her first success in a major strokeplay tournament, having won the British Ladies' Amateur Championship in 1971 and 1972. Her total was 299, her last round of 73 being the lowest of the tournament. The runner-up on 308 was Ann Irvin. Sally Westmacott was the only home player to qualify in the handicap section. Douglas Caird in his report in *Golf Illustrated* noted that 26 of the competitors were under the age of 21 – "surely a record for a major tournament in this country." He also praised the club, saying, "they did a great job and especially Mrs. Dorothy Johnson and her committee. It would be no exaggeration to describe that committee as a model for all clubs to try to emulate. It is a very happy golf club."

The eighteenth green at Porters Park as Mickey Walker holes out in the final round

Dorothy Johnson with Mickey Walker

Mrs. Johnson completed her triumphant year by presenting a cup to be played for by medal winners. She was elected County Captain for the following year, having been a member of the first team from 1969 to 1971. Further honours came in 1980 when Mrs. Johnson was Chairman of ELGA's South-East division, and from 1981-85 when she was County President. Sadly she died in office, while on holiday in Spain.

The charge for the prize fund was raised to £1, a 100% increase, and sweep money went up from 5p to 8p. The ladies complained that new holes were not being cut for their competitions, some being six days old. There were now sixty full playing ladies and forty-eight five-day ladies, twenty-one of whom still had no handicap, a matter of some concern to the committee.

In May 1974, the Ladies' Captain, Mrs. Jan Macfarlane, reported that as a result of the course being remeasured by theodolite, an extra 70 yards were required to retain the SSS of 73. This figure was sanctioned because of the degree of difficulty of the course as, in point of fact, the course was 159 yards short of the requisite length. Various alterations were proposed and agreed and the new card in January showed that 2 yards had been added to the first, 36 to the fourth, 26 to the twelfth and 3 to the thirteenth. A redesigned tenth hole gave another 8 yards and a total of 75 yards in all.

The committee was continuing to forward trophy winners names to the local press, but did not feel this had been a contributory factor to the theft of the Dorothy Johnson and West Grove Cups from a member's home.

When they asked the members for their views at the A.G.M., the practice was abandoned. These trophies were quickly replaced, however. China cups were also on that agenda, when it was proposed to provide a china tea service for match teas, with the club committee's assistance and a little self-help by way of a bridge drive.

The most exciting achievement of 1977 was sixteen years old Julie Smith's victory in both the County Girls' and Ladies' Championships, when she beat Mrs. Valerie Tupman 2 up at Knebworth. She retained the trophy at Hartsbourne a year later, beating Rena Turnbull 3 & 2, but failed in her hat-trick attempt, being knocked out in the first round in 1979. She did win the Consolation Plate for first round losers, though. Julie Smith became a professional golfer in 1980 but Miss Nicola McCormack, sixteen years old as Julie Smith was at the time of her first victory, restored the County Championship to Porters that year by beating Shirley Aylwin 3 & 2 in the final at Ashridge.

This was the year in which four ladies from Porters played for the county second team – Margaret Hall, Rosemary Watters, Janet Horne and Angela Davis. Margaret played Laura Davies in both foursomes and singles in the match against Surrey, winning in the foursomes and halving the singles. The Dixon Plate was presented by Agnes Dixon's daughter after her death. Mrs. Dixon had won the plate at the Jubilee mixed foursomes at the club in 1959. It became the consolation plate for first round losers in the Nathan Singles Knockout Cup.

On 12th and 13th August the club hosted the ELGA Under-23 Strokeplay Championship, a 54 hole tournament with a handicap limit of 9. 36 holes were played the first day by the 60 entrants, including Laura Davies. However, the winner was Miss B. Cooper with a score of 226, Miss Sandy Cohen being runner-up one shot behind her.

Rosemary Watters played her first match for the county first team in 1981 and played regularly until 1991; after a gap of five years she regained her place. She was our Ladies' Captain in 1983, when she presented The Golfer of the Year Trophy. Mrs. Watters reached the final of the county championship in 1989, losing on the sixteenth to Hilary Kaye, who had also beaten Nicola McCormack in the final in 1985. Rosemary was a member of the 1990 winning English Seniors Team championship held in Germany. She has been England Team Manager, under Angela Uzielli's winning Captaincy, for two Home Internationals held at Hermitage, Ireland in 1992 and Hamilton, Scotland in 1993, as well as the European Amateur Team championship held at Milan, Italy in 1995, which was won by Spain. Other involvements include the SE ELGA Representative between 1989-93 on the Training Committee. She has won the Club Championship eleven times up until 1998, one short of Pam Lane's record.

Nicola had been selected for the national A squad in 1984, when the ladies felt that any restrictions on her playing at weekends should be lifted. Eventually a reply was received from the men to the effect that all restrictions on her playing at weekends were removed. Twelve months later Nicola informed the Ladies' Captain of her decision to turn professional.

The club was invited to participate in the inaugural Letchworth Salver, which involved two mixed foursome pairs from each club.

Proposals were made for a new ladies' clubhouse and Marion Thomson, a qualified architect, was not only invited to inspect and comment upon the plans but was co-opted on to the development and planning committee. By the time the plans were displayed in the clubhouse in May 1986, Mrs. Thomson was half-way through her year as Ladies' Captain.

Prior to this, the fourth hole was reported as measuring 424 yards from the ladies' tee – 11 yards shorter than the measurement on the card. The LGU marker was replaced in its original position, giving a length of 430 yards and this figure appeared on the new cards.

A change in the format for the West Grove Cup was also made, the committee deciding that from 1986 it be presented to the lady returning the best nett aggregate score in the May and October medals, entry being optional. This would also allow the morning rounds of the Spring and Autumn Meetings to be Stablefords. The handicap restriction was lifted for these meetings enabling ladies whose handicaps had gone back up to 36 to participate.

More serious rule amendments were put forward by Mrs. P. Rawlings and Mrs. S. Farquhar who suggested that ladies could be voted onto the main committee and that ladies with handicaps up to 24 should be permitted to play in three and fourballs on weekend afternoons.

The late Dorothy Johnson's husband presented money for a suitable memorial, which took the form of a handicap board. This was purchased in July 1986.

Mrs. Peggy Rawlings took over as Ladies' Captain and the first innovation under her stewardship was the experiment that the April medal should be used as a qualifying competition for the Club Championship, the first fourteen to join the finalists from the previous year. A request that the number of five-day lady members be restricted to fifty was approved by the main committee.

In addition to the two silver plated vases donated by Mrs. Rena Connell and Grace Wadey for the High Low competition, Malcolm Reid presented the section with a cup won by his step-mother, Mrs. Pearl Reid, in 1949. It was decided to use this as the Club Championship trophy and a suitable plinth and inscribed plate were obtained. The cigarette box used as the trophy up to that time was demoted to runner-up.

The ladies continued to support the club's professional and raised £877 for Jack Ramsden's testimonial by holding a tombola and raffle. Further celebrations were held the following year when Mrs. Albany's ninetieth birthday was marked with a tea party. She unfortunately did not reach her hundredth, dying in 1997, but Mrs. de Paula did on 27th May 1989. She had been a tireless worker for club and county golf, Ladies' Captain in 1936 and County Captain ten years later. She presented the trophy for the Herts Junior Championship in 1937, which became known as the De Paula Cup in 1950.

There had been an improvement in the standard of the golf in 1988: in February the silver division comprised 17 ladies, of whom 6 had single figure handicaps. By August there were 25, with 10 off single figures. However, new handicapping regulations were to come into force the following February and Alternative Day ladies were granted permission to play their medals and Stablefords at weekends. Further concessions were forthcoming in November when ladies were permitted to tee off from 11.30 onwards at weekends.

Part of the dining room was partitioned off to allow the ladies changing facilities while the new building work in their locker room began in September 1990.

Perhaps even more encouraging a year later was the fact that the Ladies' Vice-Captain, Mrs. Myra Wilson, was attending the club's committee meetings and in September Mrs. O'Gorman was proposed as a candidate to sit on the new club Board. In the event, Mrs. Janet Horne was elected. On becoming Ladies' Captain Mrs. Wilson sat as an ex officio member of the general committee and was asked to sit on the membership committee. The Vice-Captain became an ex officio member of the golf committee.

Rosemary Watters and Janet Horne

The Ladies' section purchased a Business Ladies' Cup as some ladies were unable to compete on weekdays and fourteen business ladies played for this cup in September 1992. During this year Janet Horne captained the county second team, a position she held in the following year.

When Myra Wilson succeeded to the captaincy she organised a

charity drive-in prior to the Xmas Fayre and this has become a regular event.

The ladies over sixty had three matches home and away with other clubs and the Ladies' Open was revived after a long lapse. The LGU ruled that the full handicap allowance would be given in Stablefords, and the extra day book would be abolished, thereby allowing an unlimited number of extra day cards to be submitted.

A further gesture in 1993 permitted all lady members to play in fourballs on weekend afternoons. In March of the following year handicaps were installed in the computer. The ladies' committee requested that handicaps should now be administered by the club management. The manager, Mr. Springall, agreed to take over the system in May 1996,

COURSE RECORD

COMPETITION: LADY CAPTAIN'S DAY – STABLEFORD
Please indicate which tee used. PAR 70 / SSS 70
DATE: 20-6-95   TIME: 12.54   Handicap: 3   Strokes Rec'd
PAR 70 / SSS 70
Player: FIONNUALA SMITH
PAR 70 / SSS 69

Hole	Marker's Score	Blue Yards	White Yards	Yellow Yards	Par	Stroke Index	Score	Nett Score	W+ L= H−0 Points	Par	Stroke Index
1		254	254	237	4	18	3		3	4	18
2		356	356	339	4	13	4		2	4	13
3		411	411	406	4	4	4		3	5	7
4		453	453	434	4	1	5		2	5	9
5		384	384	372	4	9	3		3	4	4
6		149	149	133	3	12	4		1	3	11
7		398	398	386	4	7	4		2	4	5
8		425	411	397	4	3	4		3	4	1
9		155	155	136	3	16	3		2	3	15
OUT		2985	2971	2840	34		34		21	36	
10		489	484	469	5	14	5		2	5	6
11		432	432	417	4	2	5		2	4	2
12		205	196	175	3	11	2		3	3	12
13		511	502	478	5	8	4		3	5	10
14		160	160	142	3	17	3		2	3	14
15		360	338	299	4	15	4		2	4	16
16		418	411	399	4	6	5		2	4	3
17		385	385	376	4	10	5		1	4	8
18		450	434	425	4	5	4		3	5	17
IN		3410	3342	3180	36		37		20	37	
OUT		2985	2971	2840	34		34		21	36	
TOT		6395	6313	6020	70		71		41	73	

PLEASE AVOID SLOW PLAY AT ALL TIMES

Holes won: STABLEFORD POINTS OR PAR RESULT 3
Holes lost: C.G.S. 68
Result:
H'CAP
NETT
Markers Signature   Players Signature: Fm Smith

Fionnuala Smith's course record scorecard

but although he entered competition results for a few weeks he did not take over the handicapping system leaving the ladies to continue the work.

While a ninetieth birthday for both Joan Hopkinson and Gwennie Parkes had been a great success, the ladies were less impressed when they learned that the men were using their changing room as a hairdressing salon.

1995 was a busier and more exciting year for the ladies. On the golf course, Fionnuala Smith set a new ladies' course record of 71 on Ladies' Captain's Day. ELGA held the English Girls' Championship at Porters in July, Rebecca Hudson defeating Gillian Nutter in the final, and Lorna Nelson won the area final of the *Daily Mail* Junior Golfer of the Year competition, her prize being a trip to Lake Nona in Florida. Lorraine Beardwell completed a full hand of holes in one on each of the par 3s.

Off the course, a communication from the Board asked the ladies' committee if the section was happy with the status quo regarding the status of women in the club and proposed that no changes be made in the current arrangement for ladies' membership. The ladies' committee felt it was necessary to consult the ladies about this before accepting the Board's resolution. A meeting of lady members was held in December where they voted against the Board's proposal to maintain the status quo and proposed the setting up of a working group to examine equality at the club. They requested that:

a) The working group should be formed consisting of three women and three men.
b) The men should be chosen by the Board but should include one member of the Board and one member of the general committee.
c) All the members of the group should agree that women are equal.
d) It would be helpful if one member of the group had financial expertise, particularly with regard to Porters Park Golf Club.
e) The working group would present their recommendations to the Ladies' section, who would then agree on a proposal to be put to the Board.

The Board and committee had other ideas, however, not wishing that any of their members sit on the working group, but being happy for the ladies to have their own working group. The ladies considered it was part of the Board's responsibility to participate in the discussions. However as the Board was disbanded at the end of 1996 the matter went no further, although the Chairman of the Board had agreed that the matter of women's status would be discussed. The committee gave a hint of what may have been the outcome when it rejected the idea of aerobics classes, without giving a reasonable objection. The Ladies' Captain immediately took this up and the first classes were held in October.

The Board decided to circulate a forward-planning questionnaire and the ladies were asked to comment on the second draft, although they had no input into it. It was sent out unamended and any further discussion on ladies' status awaited the results, although the ladies were assured that they would be included at the consultative stage.

The ladies pursued their own idea of equality within the section, proposing that the five-day ladies could vote at the Ladies' A.G.M. and also join the ladies' committee. They could not be captain or vice-captain, though. Diana Barry was elected to the general committee at the club's A.G.M., and the Ladies' Captain was automatically part of this body, so there were now two women on the general committee for the first time. By 1997 Mrs. Margaret Nelson was on the green committee, Fionnuala Smith on the golf committee, Mrs. Rowena Hemmings on Front of House for a second year, joined by Mrs. Dorothy O'Gorman. So, finally, the ladies have some input into the running of Porters Park Golf Club.

Within the section another constitutional change was made in 1996 when the ladies' committee, at the request of Mrs. Liz Copley, made during the 1995 A.G.M., clarified the ladies' procedure for choosing a vice-captain. After much debate it was decided that the incoming captain would discuss the nomination of a vice-captain with each member of the committee before she put a nomination to the committee for approval.

The first Ladies' Dinner was held on 28th February 1997, after an initial postponement due to a lack of confidence in the club's catering. Liz Kahn, golf journalist and lady member of Porters Park, agreed to speak and donated her fee to the Ladies' Centenary Fund.

The most recent honour for a member of Porters Park Ladies was the election of Fionnuala Smith as county second team captain for 1998.

Chapter Thirteen

The Juniors

THE JUNIOR section of any golf club tends to be the last one to gain any concessions from the main committee and for the first fifty years there was no exception to this at Porters Park, although "Juveniles", over the age of twelve, were admitted from the earliest days of the club. Younger potential golfers were frowned on and were not permitted access to course or clubhouse. This was confirmed again in 1950. Several minutes refer to members sneaking their younger offspring onto the course only to receive reprimands from the committee. Indeed one of the club's most distinguished members recalled being ordered off the course by Mr. Richmond, the secretary.

The lot of the juveniles improved after the Second World War, for in January 1946 they were permitted to play at weekends and on Bank Holidays at the discretion of the secretary. A year later Mr. J. Darroch presented a cup for a Juvenile Tournament, 18 holes knockout. Two cards over nine holes were to be submitted to obtain handicaps.

By 1948, with the course being used more heavily at weekends, the 1946 ruling was changed; juveniles were only permitted to play after 4.30 p.m.

A more lenient attitude was evident in 1949 when Eddie Whitcombe offered free tuition in the Easter and summer holidays and the committee decided to extend this offer to include the children of existing members who were not yet juvenile members of the club.

The prime requisite to facilitate the successful running of any section of a golf club is the appointment of a committed and capable organiser and this is especially important with a junior section. No matter how lacking the etiquette of adult members may be, junior members unversed in this section of the rules of the green may expect the full wrath of the whole membership in the event of the slightest deviation from the code. Fortunately such a man was available and ready to shoulder the responsibility at Porters Park. Much has been written already about Malcolm Reid and his long service not merely to the club but to the game of golf in general. He was elected to the committee in 1949, being assigned to the handicap committee.

He arranged the club's first junior golf day in 1950, played in conjunction with the Darroch Cup, which was an 18 hole bogey competition. Malcolm consulted parents to ascertain the most suitable date and it appears that the event took place in September. Malcolm received a vote of thanks from the committee for his work and he requested that the secretary be included; it appears that the day was a great success and much appreciated by the juveniles. The following year the juveniles were permitted to invite guests to the event.

Always ready to encourage and foster young talent, Malcolm proposed Eric Holt and Cyril Ostler for junior membership, the former becoming first team captain twenty years later. The ladies, too, played their part, organising a Christmas party for children. They also suggested that the age limit for juvenile membership be lowered to ten years and this was accepted by the committee in

Brian Chapman aged fifteen

July 1952. This led to a number of elections of juveniles. The committee also agreed to cover the cost of a cup for the Junior meeting up to £15 of the £26 required. Malcolm Reid continued to raise the profile of the section by organising a Christmas Foursomes competition.

Angela Davis, née Henderson, recalls the early days of the development of the section, when she and several lads, including Paul Orchard-Lisle and Tony Taylor, were sent out with instructions to mark and return three cards. Malcolm Reid then assigned handicaps; Angela remembers that she was given 84! Small wonder then that she, the only girl competitor, won the six wrapped Dunlop 65's Malcolm had provided and which were presented at the Junior Open Boys meeting of 1952.

Having served his term as Captain in 1953, during which period he arranged for a box to be placed in the clubhouse for donations towards prizes for the Junior Open, Malcolm Reid's next step on a ladder that led to his becoming the greatest advocate the junior game may ever have had was his appointment in 1955 as the club's liaison officer with The Golf Foundation. This body was founded in 1952 expressly to encourage the development of junior golf by subsidising coaching by professionals for school-children, students and junior club members. Competitions are organised on a national scale, with the help of generous sponsorship, for teams from schools and for individuals from clubs in The Weetabix Age Group Championship.

The 1954 Junior Open attracted 61 entries, 21 more than the K.G.V., and was won by M.M.D. Laidlaw of Chigwell with a score of 157. The club committee agreed unanimously that the success of this event fully justified the decision taken in 1952 to institute this as an annual event. The following year the competition was held in April and was not completely free from problems. On the practice day a young competitor assisted in the putting out of a fire behind the sixteenth green, suffering damage to his trousers. His enquiry into possible cover under the club's insurance met with a negative response, though ironically it was reported at the next committee meeting that the first fire damage contract had been completed. Both the Junior Open and the K.G.V. had been run at a loss and it was the latter which was dropped from the following year's fixture list, a members' invitation meeting being proposed in its place.

The question of a hut being converted into a games room for juniors was deferred but was raised again subsequently.

As a result of Malcolm Reid's work with the Golf Foundation, boys from Aldenham School began receiving lessons at the club in 1957 and were able to play on the course during the week. Later in the year he offered an honours board for the Junior Challenge Cup. The event continued to run successfully and in October 1958 it was decided that a sub-committee be formed, consisting of the Captain Mr. M.A. Dick, Mr. A. Randall, Malcolm and Mr. R. Baucher. It should be remembered that Malcolm was practising law at the time so he doubtless welcomed the extra assistance, particularly as he had now become associated with the County Boys' team and requested permission for a match between them and the County Men to be held in September 1959. He was also back on the club's committee and Chairman of the Green as well as a member of the Open Meetings' sub-committee.

He would no doubt have supported Mr. H.A. Chapman's suggestion in September 1960, that children aged from eight to ten be admitted as child members at £1.1s. per year, subject to their receiving lessons from Bill Large and that they be accompanied by an adult member, playing only on weekdays. This was to be put to the members at the 1961 A.G.M. but appears to have been overlooked, as the May committee meeting in 1961 gave only guarded support of the proposal. However, children in this age group could be intro-duced into the clubhouse at weekends *provided they were properly controlled.* Later evidence suggests that the idea was not ratified by an A.G.M.

Malcolm was put in charge of the Herts Golf Union Colts section in 1962, the year in which the Golf Illustrated Junior Silver Vase was held in May at the club. This tournament was for players between the ages of sixteen and twenty-two and was won by Ian Stungo of Wentworth. The trophy, a replica of the Gold Vase awarded by the same periodical, was presented by Mr. Chapman; by a happy coincidence his son, Brian, had won the main trophy a month before at Sunningdale, from a field including Michael Bonallack and many other leading amateurs now prominent in the administration of the game. When the Silver Vase returned to Porters in 1974 a large proportion of the field went on to distinguished professional careers, including a lowly placed N. Faldo of Welwyn Garden City. The tournament was won by Nicholas Brunyard of Pontefract on this occasion. Once again Malcolm Reid was chiefly responsible for the club's arrangements.

The tournament obviously attracted support from the Porters junior members. Brian Chapman had agreed to take charge of the increasing numbers and the Captain felt the need to form a sub-committee to look into their playing rights and times. By July the section was so large it was felt that entry would have to be restricted to the children of members. In the meantime the club had donated over £100 to the Golf Foundation, the largest amount from a Hertfordshire club.

By September the following regulation was confirmed: a junior member attaining a handicap of 9 or better could enter club competitions, but not the sweeps. Peter Townsend had won the British Boys' Championship as well as the club's Junior Open meeting and was presented with a club tie at that event in recognition of his achievement. Malcolm was once again congratulated for all his efforts and it was recognised that an official junior organiser would have to be appointed to run the section's competitions in the summer holidays. Mr. Overton accepted the invitation to undertake the task. One of his new charges in 1963 was Campbell Boal. Mr. Overton ran the section for two years and then Paul Orchard-Lisle took over at the beginning of 1966, during which year Nigel Notley joined the club. It was suggested to Paul that he seek any advice about junior golf from Malcolm Reid. With the added assistance of Jack Everington these two ran another successful Junior Open meeting, which was attended by Michael Bonallack, who presented the prizes.

By the middle of the following year the club had 56 junior members, 6 of whom were girls. It was felt that this was a situation that needed watching, but even so five more juniors were elected in July.

During this year Malcolm Reid earned still further recognition for his work on behalf of junior golf when he was elected Chairman of the English Golf Union's Junior Golf Committee. He remained on that committee until his death in 1996 and served as a national selector until 1995. In 1988 he presented a salver which would be awarded to the boy with the best aggregate score in the Peter McEvoy Trophy and the English Boys Strokeplay Championship, better known as the Carris Trophy. The Malcolm Reid Trophy at Porters Park was adopted by the EGU in 1996 as the national under-14 championship, having previously been awarded for the club's Junior Open championship. That his obituary appeared in *The Daily Telegraph* is some indication of the high regard in which he was held and how much his work was appreciated. Carl Duke's words in the chapter on notable players probably explain why every one who came within his field of influence felt that way. He was made an Honorary Life Member of the club in 1980.

Another trophy presented by Malcolm for domestic use was the Christchurch Holiday Club Cup, which the club gratefully accepted in June 1968. However, prior to that the club's Junior Open Meeting was proving so popular that the Captain suggested that perhaps a handicap limit should be imposed. Paul Orchard-Lisle begged leave to discuss the matter with the elder statesman, while the President pointed out that it had become a prestige event and a valuable asset to the club. Added incentive to younger players was the Peter Townsend Trophy, presented by Malcolm Reid for the best score by a boy under sixteen. A handicap limit of 15 was agreed and duly recorded at the January meeting in 1968, at which Orchard-Lisle also reported a turn-out of twenty-two players for a junior meeting on 4th January and that Nigel Webb and Campbell Boal had been appointed junior captain and secretary, respectively. He planned to arrange a knockout, an eclectic and three medal competitions during the year, one of which would be for the Darroch Cup.

The list of sub-committees in 1969 lists the junior section for the first time, Paul Orchard-Lisle being joined by Mr. Ian Judge and Jack Ramsden, the professional, junior captain Campbell Boal, who graduated to brevet membership in March and full membership in November, and junior secretary Tony Moore.

A school friend of Nigel Notley's, Neil Elsey, joined during the year. He became a golf journalist and edited *Golf Weekly* and then *Golf World* before his tragic premature death from cancer in the early 1990s.

As the increasing number of juniors was being monitored, a suggestion was made that the lower age limit be raised to twelve. Fortunately this was emphatically rejected but boys proficient enough to be allowed on the course at all times were to be issued with a badge for identification. The Open meeting again proving popular, handicap limits were proposed for the following year, seventeen year olds must play off 8 or below, sixteen year olds, 10, and under-sixteens, 12.

Hillside School's request for block membership was refused but pupils were informed that individual memberships were available. So by January 1970, when Mr. P.J.R. Marsh took over the section , there were 56 boys and 5 girls. It was decided that no limit would be imposed but the lower age limit would remain at ten. By October the following year the club had 78 junior members and the committee mooted a limit of 75. Such was the support for the Open that a handicap limit of 8 was imposed and the prizes were for scratch scores only.

As junior numbers fluctuate when children become adults it was perceived that careful monitoring of regrading from junior to full membership was necessary, only juniors with handicaps being offered the opportunity to progress. By April 1972, there were just 63 boys, 24 of whom had handicaps and were taking lessons with the professional under the aegis of the Golf Foundation. This increased to 38 in the summer holidays, although Mr. Marsh reported a poor standard of play in the Darroch Cup. The boys' captain, Anthony Coral, was runner-up in the Herts Boys Championship that year and led his team to victory in the Inter-Club Championship. The first record of a junior inter-club match also appears in August of this year. The boys also played a match against the club, Mr. Marsh requesting that the club field the best possible players rather than fathers and committee members. "This would act as a stimulus to encourage playing standards and boost the amour propre of the junior section." Happily, the committee agreed with him.

His energetic leadership inspired 29 entries in a medal at the beginning of January 1973, followed by the juniors' A.G.M. and a film show. He went on to organise medal competitions in two divisions, a matchplay knockout and home and away matches with Moor Park and West Herts. Porters won all four. £5 vouchers were awarded to the winner and runner-up of the matchplay and the committee agreed unanimously to concessionary green fees for single figure handicap juniors from other Herts clubs, as part of the county scheme.

Mr. Marsh prepared a full report on the section for his successor, J.F. Reid, who requested monthly strokeplay competitions, to be held on Saturday afternoons and for which there would be a tee reservation. He increased the number of matches with other clubs, adding South Herts, Bushey Hall, Knebworth and Berkhamsted to the fixture list. He also sought an increase in the number of juniors and by holding regular interviews achieved a full quota by the end of the year.

Bad weather restricted play in the Junior Open to one round this year but the Peter Townsend Trophy was won by a home member, Chris Grant.

Much the same programme was implemented in 1975, but there was an unhappy occurrence when the junior captain, Paul Ramsden, was involved in a road accident. It was reported to the committee that, "his injuries were not serious, but entailed having one toe amputated".

J.F. Reid handed over to D.G. Johnson in 1976 and he maintained the same pattern, assisted by Malcolm Reid, now President, who arranged for no less a personage than Gerald Micklem to attend the Boys' Open and present the prizes. Mr. Johnson only ran the section for one year and was followed in 1977 by Nigel Notley, whose immediate policy was to introduce more strokeplay competitions and inter-club matches and to improve communication by having a bigger and more accessible notice board and listing juniors' dates in the club's fixture card.

Nigel also conceived another project, suggesting that a part of the trolley shed be made into a juniors' club room. He also mooted the idea of a pitch and putt course between the eighth green and eleventh fairway, a suggestion Donald Steel addressed in his report later that year. The committee were concerned about the cost of the latter but showed more inclination to pursue the idea than their predecessors, for such a scheme had been put forward previously.

Nigel presented a lively report to the committee in September; more than half of the competitors in the Darroch were the children of non-members; the average entry for medals was between 12 and 24, but 30 juniors were participating in the eclectic. Similar enthusiasm had not been shown in the knockout, however. His plea for a bigger notice board had led to one being placed in the lounge, which meant juniors had to contravene club rules to read it and arrangements for the juniors to buy soft drinks in the mixed bar were also unsatisfactory.

The fifteen year old Andrew Cotton was appointed junior captain in 1979 in the absence of suitable older candidates, the unfortunate David Keller being due to turn eighteen the following February and thus becoming ineligible for junior competitions. Since then the more sensible rule whereby the qualifying age is determined as of 1st January of the year in question has been adopted for virtually all important competitions.

It was sensed that a certain animosity existed between the juniors and the Ladies' section so a match between the two sections was proposed. Other matches were played in the newly formed Ver League but sadly the club occasionally had problems in raising a team. A family foursomes was also instituted and was reported to be a success.

Mr. L. Major took over as chairman of the junior sub-committee in 1985 and reported that 24 boys and girls had attended three coaching days. The club finished second in the Herts Championship and Wayne Henry, a new member, won the Malcolm Reid Cup. Six inter-club matches were arranged during the summer holidays.

It was thanks to Mr. Major's successor, Mr. Tom Oxenham, that the juniors were finally admitted to the clubhouse and he earned another feather in his cap when Wayne Henry was made Captain of England Boys at the age of sixteen, rather than the honour going to a seventeen year old. Mr. Oxenham was further rewarded by the popularity of the parent/junior events and the success of junior events during the summer earned the approval of the general committee.

In 1987 Mr. Oxenham recommended that 48 juniors rather than 55 should be the limit for the section, a figure which would be achievable due to the forthcoming regrading of 15 boys to student or full membership. Three of the boys were also members of Batchwood and having failed to take the appropriate steps to name Porters their home club were obliged to represent the former club in the Herts Boys Championship. However the required number was reached and only sons and daughters of members were considered during the latter part of the year.

In November Malcolm Reid had a meeting with the captain and the vice-captain to suggest a new format for the Juniors' Open. The English Golf Union had adopted the Carris Trophy as the National Under-18 championship and proposed moving it around the country to different venues each year. The club's own Junior Open had been played as a curtain raiser to this event. Malcolm proposed that a new event be initiated, the Porters Park Inter-club Open Junior Tournament. Two boys, one aged fifteen, his partner aged sixteen would represent each club, playing 36 holes medal off scratch, the trophy going to the lowest 36 hole aggregate score. A maximum of 30 clubs would be accepted. A new trophy, The Reid Trophy, would be purchased and the existing Junior Open Trophy, Townsend Trophy and Stewards Salver would be used for runners-up and first and second individuals. The event would be held at the end of July in 1988 but subsequently moved to five weeks prior to the Carris.

Malcolm boosted interest in the tournament by offering the county union £200 towards coaching for boys under sixteen and a practice net for the winning team, to be purchased through David Gleeson. Malcolm also requested that the bill for printing the entry forms be sent to him.

Tom Oxenham had been busy as well. He reported that out of 55 juniors, 30 were keen golfers. The team lost by one point in the semi-final of the Ver League. Gregory White won the London Boys' Junior Open at Richmond, with James Wright, who had won the Darroch Cup, second. Wright and Chris Jones also played for the Herts Colts and the club first team and entered the K.G.V.

Oxenham's successor, Dennis Lamond, who had briefly been juniors' chairman in 1980, reported a less satisfactory situation a year later as only 26 juniors out of 60 were really interested and he requested permission to raise the number to 70 and to circulate schools about recruitment. The situation does not appear to have improved much by 1991 when Paul Tolley took over the running of the section and suggested that more competitive golf might be part of the answer. He proposed monthly medals in the summer and Stablefords in the winter and that junior tees be provided as even the yellow tees presented a daunting proposition to young golfers.

Later in the year he felt that serious consideration should be given to reducing the entry fees for juniors, particularly if "we wish to continue as a caring kind of club". Accordingly it was suggested to set them at 40% of the full entry fee and payments could be staggered. In the event a reduction of 15% at all stages of the juniors' development was accepted. So by 1992, the juniors were taking their share of the responsibility in restoring the club's financial situation, a member of the section playing his part, and whose exploits are recorded elsewhere, being Carl Duke.

Under Mike Paterson's stewardship from 1992-95 the Junior section enjoyed some success and improved recognition within the club. They won the Ver Plate, got eleven boys into the Boys' County Championship and received support from the membership in the form of shirts, sweaters, equipment and the donation of prizes and trophies. Attendances in competitions went up and playing standards improved as did their playing privileges.

The Porters Park Inter-club Open Junior Tournament was not the anticipated success and Malcolm replaced it with a National Under 14 tournament. Finally the English Golf Union adopted this as the Malcolm Reid Trophy for boys aged under fourteen in 1997, the winner being Craig Stevenson from Staffordshire.

174

Chapter Fourteen

The Past Captains' Circle

THE MINUTES of this select body read like a rolling time capsule. Indeed, those of the first meeting of The Past Captains' Circle on 1st October 1934 were circulated to all the members, so there is no breach of confidentiality in revealing what went on at these jovial gatherings. A few choice samples will convey the atmosphere.

Thirteen Past Captains attended that first gathering, thought to be only the third such association in the country. "Coley" Colebrook, a founder member, who held the office in 1904, was one of eight who played in the afternoon's bogey competition, which was won by J.P. Hall, 1 up on bogey and so taking the sweep.

"After the meeting, the company assembled in the club anteroom, where, under the influence of many cocktails and much sherry, the members exchanged delightful reminiscences of past glories and successes, prior to partaking of an admirable dinner arranged by Capt. Lawrence, the secretary, and graciously presided over by the senior Past Captain, namely A.E. Colebrook.

"'Coley' was in admirable form and in a felicitous speech to those who will succeed him in the Chair, said that he considered the idea of a Past Captains' Golf Circle an admirable one, and he would be prepared to give it every possible support. (Applause from the assembled party.)"

"Coley" it was who laid down the ground rules of the Circle, stipulating two annual meetings, later reduced to one, when the senior Captain would preside at each subsequent meeting and the club Captain of the day would be an honoured guest. It was quite literally a circle, for "On the presiding Captain's right hand, there will sit Captains in order of seniority. At the first meeting, therefore, on the presiding Captain's left hand will be the Captain for the current year. The Captain vacating the Chair each year will move to the left of the table." With a few modifications "Coley's" rules are still strictly adhered to, including the appointment of The Scribe from amongst this number.

Back in 1934 Major Burton was duly installed in this honorary capacity and duly acknowledged "the gracious compliment". He was expected to act as accountant as well, as the dinner was a "Dutch Treat" – each man paying for himself.

The speakers at the meeting included all members present. Only the Scribe's own words can be used to describe the next item:

"Colebrook brought with him the famous Grace Cup (given by the owner of the Park on the formation of the club) and most kindly offered the trophy for competition yearly amongst the Captains. This Cup had been won outright by Colebrook, and the members, whilst very conscious of Colebrook's delightful gesture, felt that he should not be deprived of it. It was suggested, however, that Colebrook might produce the Cup every year to grace the Captains' table. Colebrook at once accepted the suggestion, and at future meetings the Grace Cup will occupy an honoured place."

Indeed, it still does as do other trophies associated with the Circle.

The Circle was in abeyance during the war and immediate post-war years but was vigorous again in the 1950s. That traditions continued is clear from the mid-1960s when thirteen Past Captains assembled and the current Captain, J. Stewart Ross, with four others, was required to delay the start of play for the Past Captain's Salver whilst Dick Bott watched the Coronation Cup from Epsom. "Eventually five Past Captains (including Bott) got away without further fuss … some played golf, some at it. The Salver was won by Dick with the very fine bogey score of all square, which gave him the privilege of paying for the port at the dinner. Reggie (Baucher), in danger of repeating his 1965 victory, was seen discreetly to play a few 24 handicap shots towards the end of the round, which brought him safely into second place with a score of 2 down."

A more serious note was struck when, according to tradition, the assembled company stood in memory of Edward Dix who had died during the year. Then the fun – and the fines – started. This system had been instituted to set up a reserve fund to finance various developments and even an exhibition match with the four Whitcombes, and any pretext would seem to justify a fine being levied.

"It came as no surprise that the first offence was committed by Dick Bott – criticising the Chairman for shouting while Dick was shouting – and for which he was smartly fined 10/-. Max Dick's misdemeanour of proposing the health of the Chairman before the Loyal Toast and in the middle of the roast beef caused embarrassment to the Chairman and the loss of 2/6 by Max.

"Boy Sherriff, on being fined 5/- for not making such an infernal nuisance of himself as usual and a further 5/- for not paying quickly enough, tried unsuccessfully to avoid payment by asking the Scribe for change for a £5 note.

"At this point, when the innocents were congratulating themselves, some clot (or Bott) proposed that all Past Captains present who had not been fined be mulcted of 10/- for their misconduct. The Chairman so ruled.

"The Chairman then took the unusual step (possibly apprehending what might be coming to him if he didn't) of fining himself £1 for shaving off the beard which, at his last attendance, he was fined for growing.

"Mr. and Mrs. Collinge were called in for a glass of port. The Chairman proposed a toast to them and all present joined him in thanking them and their staff for a truly excellent dinner.

"Some endeavour was then made to get down to business. Ignoring all protests, the Chairman declared the minutes were taken as read and signed them first shot."

Even absent friends were expected to donate, such as Arthur Franks, Gordon Boggon, who mentioned Derby Week and Charles Green who wrote from Rhodesia to point out "were my account in England not frozen I should have sent you a cheque (value ½d) with a request that the health of your Prime Minister be drunk at my expense". All made payments, as did Mervyn Orchard-Lisle who had an appointment as President of his Old Boys' Association which cost him £1 and further 5/- for being a past Scribe.

The Scribe announced that there was now £35. 3s. in the kitty. "There were no accounts and they would have to take the ex-Scribe's word for it. (Opposition jeers)." To this sum was added the evening's fines, amounting to £8.15s.

For their £3.15s. as well as their pre-dinner drinks, the Past Captains got: Turtle Soup, Smoked Salmon, Roast Beef and Yorkshire Pudding, Roast and New Potatoes, Cauliflower au gratin, Creme Brulee and Strawberries, Stilton cheese, biscuits and butter and coffee.

Max Dick made his mark early at the corresponding function in 1969, when "in no way abashed by not wearing the right tie, [he] helped himself to port at the sweet course. He was smartly booked by the Chairman, who rejected Max's defence that he liked port with strawberries.

"The older members were somewhat apprehensive of the euphoria of the "goodwill toward all men" demeanour of the Chairman (Mervyn Orchard-Lisle) which pervaded until the circulation of the port provided by Ken Whitworth. How right they were; no sooner had the Loyal Toast been drunk than the Chairman assumed the role of the Mikado, announced that he was going to administer justice and injustice, with emphasis on the latter, and read out a list of fines (happily not too swingeing) at such speed as to make it impossible for the Scribe, who is no shorthand writer, to record them fully."

But Tony Randall, accused of shooting a line and informing the Press, among other things, about his holing out in two shots after driving out of bounds on the thirteenth, had to stump up 10/-. Pat Graham was fined 10/- for being knighted (following elevation to the High Court Bench) and a further 5/- for his absence.

Dick Bott was fined 10/- for recovering from his operation, while Ken Whitworth incurred two penalties of 5/- for winning the Past Captains' Salver two years running and for being recorded on the Salver (through no fault of his own) as Captain of the club.

Even today the tradition of taxing success and penalising failure continues. Attendances at Circle dinners invariably number twenty with half managing to compete in the Salver. Old friends come from far away and those unable to make it send suitable donations. Behavioural problems at table inevitably invite and receive immediate retribution so that funds in the Circle's reserve continue to swell to meet the plan to present to the club a suitable feature to mark its centenary. Yet above all, hopefully the foregoing gives a glimpse of a vibrant club where old friendships are truly never lost with the passing of the years.

Chapter Fifteen

The Professionals

I N THE formative years of most golf clubs, once a professional had been appointed, he was expected to do a lot more than play and teach golf and make, mend and sell clubs. He was usually required to work on the course and, if married, assist his wife in the clubhouse. Our first professional, Arthur Long, was no exception to this general rule.

As the club grew it became necessary to appoint a full-time steward and Long and his wife were relieved of this duty and also of the house which went with it. His wages were increased and he earned extra money by acting as caddie master. His playing time was restricted because of his work on the course but this could not have been entirely satisfactory as it was Butchart rather than Long who was asked to recommend and construct the new bunkers and remodel parts of the course. Long was dismissed in February 1905, but the dismissal was deferred until a replacement had been appointed. When he finally departed in May he took a testimonial with him from the Captain. However, he does not appear to have gained another club position until 1908 when he took the professional's job at Verulam. We have no idea of how good a golfer Long was but we do know that his successor, James Bradbeer, had a sound golfing pedigree. He had been the professional at Ivythorne Golf Club, Glastonbury, from 1897 to 1900 when he moved to Finchley where he remained until his appointment at Porters in 1905.

The Bradbeer family hailed from the West Country and nine out of ten brothers became professional golfers, founding a dynasty that continues to this day. James was born in Berrow, close to Burnham-on-Sea, Somerset, in 1879. An original member of the PGA, which was formed in 1901, he also patented steel-faced woods. It appears that he was spared greenkeeping duties but had responsibility for the caddies.

He was one of the professionals invited to play an exhibition match in the spring of 1906, with James Braid, J.H. Taylor, Tom Vardon, (Harry's brother) or A. Toogood if Vardon was unavailable. 5th May was confirmed

as the date; a medal round was played in the morning at 10.45, the winner receiving £10 and the runner-up £5. At 2.30 there was a fourball match, the winners earning £10 and the losers £5. Members were asked to subscribe to the prize fund and ten local clubs were invited to send spectators at a charge of 2s. 6d. per ticket.

Golf Illustrated reported the event: "an interesting day's golf ... The course, an undulating one with excellent turf and sub-soil of gravel, was in first class order." Bradbeer played particularly well and won the morning medal round with 72. Tom Vardon went out in 35 but took 6 on the fifteenth, having putted weakly and this unsettled him, resulting in a 75 and a tie with Taylor. Braid's driving was erratic and he finished with 76. However in the afternoon fourball, Braid asserted himself and with Taylor beat Bradbeer and Vardon 4 & 3, despite Bradbeer's carding 71. The home professional and his partner won the bye, however, so there was plenty of excitement for the considerable crowd.

In August photographs of the players were framed for display in the clubhouse, where they can still be seen.

In 1907 Bradbeer was given permission to play in the London Professional Foursomes tournament which was held at Porters Park. The committee also agreed that the club should supply his lunch and tea. Later in the year he was given £5 towards his expenses at the Open Championship, which was held at Royal Liverpool and won for the first time by an overseas player, Arnaud Massy, who successfully broke the monopoly on the Open held by the Great Triumvirate. Bradbeer finished joint twenty-first with a score of 330, 18 shots more than Massy.

He improved on his score in 1908, but 329 was 38 shots worse than Braid's winning score and joint fifty-first a disappointing result. His entry is listed as from Radlett, as it was in 1920 at Royal Cinque Ports when he again finished well down the field on 328. In the other years in which he qualified his entry was registered from Porters Park. His most successful attempt in the Open was in 1913 at Hoylake when he finished joint seventh with Massy, James Sherlock and Tom Williamson on 317, J.H. Taylor having holed the Royal Liverpool course in 304 strokes.

That Porters Park had become a busy, competitive club may be inferred from the committee's discussions with Bradbeer in August 1908. It had been decided that a caddie master should be employed, relieving the professional of responsibility for caddies. It was put to Bradbeer that he accept a cut in his salary of fifteen shillings but increase his playing and teaching fees. The alternative was retention of the original salary with no increase in his fees. He opted for the former which suggests he was in demand as a partner in matches and as a teacher.

Bradbeer must have enjoyed some popularity with the members, for when the Charing Cross Bank failed in 1910, causing the professional to lose a considerable amount of money, permission was given to Miss G. Kell to raise a subscription to assist him. However, in February 1911, he was asked to appear before the committee who were not happy with his charges nor with his attitude to the members. "If he thought the place was not good enough for him he had better go elsewhere." The outcome of the meeting was that he was to be paid £1 per week and could charge 2s. 6d. for playing with the members. He was required to be in attendance at the club no later than 9.30 a.m. and remain until all had gone home and was given Monday off. The club continued to assist him with his expenses for the Open Championship and supported him in January 1914 when the Professional Golfers' Association wrote to him, not the club management, to ask if the club could hold either the *Sphere* and *Tatler* Qualifying Competition in April or the News of the World Qualifying Competition in September. They opted for the *News of the World* and thereby set up an association with that prestigious tournament which continued after the war. Unfortunately the 1914 tournament was postponed because of the hostilities.

Bradbeer married Winnie Peasgood, the steward's daughter, in 1914 and Revd. Gotto, supported by C.L. Richmond, proposed that a fund be set up to purchase a suitable wedding present. Winnie continued to assist her father and was dismissed with him in 1917 for "continued insubordination" as we have recorded earlier. This resulted in the professional's position being jeopardised but it seems correspondence between him and the secretary arrived at an amicable settlement.

James Bradbeer may not have been too aware of the situation at the time as he had enlisted in the Second Sportsman's Battalion of the 24th Royal Fusiliers in 1915 and had been gassed at the front at Cambrai in 1918 before becoming part of the First Army of Occupation at Dormagen near Cologne. The club paid him an allowance of £1 during the war, from which he had to find 5s.0d. towards the wages of Joe Garigan, his assistant, whom the club were also paying £1 per week, as they did not consider that a living wage. Bradbeer acknowledged the committee's generosity and authorised them to give the money to Garigan, who enlisted in his turn in 1916, a sum of 5s.0d. per week being paid to his wife.

James Bradbeer survived the war and returned to Porters Park in 1919 at an improved salary of thirty shillings per week. He was allowed to charge 5s.0d. per round for playing and 3s.0d. per hour for teaching and a new shop was built for him. In November 1920 he played in the bogey competition marking the formation of the Hertfordshire County Professional Golfers' Alliance, which had been set up at the suggestion of Lennox Richmond, who became the Alliance's first secretary. The club subscribed to a trophy, The Porters Park Bowl, which was to be played for by the professionals of the affiliated clubs, each with an amateur partner, playing the better ball against bogey. The winners' club was to be responsible for staging the following year's contest.

Harry Vardon's golf and cardigan drew the most attention from the press and he finished 6 up with his partner from South Herts to win the event. This success came immediately after a strenuous tour of America which had left Vardon, who never enjoyed the best of health, exhausted. He appears to have had little assistance from former England international Mr. A.C. Lincoln, his partner, whose play was amusingly described by George Greenwood in *The Daily Telegraph*: "There was a fatal tendency on the part of Mr. Lincoln to top his tee shots; not just low, skimming shots but wholehearted blows on the head. I recollect three or four of these where the ball dived into the long grass in front of the tee and then hopped and fluttered a few yards like a winged partridge."

Bradbeer and his Porters Park partner, Mr. R. Foster, finished 3 up in third place. The following year the event was held at Totteridge and Bradbeer had Captain Mears as his partner. They finished 7 down in terrible conditions, the winners having finished 3 down.

Permission was given for the *News of the World* Qualifying Competition to be held in September 1921. The first 25 professionals would qualify for a matchplay tournament to be held at Oxhey a fortnight later. This attracted a large and distinguished field: Braid, Ray, Taylor, Duncan, Boomer, Jack White, Tingey and Alec Herd. It was the last-named player's son who stole the honours in the first round, however, with 72. Bradbeer was well-placed with 76, alongside James Braid and his brother, C.W. The next day Braid, whose first round had been marred by bad putting, set a new course record of 69 with scintillating play, which left him one shot behind the leading qualifier, Ted Ray. Bradbeer finished joint fifth on 148.

J.H.Taylor failed to qualify and Greenwood, who seemed to enjoy his visits to Porters Park wrote, "Much of the joy derived from watching Braid dragging himself from the mire was turned into bitter sorrow at the sight of the great Taylor battling courageously, yet hopelessly, against cruel misfortune … There was a tragic note in it. At one moment the wedding bells were ringing for Braid; at the next they were solemnly tolling the death-knell of Taylor."

Robert Herd, the overnight leader, faded away and Jack White just managed to get into a six-way tie for a play-off for twenty-fifth place. This clearly upset him, for his behaviour was the subject of serious discussion at the club's next committee meeting, the outcome of which was not recorded.

Bradbeer finished third in the Hertfordshire Open Championship the following year, which was won by Ted Ray. This tournament was held at Porters Park in 1924 and Ray won again, breaking Braid's record by two shots; Harry Vardon was second and Alec Herd, third. Bradbeer finished 14 shots behind the winner on this occasion. With the wealth of talent competing in these events interest must have been high and the Hertfordshire events received good press coverage.

Earlier in the year, George W. Greenwood reported in *The Daily Telegraph* on the Alliance, which was cancelled due to the atrocious weather, the sleet being so thick that umbrellas froze and could not be shut once the safety of the clubhouse had been reached. Conditions improved sufficiently in the afternoon for a nine hole consolation competition in which Bradbeer and Mr. E.H. Baucher tied with three other pairs for first place. An unlikely highlight was "Vardon looking for all the world like a deep-sea diver, in a mackintosh suit – knickers and a coat that filled out with the wind like a decent sized balloon."

In the 36 hole better ball tournament promoted by the Alliance at Porters on a windy February day in 1925 Bradbeer and his partner, Mr. J.P. Hall, achieved a commendable score of 6 up to win the event, Greenwood reporting that Mr. Hall, "receiving three strokes, came to Bradbeer's assistance on three occasions" in their "well-deserved victory". Greenwood's comments on the professionals' attire are well worth reading, as Herd appeared in plus fours "of ample dimensions" and a "pull over jersey", the ensemble completed by grey stockings whereas Vardon wore a soft leather coat, apparently the latest fashion.

The following year the event was held a month earlier and the conditions that caused the abandonment of the 1924 contest returned to torment the contestants. Greenwood's account is worth quoting in full:

PLAY IN A BLIZZARD
PUTTING WITH MASHIES

A blizzard, accompanied by an intensely cold wind, swept the Porters Park course at Radlett yesterday during the progress of a Herts County Alliance tournament, and at three o'clock, when the last of the competitors, almost frozen to death, concluded an adventurous round, there were over two inches of snow on the ground. The average time occupied in finishing the eighteen holes was three and a half hours – a period of misery and self castigation for being so supremely foolish as to play golf in such distressing conditions. That thirty-two couples made the attempt and that ten actually holed out on the last green, shows clearly that the race of heroes is not dead. How they managed it is a mystery, for I calculated that at least fifty perfectly good balls were swallowed up by the snow and never found. It was very tantalising to see a nicely-struck shot go sailing straight down the course, and then to defy search on the part of four players and their caddies. Some gave up in disgust after playing half-a-dozen holes, returning, with teeth chattering, to the warmth and comfort of the club house.

Vardon and his partner, whom I saw struggling painfully over the snow-clad ground, consumed one hour and a half in playing five holes – an average of eighteen minutes per hole – and then, like discreet men decided that it wasn't good enough. But Vardon hated the thought of capitulating, because it was the first time in an active golfing career of thirty-five years, in the course of which he has played thousands of rounds, that a round once started had not been completed. So it was with Alec Herd; never before in a life of forty years on the links had he been beaten by the weather or any other agency. I rather suspect that even yesterday's appalling conditions would not have deterred him, but the fact that his partner lost the only red ball he possessed, and positively declined to go any further, left poor Herd with no choice in the matter. Although he had packed up his clubs and sent the shivering caddie back to the clubhouse, Herd tramped the remaining thirteen holes in the blinding snowstorm as marker for the West Herts couple, Mr. R.T.

Campbell and Bellworthy. They returned a very meritorious 82, only to be beaten on their post by a stroke.

A Remarkable Finish

In the circumstances Bellworthy's finish was remarkable. At the last two holes, each well over 400 yards, he reached the green with two full wooden club shots, taking the precaution to send a caddie forward to stalk the ball immediately it dropped to ground and to stand sentinel over it. At the seventeenth he discarded the putter altogether, as it was physically impossible to drive the ball through the snow, and instead, chipped the ball up to the hole with a mashie. At the eighteenth he holed a mashie chip-putt of six feet for a wonderful 3. Three strokes under the bogey score for the last two holes was certainly an achievement, if a trifle lucky one. The side's stock of ammunition was only depleted to the extent of a red ball, Bellworthy losing one at the eighth, where the ball plunged into a ditch and vanished.

The winners of this eighteen-hole better-ball medal round were Mr. G. Allison and J.S. Fernie, representing Old Fold Manor, who returned a highly creditable score of 81. They thoroughly deserved to win, for they battled through the worst of the storm with the snow creeping down their necks and finding an entrance through the tiniest apertures in their clothing. Like the others, they encountered many difficulties, but the worst experience was in obtaining a satisfactory foothold, and with the snow caked on their boots the sensation was the uncanny one of walking about on stilts. For the first nine holes Mr. Allison played so well as almost to surprise himself. He accomplished a 2, several 4's, and so laid the foundations of the side's success. In the second half Fernie played his part nobly. Mr. Allison was one of the very few competitors who had the satisfaction of saying at the end of the round: "I did not lose a ball."

Bradbeer and his partner Mr. J.R. Grundy finished in seventh place with 87, at 4 down. Later in the year, in October, he won the Herts Alliance Open Championship on his home course with rounds of 73 and 70, and Mr. Stanton Seddon of Porters Park won the Amateur prize with 80 and 72, two strokes behind Harry Vardon. Their combined efforts won the team prize for Porters Park. Despite his record Bradbeer was only awarded £10 towards his Open Championship expenses in 1927, even though it was at St Andrews. He failed to qualify but if Bradbeer was dissatisfied he let his clubs do the talking for him later in the year.

An invitational Professional Competition arranged by the Captain in September was won by C.A. Whitcombe, with Bradbeer in second place. The field was a distinguished one, with Braid, Taylor, Vardon, Compston, Duncan,

Jas Braid

Jas Bradbeer

J.H. Taylor

A. Herd

Harry Vardon

T.H. Cotton

Herd, Havers, Ray and the young Henry Cotton: six were already Open Champions and Cotton was later to join that exalted company. What a feast for the members!

Bradbeer and Captain Lawrence came second in the Herts Challenge Cup, a foursomes event, four shots behind the winners.

The grant towards his Open expenses remained at £10 in 1928 and was increased by 10s.0d. the following year. As it had been some time since Bradbeer had actually qualified for the final rounds perhaps the committee's generosity was being somewhat tested; after all the professional was now fifty years old and the Americans were beginning to dominate the Championship. It is therefore pleasing to record that Bradbeer did complete the full tournament in 1930, the year of the Bobby Jones "grand slam". He finished joint thirty-seventh, 21 shots behind the man many regard as the greatest of all time. This would appear to have been his final attempt, as no further references to his expenses appear in the club's minutes.

Whether he needed to augment his finances or not, Bradbeer incurred the disfavour of the committee in 1932, when he installed a gaming machine in his shop. The secretary was instructed to order him to remove it from the shop "forthwith".

Having done so, he played an exhibition match with Abe Mitchell against Arthur Havers and Ted Ray on 22nd May, Havers and Ray winning by 3 & 2.

Four Ball Foursome (36 Holes) Porters Park Golf Club Sunday, May 22nd 1932. Arthur Havers and Ted Ray v. Abe Mitchell and Jimmy Bradbeer. Won by Havers and Ray 3 and 2

He was back in favour with the committee the following year when he needed a surgical operation, the club paying the fee of £19.7s.0d. Clearly his playing career was drawing to a close and in 1935 he completed thirty years' service at Porters Park. A benefit fund was set up on his behalf and he was elected an Honorary Life Member of the club. At a ceremony in the clubhouse, attended by over 100 members, on July 14th, Bradbeer was presented with a cheque for £325 and a signed autograph book, expressing the high regard in which he was held by the members. He continued to serve the club for another two years and retired in 1937.

James Bradbeer died in August 1937, after a short illness while on holiday at Burnham-on-Sea. He always took his annual holiday there, never having lost his love for his birthplace. His funeral, which was attended by representatives from Porters Park, was described in a three-column article in the *Burnham-on-Sea Gazette*. He was buried in the churchyard, encircled by the sandhills of the course where he first learned the game of golf.

The committee's first choice of a replacement was Abe Mitchell, to whom the Captain issued an invitation to an interview. However, one week later the committee was informed that a short list had been drawn up from which Mitchell's name was absent. He was a noted golfer and was a private professional in St Albans when he received the invitation, one of his most famous pupils being Samuel Ryder, who had earlier been a member of

Eddie Whitcombe

Porters. It is Mitchell's likeness which graces the Ryder Cup.

The choice of the new professional fell on a member of another illustrious golfing family, Eddie Whitcombe, who was retained for £2.10s.0d. per week from 18th October 1937. He was the son of Ernest Whitcombe and nephew of Charles and Reg, who won the Open in 1938. It may not be entirely coincidental that the brothers hailed from Burnham, the neighbouring village to Berrow, the birthplace of the Bradbeer clan. Ernest Edward "Eddie" Whitcombe was born at West Flagg, Dorset, where his father was professional at Came Down Golf Club, in 1913.

With Whitcombe now employed by the club, the Past Captains had the inspiration to engage the Whitcombe family to play an exhibition match in September 1938, by which time Reg was Open Champion, Eddie the losing finalist in the Matchplay Championship (to another Hertfordshire professional, Dai Rees), and Charles and Ernest were Ryder Cup regulars.

1,000 people attended this occasion to watch father and son, Ernest and Eddie, take on Ernest's brothers Reg and Charles. The latter pair won the morning fourball by 3 & 2, although only five holes changed hands during the match, a highlight of which was the holing of some long putts. The better ball scores are worth recording:

```
Reg and Charles:    Out:  3 4 4 4 3 3 4 4 3 = 32
                    Home: 3 3 3 4 2 4 4 3 4 = 30 = 62
Ernest and Eddie:   Out:  3 4 4 4 4 3 4 4 3 = 33
                    Home: 4 4 3 4 3 3 3 4 4 = 32 = 65
```

Father and son had their revenge in the afternoon, when an American Greensome was played, in which the drive selected is nominated before the players leave the tee. Ernest and Eddie won the first two holes, Eddie being the only one to escape the bunkers on the first. Charles was stymied on the second and knocked both balls into the hole. Some spectacular golf followed, Ernest's tee shot on the sixth finishing two feet from the hole. Eddie sank the putt for a 2 and repeated this on the ninth. Father and son were out in 30, against 35 from the brothers. Ernest and Eddie finished the match on the fourteenth, having taken 18 shots for the 5 holes, whilst Reg and Charles took 19.

An amusing aside on the career of Eddie Whitcombe, who generally suffered by comparison with the successes of his father and uncles, was a song composed by the music hall entertainers, Kenneth and George Western.

STRAINED RELATIONS

Uncle Charles, Uncle Reg and Dad,
You Whitcombes really are too bad!
Your little boy Eddie, it does seem a sin,
These golf competitions you won't let him go in
But who are the fellows who won't let him win?
Uncle Charles, Uncle Reggie and Dad!

Uncle Charles, Uncle Reggie and Dad,
It's happened since he was a lad,
When he was a baby, he'd lie in his cot,
Just eating his sweets, would this dear little tot.
But who would creep up and pinch all the lot?
Uncle Charles, Uncle Reggie and Dad!

189

Uncle Charles, Uncle Reggie and Dad,
You've made his life awfully sad!
Just think of his heartaches when he was a mite;
You should be ashamed of yourselves and contrite
Who played with his soldiers, kept flying his kite?
Uncle Charles, Uncle Reggie and Dad.

Uncle Charles, Uncle Reggie and Dad,
Do you want to drive young Eddie mad?
When you're in the nineteenth, he's right in the shade;
You're bound to have three, that's if each one had paid.
Who stands him outside with a small lemonade?
Uncle Charles, Uncle Reggie and Dad!

Uncle Charles, Uncle Reggie and Dad,
What chance has this boy ever had?
After all, he's a Whitcombe: he looks just like you.
So why do you treat him the way that you do?
Next time he shouts "fore", won't you please let him thro',
Uncle Charles, Uncle Reggie and Dad.

Although a very good putter, a lack of power prevented Eddie reaching the heights attained by the older generation of his family, but he did win the East Anglian Open three times between 1953 and 1964. The Second World War interrupted his career and, like Bradbeer before him, he joined the Army in 1940. Frank Scales was appointed as his deputy and later the same year was called up into the Auxiliary Fire Service. While taking part in a training exercise Eddie broke his left wrist which further diminished his power.

On his return in 1946, Whitcombe's retainer was increased to £3, plus a weekly bonus of £1.10s.0d. He was also permitted ninety days per year leave from the club to allow him to compete in tournaments. It is interesting to note, in passing, that this was the same amount of time James Braid was allowed to absent himself from Walton Heath both to compete and to design golf courses, Braid's contract having been negotiated first in 1904, when there were far fewer professional tournaments, but possibly more exhibition matches, than in the post Second World War era.

In addition to adding to his reputation as an outstanding club-maker, Whitcombe began a free coaching scheme in 1949 for juveniles who were not club members and in October was joined by Uncle Charles for an exhibition match with one of that year's American Ryder Cup team, "Dutch" Harrison and former team member Ed Dudley. This was arranged by Arthur Baucher, who had attended the biennial contest at Ganton. Charles was the captain of the home team, and Eddie's friend Ben Hogan led the

Americans and the two were soon embroiled in a dispute about the legality of some of the British side's clubs. Despite that, Baucher found the Americans a very sporting group of men and resolved to invite them down.

Sadly no record of the match result exists but Malcolm Reid recalls an incident on the second hole where Charlie Whitcombe hit his second shot across the brook to the green, stopping it absolutely dead by the pin, causing Ed Dudley to call out across the fairway, "Say, Mr. Charlie, just bring that club here for inspection".

Eddie Whitcombe left Porters Park in 1950 and Frank Scales was appointed to succeed him, but as he was in hospital at the time, he had to appoint a capable playing assistant. Whitcombe moved to Chigwell Golf Club, where he was accorded honorary life membership. He became an important member of the PGA Committee and was responsible with Bill Cox for setting up the training scheme for assistant professionals. He died in February 1997, aged 83.

Frank Scales' health problems were to continue, but he served the club for eighteen years. The wording on the Maltby Cup was changed in 1952; as Whitcombe was no longer the professional his name had to be removed, to be replaced simply by "the professional". A benefit for Scales was proposed for 1954, possibly an exhibition match. This was most probably the match involving Harry Weetman, who apparently drove through the fifteenth green, chipped back too strongly and was heard to say that it was the first time he had been short with two shots on a 300 yard hole. The committee did agree to Scales giving lessons to residents of the Aldenham Lodge Hotel in the club's practice nets, provided it did not interfere with the requirements of club members and took place only in the winter after dark!

Peter Lynn recalled that Scales enjoyed teaching and making beautiful wooden clubs rather than playing competitively. Despite his illness he was always cheerful and Peter was grateful to him for bringing his handicap down from 24 to 16.

Scales took on Tony Grubb as an assistant in 1958, but the young man was on his way in less than a year to pursue a career on the tour. Scales' shop was apparently inadequately stocked or attended and the professional was given an ultimatum: improve his service or leave. It was not realised until after he had left how serious his illness was and it was reported that he was likely to die within six months. The committee made themselves liable for his debts, paying off £300 worth, and set up a benefit fund for him. As a result £910 was given to his widow in 1960.

In the meantime Bill Large had become the professional, on a retainer of £5 per week. This was increased by £2 in January 1962, along with his lesson fees, despite adverse comments about the untidiness of his shop.

191

He received further criticism for his lack of enterprise and also a lack of interest in the golf of the Ladies' section in the long hard winter of 1963, when he missed an opportunity to hold evening classes for the benefit of the members. Nevertheless he was given £30 by the club to tide him over.

The message did not apparently sink in, for two years later the President took it upon himself to investigate the "paucity of goods" in Large's shop. The committee's solution to the problem was to offer an increased retainer of £8 and higher playing charges in return for a better stocked shop. It became clearer in January 1965 where the professional's real interests lay, as he informed the Captain that he wished to devote more time to tournament golf. Permission was granted upon Large's undertaking to maintain his stock adequately and to employ an extra assistant at the weekends. Matters came to a head when the Captain and President decided to interview Large about his intentions and were offered a letter of resignation with effect from 31st December. Although requested to defer his departure if no replacement had been appointed by then, he informed them that he was leaving for South Africa at the end of the year.

The committee decided that, in future, the ideal professional for Porters Park would be a middle-aged man with no pretensions to playing tournament golf.

In fairness to Large, he had a good tournament record and was only twenty-two years old when given the responsibility of the professional's job at Porters Park. Born in Liverpool in 1937, he reached the final round of the Open Championship in 1958 at Royal Lytham, finishing equal thirty-eighth. On the two subsequent occasions on which he qualified for the final stages he improved on this position, thirtieth in 1965 at Birkdale, a venue he must have liked for he came equal twenty-fourth there in 1971. He holds the record for the fewest putts in a PGA event, taking just 22 in qualifying for the Benson and Hedges matchplay in 1972. His best year, though, was 1968 when he finished twelfth in the Order of Merit, tied for the Alcan International Tournament and was second in the Wills Open. He won the Honda Foursomes in 1965 and tied with Peter Alliss for the 1966 Martini International. He is now the professional at another Hertfordshire club, Dyrham Park.

The committee recommended J.K. Ramsden of Hampstead Golf Club as Large's successor and further recommended that while Ramsden was at liberty to choose his own assistants, Glyn McCarthy, who had assisted Large and would run the shop if there was a hiatus between appointments, should be considered by Ramsden.

Jack Ramsden was born in Keighley, West Yorkshire on 10th March 1923. He left school at fourteen to join Sam Walsh as assistant at Bingley St Ives Golf Club. After twelve months his wages were increased by 2s.6d. to 15s.0d.

per week. He moved to Keighley Golf Club, where E.T. Large paid him double that amount. Ramsden took up an apprenticeship as a machine tool engineer in 1940, which left him little time for golf. He joined the forces in 1945 and became a P.T. Instructor in the West Yorkshire Regiment, playing rugby rather then golf. On his demobilisation in 1948 he returned to engineering and had a trial for the Yorkshire Rugby Union team. He returned to golf and E.T. Large at Keighley in 1949, first as assistant, then as partner to take over on Large's retirement.

Ramsden came south in 1957, to Tandridge Golf Club as playing assistant to A.J. Baker. He moved to Hampstead in 1959 as professional and in 1962 tied for the Middlesex Professional Championship. He was the captain of the Middlesex professionals in 1965 and 1966 and took up his appointment at Porters Park on 1st January of the latter year. He continued to participate in Middlesex events, being the Middlesex Open Champion in 1967 at Mill Hill and was runner-up in the event the following year. He became Captain of the Hertfordshire Professional Golfers' Association in 1973. He retired from Porters Park in 1988.

In 1967 Peter Townsend announced his intention to turn professional, his career being discussed elsewhere. During the same year another Peter who had enjoyed an even more illustrious career was engaged to play in an exhibition match in aid of the Variety Club of Great Britain. At the instigation of Mr. Bernard Coral, head of the well-known book-making firm, Peter Thomson, the five-times Open Champion, was joined by Gary Player, who claimed the Claret Jug on three occasions, replacing Billy Casper, the original choice, on 16th July. A sub-committee was formed, co-opting Mr. Coral, to handle the arrangements. It was a most successful occasion, which raised over £3,200 for the charity.

The match took place the day after the completion of that year's Open Championship which was played at Hoylake and won by Roberto de Vicenzo. Player tied with Clive Clark for third place and Thomson finished three shots behind him. Player also prevailed in this encounter, scoring 66 to Thomson's 69.

Gary Player holes out in 66 to beat Peter Thomson by 3 shots

193

Thomson led in the match up to the turn but was suffering from hay fever and lost on the sixteenth. Player was accompanied round the course by actors Stanley Baker and Sean Connery.

Some older members still have memories of the match: Tony Mills remembers Player's caddie, Alf, giving him an 8-iron for his second shot to the eleventh. Player claimed he would be short with this club and when the ball finished six inches short of the hole apparently said, "I told you I'd be short." John Van Gelder, acting as a steward at the event, recalls this slightly differently. The drive on the eleventh was never more than six feet above the ground and finished level with the twelfth tee. He then hit a lofted iron to the green and told John that it was a 9-iron. John informed him it was quite a difficult hole but Player disagreed, maintaining it was one of the easiest and duly holed the birdie putt, from six feet according to Van Gelder.

A film was made of the occasion, which was not shown to members until the following year, after it was realised that the film had been shot but nothing further had been heard of it. Eventually correspondence with Mr. Coral enabled the members to relive the day. Unfortunately this film has subsequently been lost.

Peter Townsend had also volunteered to play an exhibition match and a challenge was issued to Clive Clark who picked up the gauntlet on 13th July 1968. Townsend, struggling with his re-styled golf swing, showed immense powers of recovery and putting superbly, scoring a record 64 to Clark's 71.

PORTERS PARK GOLF CLUB
RADLETT ☆ HERTS.

£200 CHALLENGE MATCH

PETER TOWNSEND
(Porters Park)

v.

CLIVE CLARK
(Sunningdale)

SUNDAY, 13TH JULY

GOLF CLINIC 2-15 p.m.   TEE–OFF 2-30 p.m.

MEMBERS BADGES – 7/6   .   FREE CAR PARK

On the retirement of Jack Ramsden, our present professional David Gleeson was appointed. Born in 1954, he took up his duties at Porters on 1st May 1988. David first took up golf at the age of fifteen at Royal St Georges. He clearly possessed a very natural aptitude for the game, turning professional one year later with a handicap of 1. He had already caught the eye of past Walker Cup Captains, John Beck and George Hill, and they acted as his sponsors into the Professional Golfers' Association. His performance in the 1970

Under-25 Tournament also helped as he was the youngest player to qualify for the final round. A year later he was the youngest fully qualified professional at the PGA School and continuing to exploit his youth became the youngest club professional in Kent in 1977 when he was confirmed in that appointment at Walmer and Kingsdown.

Rather than seek fame as a player, however, David devoted most of his time to teaching and making and repairing golf equipment, thereby continuing the traditions of the true club professional. He is now developing the teaching side of his career by studying for a degree in Sports Psychology.

A family man with two sons and a wife who works as a nursery nurse, David is aware of life beyond the golf course, holding office as a school governor, his responsibility there being leadership of the Special Educational Needs team.

CHALLENGE MATCH.

MEN'S MEDAL TEES.

Player PETER TOWNSEND   S.S.S.—70

Handicap ....

Strokes Received ....

Marker's Score	Holes	Stroke Holes	Yards	Par	Player's Score	Mark Won + Lost − Halved 0	Marker's Score	Holes	Stroke Holes	Yards	Par	Player's Score	Mark Won + Lost − Halved 0
	1	18	259	4	3			10	6	479	5	4	
	2	11	352	4	4			11	1	437	4	4	
	3	2	415	4	3			12	14	191	3	3	
	4	5	450	4	5			13	8	480	5	3	
	5	9	389	4	4			14	16	163	3	3	
	6	13	160	3	3			15	17	312	4	4	
	7	7	402	4	4			16	3	415	4	4	
	8	4	416	4	3			17	12	385	4	4	
	9	15	138	3	2			18	10	440	4	4	
OUT			2981	34	31		**HOME**			3302	36	33	
							OUT			2981	34	31	
							TOTAL			6283	70	64	
							HANDICAP						
							NET SCORE						
							RESULT						

Marker's Signature FOR PORTERS PARK GOLF CLUB

Player's Signature .... J. Stil

Date 13th July 1969 .... Secretary.

A stroke should be taken at each Hole opposite which the red figure is equal to or less than the Handicap Allowance.

Peter Townsend's Professional record scorecard of 64

David Gleeson

Chapter Sixteen

The Artisans

ARTISAN CLUBS have long been associated with a considerable number of prestigious and less well-known clubs in England and many fine golfers have emerged from the ranks of their members. The idea behind the movement was to allow "the working man" the opportunity, which he might otherwise be unable to afford, of playing the golf course at times less popular with members from more leisured backgrounds, in return for duties on the course or maintenance of the clubhouse and associated buildings, thus freeing the greenstaff for more urgent tasks. By 1921 there were sufficient artisan clubs to sustain a national association, founded by J.H. Taylor and Fred Hawtree sr. By 1923 the best players were competing for the Sandy Herd Memorial Trophy in the Artisans Championship.

The first time the formation of an Artisans section at Porters was suggested was in 1929, when it was considered unnecessary. The issue was raised again in 1941 but shelved again until 1944, when E.S. Markham, J. Everington and J. Macdonald were appointed as a sub-committee to investigate the possibilities, based on information already received. A representative of the artisans attended the committee meeting in October and it was explained to him that before a section could be founded the club's members would have to agree to the idea at the next A.G.M.

That they did is borne out by the fact that very quickly after that meeting the sub-committee, augmented by Mr. J.L. Darroch and C.K. Cotton met the representatives of the Artisans, Messrs. McClafferty and Longman, and spelt out the rules.

The first subscription was 10 shillings per annum, payable on 1st June. Membership was limited to 40 but only 20 vacancies could be filled immediately, the remaining 20 being reserved for men in the forces who might wish to join on demobilisation. The names of the first members were to be submitted to the club committee by 25th April to enable the section to begin operations on 1st June. Cotton had already had rule books and application forms available and for their part, the artisans had already appointed their officers.

25 applications were submitted to the club in April, of which 19 were accepted, the remaining six being turned down on the grounds that they owned their own businesses and therefore were not, in the strictest sense, artisans. This decision was reversed in May after an appeal by the artisans' committee. Up to this point, no mention had been made of the duties expected of the section.

Having permitted the election of a number of artisans, when faced with a list of six ex-servicemen in February 1946, the committee referred their election back to the artisans' committee, which suggests that the club was satisfied with the way the artisans' affairs were being conducted, though subsequently they retained approval of the section's recommendations. They also approved a request to hold matches with other artisan clubs, within the allotted hours. A further experimental concession was made in October when the artisans were allowed to start from the first tee on winter Sundays between 12.15 and 1.00 p.m, provided they played nine holes only and in twoballs. This privilege was extended the following winter when permission was given to play twoballs on Saturdays, Sundays and Bank Holidays after 3 p.m.

The club committee viewed less favourably the suggestion that not all the artisans were making full use of their membership, and if that was the case those members should resign and make way for others. A request to sell beer to members in their club room was granted on the understanding that the artisans would obtain the necessary licence and order the supplies themselves.

The old Artisan clubhouse

198

In 1949 the limit of 40 artisans was modified to allow members of the club's greenstaff to play as artisans, as long as they remained employed by the club, without counting among the 40, unless they ceased to work for the club, in which case they would have to seek election, if so desired, to the artisans and would then be included in their limited number, if elected.

The first mention of the artisans being asked to assist on the course came in June 1950, when it was suggested that they could undertake to keep the stream clean and tidy. Their reply was not recorded but the very next month they were given permission to sign in a maximum of 80 fellow artisans a year as guests, within their allocated weekday times. The club also gave permission for the North London Artisan Golfers' Alliance to hold a meeting at a future date.

It was in this year that Mr. Percival of the parent club presented the section with a "beautiful" trophy, which it was decided to award for success in a matchplay knockout.

In 1951 the section began the year with three vacancies: Mr. McClafferty had been made an honorary life member of the section, a Mr. Brennan had been expelled and another member resigned. However, the artisans seemed to be running their affairs more successfully than the parent club, whom, it will be remembered, were experiencing severe financial constraints, so when the artisans very tactfully suggested that they would like to make a £50 donation to the parent club's funds, in view of their attitude to the artisans' section, the offer was gratefully accepted. When Mr. J.P. Hall reported the offer to the committee he also offered to sound out the artisans concerning their possible willingness to paint the exterior of the clubhouse. They were – if they were paid to do so – and it was left to the secretary to make the necessary arrangements.

To try to alleviate the parent club's financial difficulties it was suggested that some of the more "well-to-do" artisans might be offered full membership of the club, but after some consideration the idea was shelved.

In the 1950s one artisan golfer, Jim Rogers, attained a plus handicap, while others improved their golf thanks to the assistance of Eddie Whitcombe, who gave them lectures as well as lessons. When he moved to Chigwell the artisans presented him with a gift to commemorate their association. The section then continued to support Eddie's successors.

The first mention of the annual match against the artisans appeared in the minutes for the meeting of September 1951, so worded that it suggests that this had already been instituted on an annual basis (it had in fact been going since 1946). Similarly, appreciation for work done on the course by the artisans was noted for the first time in June 1952.

A request that artisans might play at the weekends in winter outside their normal playing hours on payment of a green fee was granted in

October 1953, on an experimental basis, so they were allowed to play a full round for five shillings. To ease the membership situation it was agreed to consider applications for full membership from artisan members. The section was also invited to hold its annual dinner in the clubhouse and this was so successful that the Captain suggested that this should become a permanent arrangement if the artisans so desired; as it appears from later minutes, they did. The success of the evening was probably enhanced by the provision of Benskins bitter in place of Watneys, which the membership had not found to their liking.

When the Hertfordshire Artisans' Golf Union was formed in 1954, its President, Dick Bott, wrote to all the clubs in the county requesting a subscription towards a championship trophy and Porters Park duly contributed five guineas. Porters was the venue for a fourball bogey competition involving pairs from clubs and artisan clubs organised by this body.

It was the artisans' turn to experience financial constraints a year later. They advised the club that because of their own difficulties they would be unable to make their usual donation as they needed to make provision for a new hut, for which purpose they opened a building fund. Mr. Everington advised the club that it should not be responsible for providing or erecting a hut as this might prejudice relations with the Middlesex County Council with whom the club were in negotiation over the purchase of the course. The club had made a donation in 1950, utilising the surplus from the J.P. Hall memorial fund, in aid of a similar plea.

On a lighter note, the ladies entertained the artisans to a match during the year, which in turn led to a request in 1956 from them for a return match to enable them to reciprocate the hospitality. The request for a Saturday afternoon was frowned on by the committee, mindful of members' objections to weekend matches. Nevertheless, they agreed to pass the request on to the Ladies' Captain with the proviso that such a match must be played during the agreed times for the artisans, or alternatively, on a weekday evening. That good relations have always existed between parent club and the artisans is borne out by the number of distinguished members who accepted the annual invitation to attend the artisans' annual dinner, held for some years at the Red Lion at Radlett and then in the clubhouse with the advent of Mr. Collinge as steward and as a member of the section.

The section was permitted to enrol five junior members in 1958, as long as they played with adult members and not on Sunday mornings. It is clear that there had always been a good relationship between the parent club and the artisans and a further illustration of this is the club's decision to provide half the cost of a rotary scythe which the artisans wished to purchase to enable them to give better assistance with the upkeep of the course.

The first rumble of discontent was heard in 1961, when the Captain reported that he had received complaints that artisans were holding up play, possibly because they were not starting early enough. He decided to speak to the Artisans' Captain and in the meantime it was suggested that the artisans' last starting time be brought forward to 8.30 a.m. Four members of the committee were deputed to keep an eye on things. However, the times remained unchanged and there were no further complaints until October the following year. This time the President undertook to persuade the artisans to make an earlier start.

The problem seemed to recur at infrequent and irregular intervals and the club received assurances that members would not be inconvenienced. Indeed, the annual dinner, supplemented by a social evening with club members, and regular competitions organised by the County Artisans' Golf Union continued without annoying anybody.

A club character arrived at Porters Park in 1963, when Doug Brown, then a member of the greenstaff, joined the artisans. He subsequently became the locker room attendant and used his position to raise considerable amounts for charity, for which he received the British Empire Medal in 1995. He retired in 1998.

What began as an enquiry into the artisans' hours of play in 1966 became a full report on the terms and activities of the section. It was noted that the artisans were not actually required to work on the course, so clearly all previous work had been of a voluntary nature. Little effective work had been done on the ditch which had been assigned to the artisans as their responsibility and Mr. Ross, the Captain, suggested a re-appraisal of the conditions governing the section was due. Selective Employment Tax might have influenced any decision the club might have taken on altering the hours of play. The artisans, for their part, responded by disciplining any member who failed to honour his obligation to work on the course, which, at times, led to a considerable turnover of members.

Dr. R.S.F. Hennessey, E.A. Judge and J.A. Randall were appointed to a sub-committee and soon produced a comprehensive report, after consultation with five other Hertfordshire clubs with artisan sections. The sub-committee saw no reason to alter the number of artisan members, who must be resident within four miles of the clubhouse and not be members of a recognised golf club. A review of starting times led to the recommendation that Porters' artisans should start no later than 8.30 a.m. at weekends and on Bank Holidays and that afternoon times should be strictly enforced. Any interference to the club's own members' golf by the artisans was attributed to three and fourball play and it was suggested that such matches be prohibited at weekends.

Matches were permissible on Sundays but could only be arranged by agreement with the club secretary. So far, then, there was little new or

201

controversial. However, as it had been noted that the artisans' services on the course had diminished in recent times, it was thought proper to request financial contributions from them, as other clubs in the area did. This contribution would go exclusively to the upkeep of the course, as it would defray the additional expense of S.E.T., amounting to around £100. Fortunately, the sub-committee could find nothing in the club's lease which would prevent the club implementing the recommendations.

The report was discussed in October and a meeting was arranged with the artisans' representatives. It transpired that only 12 of the 40 artisans lived in Radlett and it was decided that residential qualifications would have to be considered when further discussion on times and financial contributions took place. The next report was delayed by Dr. Hennessey's illness and then by the absence of all members of the sub-committee from the April committee meeting, although a report had been circulated. It was decided to re-constitute the sub-committee.

The report pointed out that the artisans had imposed their own 8.30 a.m. limit on starting since 1966 and assured the club that it was strictly observed. The sub-committee's feeling was that they did not wish to prejudice relations with the section by reducing available starting times. Comparative figures of financial contributions having been received, the sum of £3 was suggested as suitable for the Porters' artisans. The four mile residential qualification was also unchanged but the artisans were asked to give preference to applicants living in Radlett.

The final recommendation was much less accommodating than the first three, for it questioned the need for artisan clubs in the current climate and suggested that the numbers be reduced to 25, no further elections being made until that figure had been reached. As a result the election of a promising seventeen year old had to be deferred. It was decided to re-open the matter in the autumn but a meeting with the artisans did not take place until the following February, when, in what was described as a very cordial meeting, it was decided to retain the section because the benefits accruing from its existence were to the club's advantage in its dealings with the G.L.C. while negotiating the freehold of the course.

Possibly as a result of this the artisans offered to assist both in divot-filling in the spring of 1969 and with the Townsend-Clark challenge match later in the year. However, the number of members of the section was reduced to 25, but in April 1970 permission was granted to increase this to 30, on condition that these extra members were Radlett residents and only 16 players would be permitted to start from the first tee and follow fourballs from the tenth, with any additional players passing through the tenth by 8.45 a.m.

Congestion on the course on Sunday mornings was a topic of discussion again in 1974, when it was finally realised that club members starting outside their booked times was as much a contributory factor as four artisan club matches. Nonetheless, a meeting was held, resulting in a letter from Mr. Humphreys, the artisans' secretary, accepting the experimental ruling that only two fourballs play from the first tee. He also pointed out that hold-ups on the course were not necessarily the result of slow play by the artisans and that if the ruling became permanent, it would seriously disrupt their competitions. In any case the artisans imposed their own discipline on slow players.

The club Captain at the time was Mr. E.W. Cheadle, who had been responsible for many successful social events and other schemes for the welfare of members. He now acted on behalf of the artisans, being instrumental in piped water being supplied to their hut. By using a reserve fund of £60 they had accumulated, the artisans were able to supply a sink and fittings and dig a soak-away pit themselves. Thus, they celebrated their thirtieth birthday with running water.

In the same letter Mr. Humphreys also intimated that the artisans would undertake responsibility for keeping the area around the flagpole tidy and noted his pleasure that the divoting by the section had met with the approval of the club. He further pointed out that work on the ditch on the eighth and ninth holes was under way. In wishing Mr. Cheadle a successful year, Mr. Humphreys pointed out that relations between club and artisans had never been more cordial, a point borne out a few months later when the section was given permission to elect five five-day members over and above the limit of 30.

So far no mention has been made of the standard of golf within the section. In 1977 the Sandy Herd Trophy was held at Porters Park and

Martin Smith, not only a home player, but the club's head greenkeeper, became the National Artisans Champion. This was the only time this tournament has been held at Porters, but it has regularly hosted the County Artisans Championship. Martin has also been County Artisans Champion on no fewer than six occasions, having attained a handicap of 3.

Another enterprising venture was initiated in the 1970s when annual days out at such courses as Wentworth, Sunningdale, Walton Heath and The Berkshire were arranged.

Martin Smith with the Sandy Herd trophy

In 1983 the section moved to a new club room, the shell of which was provided by the parent club, but which was erected, fitted out and decorated by the artisans. The building is shared with the greenstaff and is the result of Jim Arthur's recommendation that the latter should be better provided for.

A project in 1998 is the construction of a double driving bay on the practice ground to enable the professional to give lessons even in adverse weather conditions.

Peter Phillips, the secretary of Porters Park Golf Club, has been a member of the artisans for over thirty years, and in 1995 was able to address the fiftieth anniversary celebrations of the section. He drew attention to the strict rules which applied to members and how a number had been banished for failing to meet the requirements of working as well as playing. He presented the oldest serving member, Jim Lawrence, who joined in 1953 and was Artisans' Captain in 1960, with a bottle of Scotch.

As the parent club moved to its centenary, the artisans undertook the task of repairing and rebuilding the bridges over the stream and carefully monitored the work of keeping the ditches tidy. Clearly, the section continues to play a major part in the well-being and spirit of Porters Park Golf Club.

Members who played in the Tom Waddell knockout which they won in 1989. Standing from left: Ray Hollamby, John Duke, Peter Crawford, Frank Oakley, Goff Green, Jim Lawrence, Stewart Green, Chris Carpenter, Trevor Burdis, Chris Condon, Derek Rowson, John Chappell, Andy Porter, Brian Winder. Front from left: Bill Dobson, Bill Thompson, Robert Phillips, Darren Burdis, Roy Phillips, Rob Washbrook

Chapter Seventeen

Miscellanea

The Caddies

THAT CADDIES were already a regular feature at Porters by 1903 is clear, for Mr. G.W. Jones organised a competition for them and the ground-staff. They were not allowed to work on Sundays until Mr. Raphael became President and made a condition of the lease that caddies would be available on Sundays. This met with partial agreement from the committee: caddies could not work before 1.00 p.m. and had to be over twelve years old.

By the end of the year a firm set of rules for employing caddies had been set down. They could only be engaged through the caddie master, with the engagement recorded in a book. Caddies could not be booked on a week to week basis, nor could special caddies be engaged "but the caddie master was to oblige members as far as possible". A whole day engagement was to take precedence over a half day's employment. The rule about booking caddies was later modified to permit forty-eight hours notice being given of the requirement.

These rules were expanded in instructions about the cleaning of clubs. They were to be handed to the professional after cleaning and he would place them in the members' lockers.

The original caddies' shed was converted to a caddie master's office as the result of a discussion in 1907, at which an increase in fees was turned down, but it was agreed to build a new shed and to supply the caddie master with tea and bread and butter in view of the late hours he was obliged to keep.

An insurance scheme indemnifying members against any loss sustained by a caddie employed by him, caused by the player or a fellow competitor was proposed later in the year. [This appears to have been for the members' welfare, not the caddies'.]

The following year Bradbeer handed over responsibility for the caddies to a new caddie master. He received a list of twelve rules which the caddies were to observe. This was partly to palliate a neighbour who had claimed the boys were creating a nuisance next to his property, which became the subject of an investigation by the committee. The rules were:

1. The caddie master shall keep a general register of all caddies allowed to carry clubs and arrange them according to their qualifications into first and second class caddies.
2. Boys and others desirous of becoming caddies must submit their names to the caddie master, who will place them, if approved, on the register.
3. The qualification of caddies shall be decided by their carrying capabilities, knowledge of the game and physical strength, not by their age.
4. Except on Saturdays and other holidays no one shall be employed as a caddie unless he is exempt from attendance at school. On Sundays, only caddies of fourteen years of age and over are to be employed. (An increase on the previous agreed age limit.)
5. The caddie master shall keep a book showing the names of caddies employed and the number of rounds carried daily.
6. The caddie master shall enter the names of the caddies in the order in which they arrive, but the order of their employment shall be left to the discretion of the caddie master.
7. A caddie cannot be ordered more than 48 hours before he is required. Whole day engagements will take precedent over half day engagements. If the ground men wish to carry clubs they must be treated and engaged the same as caddies. No general engagement from week to week can be recognised, no member having the right to engage any special caddie but the caddie master has instructions to please members as far as possible.
8. The caddie master shall receive and look after the clubs of members who have been playing and must see that they are properly cleaned before the caddie is paid.
9. All complaints against caddies for misconduct, neglect of duty etc, are to be made to the caddie master, who shall have power to suspend a caddie pending his report to the secretary.
10. The caddie master shall be responsible for the maintenance of order among the caddies.
11. Caddies must on no account use clubs or balls left in their charge, nor shall they be permitted to solicit employment, or loiter about the club-house or on the course.
12. The charges for caddies shall be (which includes the cleaning of clubs)

	1st class	2nd class
18 holes	10d.	7d.
9 holes	7d.	5d.

Lunch money (6d) shall be given to the caddie when he is employed in the forenoon.

On Sundays & at Prize Meetings the charge shall be 1s.1d. per 18 holes.

These charges were increased later in 1907 when the charges for eighteen holes became 1s.1d. and 9d., while for nine holes the charges remained the same.

Caddies continued to be available until after the Second World War and regular entries in the suggestions book refer to members' frustration in failing to secure a particular caddie, or even one at all. Apart from one undesirable character who was banned from the club's premises, Porters does not appear to have been served by any particularly colourful or outstanding caddie, though no doubt members had their preferences. With the increasing use of trolleys, including powered ones, the need for caddies grew less and so a body of men who were once part of the very fabric of the game has become a dying breed, save at those prestigious courses where they are still considered *de rigueur*.

Societies

As the club's reputation grew, it became a venue for society meetings. The first to be invited and given courtesy of the course was "The City Liberal Golf Club" in 1904 who played one of their half-yearly competitions. (The Tory Golfing Society didn't come until some time later.) Two years later "The Baltic Golf Club" held their autumn meeting at Porters Park and in 1907 "The Coal Exchange Golfing Society" was given the courtesy of the course under the same conditions as the Baltic Golfing Society. "The Corporation Golfing Society" was given permission to play in July, provided that extra caddies were engaged for the day. The Liberals cancelled their day in 1908 because of the "uncertainty of caddies" but The Scots Masonic Lodge Golf Club played in April. Between the wars the Diocesan of St Albans Golfing Society were regular visitors.

The Lucifer Golfing Society have been regular and welcome visitors, as have the Hazards Golfing Society. The former presented the club with a picture for the clubhouse, and the latter, presumably through the persuasion of one J.M. Reid, donated a salver to be awarded to the boy under the age of sixteen with the best score in the English Boys' Strokeplay Championship, formerly the Carris Trophy.

The Oxford and Cambridge Golfing Society have played at Porters, as have the University teams and their second strings, the "Divots" and the "Stymies".

Occasionally societies have incurred the wrath of members, which, directed through the suggestion book and the committee, has led to their deletion from the fixture card. Nevertheless the course is still a popular venue for an important source of revenue for the club.

Social Events

Since the very early days the club has held a variety of well-supported social events, dances, dinners, bridge drives, film and race nights and, more recently, casino nights. The war years enabled the membership to support a number of war charities and other charitable organisations have received help through either golfing or social occasions. The more important of these have been recorded in the appropriate places in this narrative.

The club's fluctuating financial fortunes have also had regular assistance from the entertainments committee, but occasionally things did not go quite to plan.

Sandy Steel organised a Casino Evening in 1986 and was congratulated for his work. He wryly reported that whilst it might have been a success with the members ("and even to their individual gain") it had been a disaster in financial terms as a loss of £350 was reported. "He was, however, somewhat mollified to note that the bar takings for the evening were about £400." He recommended that a cover charge of £5 be made if such an event were to take place in the future.

With this in mind a similar event was held the following year and a deficit of only £49 was recorded. Sandy Steel became Captain of the club in 1990, but should not be vilified for owning up to what is in effect a perennial fact that social functions have invariably lost money.

Prior to the Second World War, some club functions were held in London, in no small part due to the residency of the membership. More recently the club has hosted its functions in-house. The New Year's Eve dance has survived but the Summer Ball has been replaced to some extent by a Captain's Day function of the captain's choosing.

At the Men's Dinner in November 1971, Henry Longhurst was the principal guest. In 1975 this honour was accorded to Nick Faldo, the reigning English Amateur Champion. He had been given honorary membership of the club for the year, his home club being Welwyn Garden City. Another guest on this occasion was Cecil Parkinson M.P., who assured members that a proposed orbital motorway would not affect the course.

In 1974 to celebrate the club's seventy-fifth anniversary, Eric Cheadle, who as Captain had a great leaning towards social events, took the Celebration Ball to Hatfield Palace, for a highly entertaining Elizabethan Banquet. Probably the most heavily attended ball was in the clubhouse to celebrate the extension. Ironically, a marquee had to be hired to accommodate all the members!

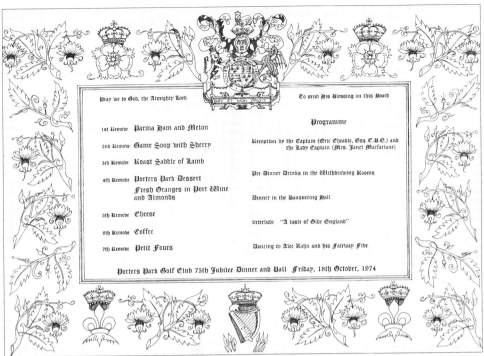

*Four Club Captains at Hatfield House for the Jubilee Dinner in 1974. Tony Randall (1968),
Dick Bott (1942), Douglas Cumming (1969 and 1970) and Eric Cheadle (1974)*

Chapter Eighteen

Random Jottings from the Suggestion Book

T HE VITALITY of every golf club is reflected in that much used, and abused, chronicle of members' ideas for the improvement of their lot. Witty, caustic, grumpy, constructive and sometimes downright rude insertions can reveal as much of a club's social history as any trawl through the minute books. Some of the more relevant suggestions appear in the appropriate sections of this story; this chapter presents the lighter side of life at Porters over the years, beginning in 1911.

"That further and more urgent admonishment be addressed to members *and* visitors in regard to replacing the turf. The number of divots one sees at Porters, sometimes lying tummy up within a few inches of the ghastly gashes from which they have been cut, is a disgrace to any club."

"That the portrait of his late Majesty, King Edward VII in the committee room be returned to the donor and one provided by the club be put in its place."

And immediately below:

"That the use of a portrait of his late Majesty as an advertisement for mineral water in the club is to be deprecated."

"That the charge of 1d. each for Virginia cigarettes is excessive and that cigarettes obtainable at the bar last autumn @ ½d be procured."

The reply: "Cheaper American cigarettes can be obtained in packets."

"That the caddie master be in attendance for members to be able to get their clubs."

"That some new arrangement be made by which members boots may be cleaned."

"That owing to the congestion on the course at weekends caused by the increasing number of visitors, to the great inconvenience of members most of whom can only play at weekends, that the green fees be increased to 5/- on Saturdays, Sundays and Bank Holidays, 10/- for those visitors not playing with a member."

"We the undersigned wish to protest against the course being given to visitors on ladies' competition days unless the visitors be notified that they must ask ladies to pass." Mrs. Beatty Smyth was one of the undersigned.

July 5th 1913: "That the time has arrived for erecting a suitable shelter for motor cars."

Reply: "The committee regret that the financial position of the club will not permit of this just now."

"That the club (either from its funds or by private subscription) provide waterproof capes and coats (which would be the property of the club) to be used by the caddies on wet days – other clubs are doing this." This suggestion was adopted.

The gentlemen who suggested the increase in visitors' green fees at weekends in 1913 had this to say the following year:

"The question of raising the green fees having been raised at the annual meeting on the 14th inst. We the undersigned (56 of them!) are strongly of the opinion that it is inadvisable to make any alteration whatever, either at the weekend or during the week. As the committee are aware, the practice of allowing visitors to pay for a single round was given a fair trial some time ago and was found to be unworkable and contrary to the best interests of the club."

To which Edward Head added: (he) "approves but suggests that this and similar questions be left *entirely* to the committee. Such questions for instance as handicaps. Where it is necessary and within his power!! he would suggest that all members' handicaps be raised 2."

Dr. Smyth replied that the committee had decided to make no change in the green fees.

March 1915: "That the question of smoking in the luncheon room – after lunch, be brought up." The committee decided that it would be undesirable to alter the existing rule.

The club's finances in the war years have been described; one gentleman suggested a remedy:

1. That 100 extra *full* members (ladies and gentlemen) be admitted at 20 gns. (entry) and 12 gns. (sub).

2. Super-tax on 4 ball matches etc (suggest 10/- per player).

3. That green fee on Sats and Suns for visitors be 10/- for 1st guest and 20/- for each subsequent guest."

While this gained the approval of another member, except for item 2, the committee only noted the suggestion.

"That ninepence (9d) for a *small* bottle of Perrier water reminds one of "profiteering"."

"That Mr. Don Langrish-Smith be given a hearing aid so that he can hear the bell at the 8th., otherwise expelled." On the reply page but not signed by an officer: "No hearing aids on issue. Expel the – – – –."

"May I suggest that it would meet the donor's ideas of keeping green the memory of our late friend Whitehead if this beautiful inkstand were used as the club inkstand & for the use of members & the winner's name be engraved upon it."

Another request for shelters for motor cars in 1922 received a similar reply to the one in 1913 and was followed by this suggestion:

"That the Midland Rly. be asked to stop the 5.50 train from St Albans at Radlett on Sundays."

A suggestion that seats be provided on every tee was considered unnecessary, as was a request to have the pond on the seventeenth netted.

"That a supply of different brands of smoking tobacco be on sale including Players smoking mixture." No reply.

A more lively exchange of views occurred in April 1923:

"We the undersigned members beg very strongly to protest against the committee arranging inter-club matches to be played at Porters Park on a Saturday thus preventing a number of members from enjoying the use of their own course on, in many cases, the only day available for them to play.

"We suggest in future these matches should be played in mid-week." The 22 signatories were referred to the reply to the next item, which was signed by another 20 members:

"We the undersigned (and also business men who can only play on holidays) beg to suggest to the committee that seeing the teams only took half an hour to get away from the 1st tee (11o/c to 11.30 o/c)and that a notice of the match has been on the board since January 10th, that the minimum of inconvenience (if any!) has been suffered by the members signing the aforegoing suggestion.

"We think these "star" matches are very good for the club and help to improve the standard of play, which is needed, by bringing good players here to play over this course & possibly the means of introducing them to become members.

"It is in our opinion to the good of the club generally & the majority of its members individually that more of these matches be played & we suggest to the committee that additional matches be arranged, if possible with the Oxford and Cambridge G.S. and the Press G.S."

The committee heartily approved of this suggestion which gained further support:

"It is suggested that the protest (against matches) obviously inspired in a moment of pique is unworthy of consideration. The loss of less than 30 minutes on two or three occasions in the year to players some of whom habitually deprive members in bulk of at least an equal period of time on most weekends by their inconsiderate selection of starting time and place

& their sluggish progress through the green, hardly merits the sympathy they apparently crave."

To which has been appended: "Hear! Hear! I know who this applies to!"

July, 1923: "That during the Summer a refreshment shed be opened, preferably near the 12th green." Followed by: "Suggest if necessary signatories finance above." The committee spared the thirsty members the expense by deeming it too late in the season to make arrangements for the year in question. They also ignored a suggestion signed "The whole club" requesting that hundreds & thousands be sold by the steward.

An unsigned and barely legible entry requested the provision of a gramophone or other sound producing equipment for use on wet days by members who did not wish to get wet playing golf and who could spend their day dancing, a benefit to the club being the resulting increase in bar profits. The suggestion does not appear to have merited a reply, however.

On the vexed and frequently repeated request for improved bathing facilities the committee continued to stall. They were more generous in agreeing to supply combs for the dressing room, and "for the comfort of the members signing the suggestion dusters have also been provided."

In 1927 one member suggested that the club colours be changed and "the subsidy to Aniline Dye Industry be cancelled." The committee resolved to await further criticism before taking any action.

More serious matters were on the minds of 8 members in October 1929:

"Why has the Committee altered the brand of club port that used to be supplied to the members and was very good? – Most of it is quite different." To which was added : "Why not have supplied the two ports and ascertain which was preferred?"

The reply : "The port on sale is identical in quality with the port sold during the last eight years, same brand, blend and strength and guaranteed by the vendors. It is however pointed out that with any wine an individual bottle is occasionally poor through defective corking."

Equally vital was the plea in 1932 from a similar number of gentlemen:

"The undersigned, having a special interest in the quality of the draught beer supplied in the clubhouse, are of the opinion that the existing source of supply should be changed. The beer at present supplied is exceedingly bitter and unpalatable and no improvement has been observed despite repeated complaints, which we understand have been brought to the notice of the brewer by the committee."

The committee appeared much more sympathetic to the beer drinkers than to the imbibers of port:

"Regarding beer at present on tap at the club, it might be worse but it is quite unlikely that it could be better having regard to the obligations placed by the Excise upon all brewers throughout the country. Perhaps the appointment of a tasting committee (ale conners) consisting of adult and experienced members of the club might serve as a provisional measure – of course free of expense to such committee!"

However other members were less sympathetic: "With reference to the suggestion dated 8 Oct, '32, the undersigned, being seasoned beer drinkers are perfectly satisfied with the beer as supplied at present, and consider that any change would be for the worse."

That the committee were sometimes of a more satirical bent than the members was demonstrated in July 1933; when a member suggested that shooting rights on the eleventh, twelfth and thirteenth holes be offered for sale with proceeds going to the Benevolent Fund, they replied, "If the committee could be assured that a few members would be shot they are willing to agree."

Presumably they were referring to the beer drinkers as the following year these comments appeared:

"That, for the benefit of the "less seasoned beer drinkers", light bottled ale might be kept." Then: "There will be no trouble in keeping the draught beer – it's awful!" to which the reply was:

"The committee wish to point out that the suggestions book is not for remarks of this nature."

However, the drinkers were not deterred:

"That the monthly competition sweepstake be 2/6 instead of the "paltry" shilling which does not buy a round of drinks and a shilling for the second round."

"Amendment: It is essential that the winner stand the aforesaid round of drinks." This attracted a number of signatures but the committee was unconvinced.

Card games have been played at Porters since the foundation of the club and occasionally given rise to comment but a number of members expressed their displeasure, writing:

"That members be asked to consider some of the other players in the card room and that they be requested to discuss their differences or hands in voices that *do not* carry all over the club house." The committee suggested that they "take no action in this matter, but leave it to the decency of the members."

This prompted the question, "Where is the card room?" and a further question, "If a member goes to sleep in the lounge – does the lounge become a bedroom?" which prompted a reply, "If the committee will provide sheets, I see no reason why it should not be so."

1938 saw the ladies demanding consideration:

"Since the ladies are now to pay one and a half guineas extra I propose that up to 24 handicaps should be allowed to play 3 & 4 ball matches on

Saturday and Sunday." The committee thought no action was necessary but one gentleman (?) thought:

"Since the men are now to pay one and a half guineas extra I propose that no lady members above 9 be allowed to play in any match on a Saturday or Sunday other than in a properly constituted 2 ball match."

As well as drink, food also became an issue:

"If we do not get our good lunches any more, we who are good eaters, most of us *very* good drinkers, will take our custom to our own homes! Please don't spoil the good name of Porters Park dining room." These gentlemen were supported by another, older member who pointed out that the members could afford good food and by another group who demanded: "We *want* treacle tart on Saturdays."

These entries were dated 1939 so it was hardly likely that the situation improved and as described in a previous chapter as a result of post-war rationing, things actually got worse. One item which was available again in 1944 was playing cards, which prompted the following item:

"As playing cards are now obtainable, we *suggest* that we should have new ones, in place of the *very dirty* ones we now play with."

Cleanliness was not just a requisite of the card school:

"That after dirty shoes have lain on the changing room floor for a minimum period of, say, a reasonable 10 days (or alternatively left dirty in the locker pigeon hole) the locker room attendant be requested to clean them and replace same."

A suggestion in 1950 regarding the "naval barrack" colour scheme in the bar prompted a further entry:

"It is suggested that in view of the deplorable state of decorative repair of the clubhouse, and in view of the urgent need for economy, that a notice be put up asking for volunteers (male and female) who are prepared to undertake painting etc, the club supplying the paint." Some ladies signed this, including Maggy Dick, who nevertheless refused to do the ceiling. However, not everyone was in agreement with this:

"While admiring the spirit of those members who have volunteered to assist in decorating the clubhouse and in no way doubting their skill, I cannot help feeling the task would be beyond them.

"I suggest that an estimate be obtained from a firm of builders to have the entire clubhouse thoroughly decorated both inside and out. And I suggest that the cost must be met by way of a "special contribution" or capital levy of say £1 per member – or whatever sum is required."

The course too attracted suggestions; these have been omitted from this section as they were duly either implemented or rejected by the green committee; however the following was not really intended for their serious consideration:

"In consideration of there being so many "rabbits" masquerading as members of the club; proposed that the committee provide step ladders for them to get down into the ditches at the risk of breaking their necks." Mr. Albany replied that this was "receiving favourable consideration."

Back in the clubhouse the wags were exercising their wits:

"It is suggested that, in accordance with tradition, the Captain's photograph not having appeared in the clubhouse prior to 31-12-52, all drinks served in the bar, should hereafter be charged to the Captain's account until such time as the photo appears." Mr. Parkes replied "An objection has been received from the Official Receiver."

A long and impassioned plea from the ladies for admittance to the men's bar after 7 p.m. on winter weekends was granted to prevent their "shivering in the fringe(?)".

The decor of the clubhouse came up for consideration again in 1959:

"In my opinion the pale blue colour of the men's bar ceiling is not appropriate and should be repainted cream or off-white", provoking an additional entry: "In view of the result of the Boat Race perhaps we may have a dark blue ceiling in the men's smoke room instead of light blue?"

A sad item was recorded in 1962: "That the club cat be renovated, or peacefully retired", inspiring secretary Albany to pen: "R*equiesc*at I*n* P*ace.*"

The inclement winter of 1962-63 caused the Football Association to set up a "Pools Panel" to determine results, which gave rise to the following, signed by Brian Chapman among others:

"That in view of the undoubted success of the recently introduced novel method of determining the results of Association Football matches –

"It is suggested that a Results Committee be established forthwith charged with the duty of arriving at the results of all club competitions. The committee which should maintain close liaison with the handicapping committee, to be comprised of: one "social" member, one "five-day" member and one "second club" member; and to reach its findings by means of its knowledge of the game, its ability to read "form", and such other impartial methods as it may deem desirable.

"Such a system has the obvious merit of doing much to relieve weekend course congestion, thus leaving the members free to enjoy their golf. In the event that the system should prove to be a success, it is envisaged that the Committee's powers be extended to cover all matches whether friendly or not. The resulting beneficial effects on bar-takings and course condition should surely render the suggestion worthy of consideration."

Reply : "Noted."

In 1967 a show case was placed temporarily along the long wall of the lounge, prompting this comment:

"That the monstrosity in the lounge, be removed as quickly as possible

216

and either placed at the back of the 11th, or await November 5th." Lieut.-Col. Steel's reply pointed out that "Due to lack of suitable drainage the suggested site at the 11th green is not feasible."

A poetic request for curtains in the men's bar is quoted elsewhere but a more sensitive issue was raised in March 1969, when a Mr. Tyler wrote, "That, in order to encourage a greater variety and number of birds on and about the course, urgent steps are taken to control and reduce the quantity of vermin and predators i.e. grey squirrels." This might be read in conjunction with a later entry:

"For rank bad behaviour & total ignorance of golfing etiquette, today's society (G.S.) could not be surpassed. I suggest societies be vetted in the same way as members!" This received a very favourable response from the committee.

May Day, 1971 elicited another entry from Mr. Tyler:

"That from this date, those golfers who are sufficiently fortunate to hole their tee shots on this course, should be guests of the club on the day that the memorable shot is struck."

The Captain replied: "This tradition already exists in the club, & the committee hopes that recipients will see fit, also as tradition decrees, to buy a drink for all players in the clubhouse that day."

A sign of the times was reflected in 1971, when Peter Halsall felt moved to suggest:

"Television – this appears to dominate the lounge, particularly volume wise. Whilst understanding some may enjoy this medium and lack of accommodation to which it may be banished, can the committee consider any alternative to what some consider an interference to peace and quiet." The committee sympathetically considered moving the offending apparatus to an alternative site.

Two more irate members penned the following in 1970:

"That the action of any person or persons responsible for destroying club property and history by removing a page from this book which for over half a century has faithfully recorded members thoughts and humour should be deplored and that the missing page be restored." The reply explained that the page was removed at the request of the members who had made the suggestion and wished it to be withdrawn.

Irascibility was frequently exercised when the vexed question of starting times at weekends gave rise to numerous complaints over the years and produced entries of great length and, not surprisingly, no great wit, as this was not an amusing matter. However one item deserves inclusion here:

"Could the club house clock be synchronised with the starter's watch on the 10th tee on Sunday mornings to avoid increasing arguments." The starters were asked to adjust their watches accordingly.

Mr. Bernard Coral issued the following protest in 1977:

"As a club member of many years standing and a founder director of Joe Coral Ltd., known as one of the major bookmaking companies in Great Britain, that the club should as its bookmaker open an account with Ladbrokes is to me most upsetting and hurtful and as such must protest most strongly."

Mr. J.F. Reid, the club Captain replied: "The committee cannot see the logic of your argument which if it is pursued to cover all supplies and services to the club would result in a state of chaos. As a point of interest the club has had a credit account with Ladbrokes for many years." (R & A recommendations on gambling notwithstanding.) This provoked further comment:

"I find it very difficult to appreciate the committee's answer to Mr. B. Coral's letter of 2nd April, '77. I have been involved in clubs of *all* sorts for a great number of years & have never seen such an answer! It was always my understanding that a club was a club, that everyone worked for the club and that the club worked for all its members. This would *not* appear to be completely true for all P.P.G.C. members – this I find hard to explain. The committee's explanation should prove interesting."

While the committee's response was to note these observations, a more succinct comment was supplied by another member who simply subscribed "Balls" to the comments.

A year later Mr. Coral's son Anthony added: "Concerning the entries on April 2nd. 1977, My father's comment was quite logical, daft maybe, but quite logical."

Motor cars also feature in a number of entries in the late 1970s:

"It is suggested in view of the entrance to the practice ground being used to bring stolen cars on to the course, that this entrance be sealed and the only entrance to the practice ground be via the main entrance to the club."

"It is suggested that the Captain's motor car be removed from the parking place in the lake on the 13th."

Reply : "Recovery of the car (not the Captain's!) is the responsibility of the owner (NOT the Captain) through his insurers. Request to do this was not received here until last Autumn after heavy rain. Because of the risk of course damage from the heavy recovery vehicle the operation has been deferred until ground conditions are more suitable."

Meanwhile back in the clubhouse other problems had arisen:

"The freedom of the press has been sadly diminished through the disappearance of *The Times*. It is suggested that the club subscribe to *Private Eye* whose causes are not unlike those which *The Times* used to pursue." The committee preferred *The Times* however and promised to restore it to circulation.

"Friday, 13th April, 1979.

"I [40 members, actually] suggest that the Chairman of the House Committee takes an early opportunity of explaining to an Extraordinary General Meeting of this club the reasons which prompted his decision to instruct the vandalistic desecration of the bar counter in the smoking room (by the installation of a cash register) to the undoubted detriment, not only of the bar facilities but also the aesthetic considerations which, I must assume, were beyond his comprehension. I should add that I entertain extreme anger that the committee in question should take upon itself the authority to despoil the heritage held in trust for the members."

In expressing their regret at the signatories' concern the committee explained that the General Committee had "unanimously decided that cash registers were essential in both bars. The options open for positioning were few and the final decision was only reached after discussion and approval with the chief steward.

"Should the signatories have an alternative suggestion for an improved position for the cash register the General Committee would be very happy to give it every consideration."

Further criticism of the committee was voiced in June 1979:

"I refer to the notice on the notice board offering a £20 reward for the name of the person wheeling a trolley through a bunker. Does the committee really believe it will induce members to INFORM on fellow members by a cash offer? Further, what impression does the committee think such a notice gives to guests and visitors. Gentlemen, this is a golf club, please take the notice down immediately as it has neither dignity or value."

The signatory does not note the impression wheel prints in bunkers might have on guests or visitors.

A more benevolent request was for a subscription of £1 per head to cover hole-in-one expenses, so that the player achieving one might receive £15 towards his expenses. This was rejected but the committee agreed to present the player with a bottle of whisky if the stroke was played in a match or stroke play event.

1981 brought a novel request:

"On the left of the 18th green there are a mass of bluebells but no one can see them as they are behind the piles of compost etc. Could these bulbs be moved so that members can get the benefit. We suggest suitable places could be on the right of the 9th tee, the area between the 5th green & 6th green & on the left of the top of the fairway just short of the 10th green & elsewhere." This gave rise to a more facetious request:

"If the previous suggestion is implemented and the bluebells disappear from their present situation, might I suggest that the "one-armed bandit" in the men's bar be moved there in place of the said flowers." Ted Hurcomb merely noted this but was more sympathetic to the flower-lovers, appreciating their comments and explaining that as the greenstaff already had a very full work load, there would be no objection to the signatories unplanting and planting the bulbs in the suggested locations.

Six frustrated members in 1982 complained, "Why do they not put the holes on the plateau of the greens instead of on the crest of hills? Porters Park is not meant to be a sporty course."

This was amplified in the next entry, which contained, among other items: "The position of the holes should offer a fair putt from all angles. Who decides on pin positions?" The answer was: "The head greenkeeper."

Thus, a source of lively debate, wit and irascibility, ably countered (on most occasions) by successive committees. References to club competitions occurred from time to time and were either acted upon or not as the committee thought suitable, maintaining a healthy dialogue throughout the club's history.

Porters Park Golf Course 1998

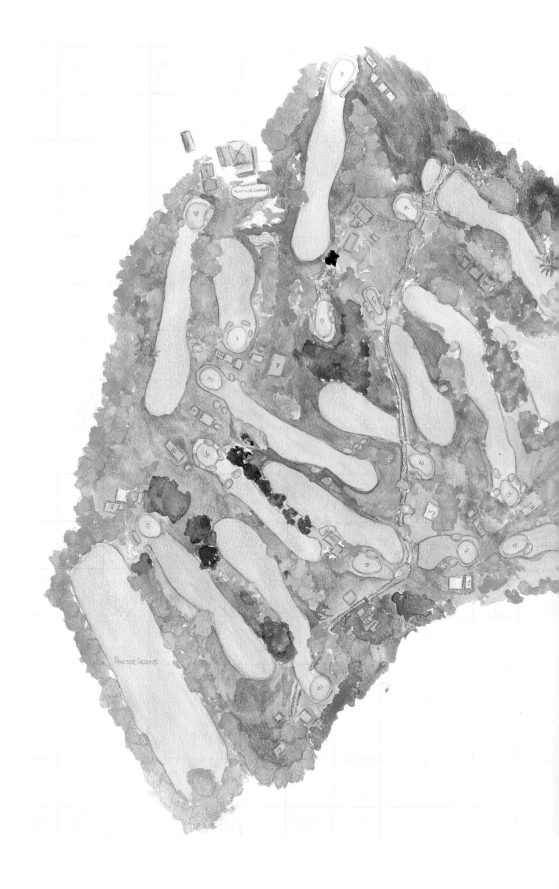

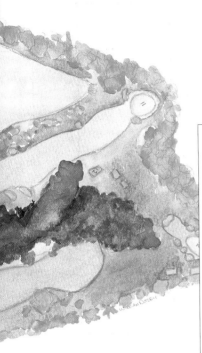

						Score		Nett Score		W = + L = - H = 0 Points			
Hole	Marker's Score	White Yards	Yellow Yards	Par	Stroke Index	A	B	A	B		Red Yards	Par	Stroke Index
1		254	237	4	18						236	4	18
2		356	339	4	13						294	4	13
3		411	406	4	4						405	5	7
4		458	439	4	1						428	5	9
5		384	372	4	9						342	4	4
6		149	133	3	12						114	3	11
7		398	386	4	7						369	4	5
8		427	397	4	3						355	4	1
9		155	136	3	16						118	3	15
OUT		2992	2845	34							2661	36	

PLEASE AVOID SLOW PLAY AT ALL TIMES

10		480	469	5	14						433	5	6
11		432	417	4	2						369	4	2
12		202	175	3	11						159	3	12
13		505	478	5	8						429	5	16
14		160	142	3	17						130	3	14
15		353	318	4	15						292	4	10
16		417	399	4	6						369	4	3
17		385	376	4	10						344	4	8
18		452	425	4	5						405	5	17
IN		3386	3199	36							2930	37	
OUT		2992	2845	34							2661	36	
TOT		6378	6044	70							5591	73	

COMPETITION

DATE   TIME   Handicap   Strokes Rec'd

Player **A**

Player **B**

Please indicate which tee used.

PAR	70
SSS	70
PAR	70
SSS	69
PAR	73
SSS	73

STABLEFORD POINTS OR PAR RESULT

C.G.S.

H'CAP

NETT

Markers Signature ....   Players Signature ....

Appendices

Presidents

1899 M.P. Grace	1944 J.P. Hall	1973 J.M. Reid
1903 C.F. Raphael	1952 J. Everington	1980 K.A. Richardson
1925 C.M. Humble	1960 R.E.A. Bott	1982 J.M. Balch
1941 R.O. Burlison	1964 R.H. Baucher	1990 P.D. Orchard-Lisle
1943 E.S. Markham	1969 J.B. Cowper	1995 H.R. Hewitt

Captains

1899-1902 C.T. Part	1935 T.C. Gilson	1968 J.A. Randall
1903 E.W. Thomas	1936 C. McKenzie D.S.O.	1969 D.J. Cumming
1904 A.E. Colebrook	1937 E.C. Dix	1970 D.J. Cumming
1905 Dr. R.V.B. Smyth	1938 E.C. Dix	1971 P.D. Orchard-Lisle
1906 E.N. Kent	1939 A. Sherriff	1972 P.D. Orchard-Lisle
1907 Maj. S.H. Creagh	1940 A. Sherriff	1973 K.A. Richardson
1908 C.M. Humble	1941 A. Sherriff	1974 E.W. Cheadle
1909 C.M. Humble	1942 R.E.A. Bott	1975 R.A. Johnson
1910 C.L. Richmond	1943 G. Boggon	1976 R.A.P. Wehner
1911 C.L. Richmond	1944 G. Boggon	1977 J.F. Reid
1912 E.W. Whitehead	1945 G. Boggon	1978 J.N. Thurgood
1913 M.J. Clayton	1946 J. Everington	1979 D.G. Johnson
1914 Dr. R.V.B. Smyth	1947 R.C.C. Green	1980 E.A. Foulkes
1915 E.A. Abram	1948 E.R. Brown	1981 E.D. Hurcomb
1916 E.A. Abram	1949 A.W.H. Baucher	1982 J.F. Tweddle
1917 J.P. Knight	1950 J.S. Scott-Miller	1983 A.D.W. Sanderson
1918 J.P. Knight	1951 E.C. Beck	1984 C.W. Capstick
1919 H.F. Thomas	1952 E.W. Parkes	1985 H.R. Hewitt
1920 H.F. Thomas	1953 J.M. Reid	1986 R.A. Barnes
1921 E.S. Markham	1954 R.H. Baucher	1987 D.M. Horne
1922 S. Chalkley	1955 M.G. Orchard-Lisle	1988 D.K.D. Watson
1923 F.R.M. de Paula	1956 M.G. Orchard-Lisle	1989 A.M. Forrest
1924 J.P. Hall	1957 J.B. Cowper	1990 A. Steel
1925 P.C. Burton	1958 M.A.H. Dick	1991 J.H. Laidler
1926 G.F. Roberts	1959 J.P. Graham Q.C.	1992 J.S. Liddle
1927 H.J. Lane	1960 J.A. Edwards	1993 S.R. Samuels
1928 J.R. Grundy	1961 R.H. Baucher	1994 Dr. P.T. Watters
1929 R.W. Needham K.C.	1962 H.A. Chapman	1995 A. Orsich
1930 R.W. Needham K.C.	1963 C.R. Glover	1996 W.F. Gelson
1931 L.J. Reid	1964 J.M. Balch	1997 J.W. Hathaway
1932 R.O. Burlison	1965 R.S.F. Hennessey	1998 T.J. Griffin
1933 A. Franks	1966 J.S. Ross	
1934 F. Goddard	1967 K.E. Whitworth	

Secretaries

1899 Dr. R.V.B. Smyth	1945 C.K. Cotton	1979 L.D. Pope
1905 W.O.J. Sergeant	1945 Maj. D. Keith	1983 M. Stamford
1908 F.G. Callow*	1952 D.E. Albany	1989 J. Roberts
1910 Maj. G.F. Walton	1954 H.P. Hinde	1995 R. Springall
1911 D.L. Cottam	1957 D.E. Albany	1997 P. Phillips
1916 C.L. Richmond	1964 Col. O.S. Steele	
1927 Capt. F.H. Lawrence	1971 J.A. Randall	

* E.W. Whitehead acting secretary during Callow's suspension

224

Trophy Winners
The President's Prize (The Raphael Trophy)
Singles Knockout Matchplay

1903 V.P. Lohr	1936 A.G. Snelling	1971 J. Van Gelder
1904 S. Brunton	1937 A.G. Snelling	1972 C.W. Price
1905 W.T. Walker	1938 F.V. Drake	1973 J.F. Reid
1906 C.L. Richmond	1939 E.K. Porte	1974 G.M. Brass
1907 W.A. Vaughan	1946 J.G. Milner	1975 N.S. Allanson
1908 W.C. Powers	1947 H.W. Singleton	1976 M.B. Peterson
1909 H.F.Mence	1948 E.P. Gray	1977 C.C. Boal
1910 A.F.W. Gourlay	1949 D. Keith	1978 P.J. Tolley
1911 P. Negretti	1950 J. Darroch	1979 D. Keller
1912 S. Thomson	1951* R.D. Henderson	1980 C.C. Boal
1913 M.J. Clayton	1952 J.R. Armstrong	1981 G.A. Uwins
1914 F.R.M. de Paula	1953 J. Sprawson	1982 E.L. Lewis
1919 D.L. Von Braun	1954 A.W. Sephton	1983 D.A. Lewis
1920 J.P. Hall	1955 R.N. Glover	1984 C.C. Boal
1921 H.J. Lane	1956 M.B. Peterson	1985 D.M. Ward
1922 R.A. Law	1957 J. Sprawson	1986 E.L. Lewis
1923 C.S. Downing	1958 E.P. Humphreys	1987 J. Warne
1924 R.E.A. Bott	1959 E. Holt	1988 C.C. Boal
1925 R.E.A. Bott	1960 R.E.A. Bott	1989 C.C. Boal
1926 Capt. G.W. Holt	1961 M.B. Peterson	1990 S.A. Masson
1927 P. Barry	1962 J.M. Reid	1991 P. Lewis
1928 J. Grimditch	1963 E.P. Humphreys	1992 C.C. Boal
1929 S. Seddon	1964 D.G. Johnson	1993 A.M. Pountney
1930 R.T. Jones	1965 I.M. Judge	1994 P.N. Tolley
1931 J.L. Baucher	1966 I.M. Judge	1995 A.M. Pountney
1932 R.E.A. Bott	1967 J. Van Gelder	1996 E. Wilson
1933 A.G. Snelling	1968 E.D. Hurcomb	1997 R. Lowbridge
1934 R.D. Henderson	1969 G.H. Dudley	1998 C.C. Boal
1935 G.F. Roberts	1970 N.F. Lee	

* Final restricted to 18 holes

Rumsey Goblets
Foursomes Knockout

1903 A.E. Colebrook & R.H. Moore	1925 R.H. Baucher & A.G. Snelling
1904 W.V. Inman & W.H.A. Gow	1926 J.H. Skelton & R.A. Skelton
1905 G.A. Cutbill & O.H. Powell	1927 L.J. Reid & R. Woodbridge
1906 P. Edgelow & R.V.B. Smyth	1928 A.W.H. Baucher & A.G. Snelling
1907 A.E. Colebrook & R.H. Moore	1929 A.W.H. Baucher & A.G. Snelling
1908 P.E. Negretti & E.C. Ackermann	1930 E.K. Robinson & R. Worssam
1908 C.M. Humble & Rev. D. Gotto	1931 S. Seddon & R.O. Hobhouse
1910 C.M. Humble & Rev. D. Gotto	1932 E.S. Markham & R. St. B. Emmott
1911 P. Burton & A. Bullock	1933 J.M. Darroch & W.A. Gray
1912 A.F.W. Gourlay & E.W. Whitehead	1934 C. McKenzie & G.A. Usher
1913 E.N. Kent & A. Wheen	1935 A.G. Snelling & R.A. Law
1914 O.P.Powell & G.A. Cutbill	1936 J.P. Graham & R.H. Burdon Cooper
1919 J.R. Grundy & G.E. Timins	1937 R.E.A. Bott & R.D. Henderson
1920 J.H. Skelton & R.A. Skelton	1938 R. Goddard & E.T. Benson
1921 R. Hogg & L. Walton	1939 A.G. Snelling & R.A. Law
1922 F.A.B. & R.M. Farquharson	1946 R.C.C. Green & R.D. Henderson
1923 G.E. Vaughan & G.E. Vaughan, jun.	1947 S.Seddon & J.G. Bland
1924 R.E.A. Bott & P. Gold	1948 F.W. Glassbrook & H.W. Singleton

Rumsey Goblets – Continued

1949	H.J. Liddiard & E.A. Judge	1974	A.C. Bynoe & P. Winship
1950	J. Darroch & J. Metcalfe	1975	P.D. Orchard-Lisle & P.J.R. Marsh
1951	F.W. Glassbrook & H.W. Singleton	1976	N.J. Notley & R.J. Nelson-Smith
1952	H.W. Singleton & J.G. Brown	1977	H.B. Pickett & J.G. Keller
1953	H.J. Liddiard & E.A. Judge	1978	K.R. Jenkin & N.P. Draper
1954	J.A. Armstrong & R.H. Baucher	1979	M.B. Peterson & P. Winship
1955	J. Sprawson & J.M. Reid	1980	D.M. Lamond & A.J. Taylor
1956	A.R. Griffith & W.F. Gelson	1981	A.T. Burton & N.J. Notley
1957	F.A. Rotherham & A.E. Potter	1982	E.L. Lewis & R.J. Dew
1958	J.M. Balch & R.D. Hyde	1983	C.C. Boal & M.J. Broad
1959	H.A. Chapman & B.H.G. Chapman	1984	D.M. Ward & D.C. Griffiths
1960	P.A. Strong & A.H.M. Hely	1985	R.J. Dew & E.L. Lewis
1961	R.C. Wood & R.P. Chappell	1986	S.M. Cox & J.D. Helliwell
1962	I.S. Anderson & M.J.S. Robertson	1987	P.J. Tolley & N.F. Lee
1963	N.A. Townsend & P.M. Townsend	1988	P.J. Tolley & N.F. Lee
1964	E.D. Broom & T.P. Stephenson	1989	P.J. Tolley & N.F. Lee
1965	J. Van Gelder & C.L. Reynolds	1990	R.J. Dew & E.L. Lewis
1966	J. Van Gelder & C.L. Reynolds	1991	C.C. Boal & P.R. Robinson
1967	R. Neill & E.C. Holt	1992	P.T. Watters & E. Stanbury
1968	B. Coral & A.K. Mercer	1993	S.A. Masson & M.D. Friend
1969	G. Sheffield & A.D.W. Sanderson	1994	C.C. Boal & D.A. Lewis
1970	C.C. Boal & N. Webb	1995	R.J. Dew & E.L. Lewis
1971	K.R. Jenkin & G.H. Dudley	1996	N.R. Cameron & M.A. Collin
1972	I.M. Judge & W.F. Gelson	1997	B. Ransley & R. Nicklin
1973	I.M. Judge & W.F. Gelson	1998	B. Ransley & R. Nicklin

Ernest Thomas Cup

36 hole medal (except for 1911) until 1920. 1921: 2 best medal scores throughout year.*
From 1922: 18 hole medal. Instituted in 1904 as Thomas Cup,
became Ernest Thomas Cup in 1932

1904	A.A. Rumsey	1931	W.A. Gray	1961	L.C.J. Ambrose
1905	E.S. Markham	1932	R.J. Fleming	1962	G.W. Murray
1906	R.V.B. Smyth	1933	A.G. Snelling	1963	R.N. Glover
1907	K.N. Stephens	1934	E.R. Brown	1964	P.M. Townsend
1908	C.L. Richmond	1935	G.A. Usher	1965	P.D. Orchard-Lisle
1909	A.E. Phillips	1936	H.D. Roberts	1966	J.G. Jarvis
1910	K.N. Stephens	1937	R.D. Henderson	1967	J.M. Reid
1911	K.N. Stephens*	1938	A. Sumner	1968	H.R. Hewitt
1912	P. Negretti	1946	H.W. Singleton	1969	M.J. Broad
1913	M.J. Clayton	1947	G. Usher	1970	A.K. Sutcliffe
1914	W.H. Lynch	1948	R.D. Henderson	1971	M.J. Broad
1919	G.E. Vaughan	1949	R.J. Sykes	1972	A.W. Murphy
1920	C.C. Arnell	1950	J.S. Scott-Miller	1973	V. Humphrey
1921	M. Brunton	1951	R.E.A. Bott	1974	G. Mckenzie
1922	P.C. Burton	1952	J. Darroch	1975	A.J. Murley
1923	R. Worssam	1953	R.E.A. Bott	1976	E.L. Lewis
1924	F.A.B. Farquharson	1954	H.T. Nicholson	1977	C.C. Boal
1925	S. Seddon	1955	W.F. Gelson	1978	K.G. Blythe
1926	G.E. Vaughan	1956	J.F. Darroch	1979	J. Connell
1927	G.F.M. Haines	1957	J.R.N. Holdsworth	1980	A.P.O. Cotton
1928	L.L. Binnie	1958	T. Neville	1981	P. Williamson
1929	C. Mckenzie	1959	H.A.C. Edwards	1982	R.D. Ransley
1930	R.E.A. Bott	1960	A.R. Griffith	1983	P.R. Hills

226

Ernest Thomas Cup – Continued

1984 C.W. Capstick	1989 T.C. Oxenham	1994 D.A. Lewis
1985 H.G. Green	1990 F.A. Smith	1995 J. James
1986 A. McCallum	1991 E. Wilson	1996 W. Cooper
1987 J.H. Laidler	1992 M. Peterson	1997 G. Brandt
1988 J. Winship	1993 J.H. Laidler	1998 D.J. Tricker

* 18 holes so did not count as one of the years for outright win

Richmond Scratch Challenge Cup
36 hole medal, except 1923-4, 1934-38: 18 holes

1908 A.E. Colebrook	1946 R.E.A. Bott	1973 R.J. Dew
1909 not played	1947 B. Nordon	1974 A. McCallum
1910 A.E. Phillips	1948 R.E.A. Bott	1975 R.J. Dew
1911 A.E. Phillips	1949 D.M. Keith	1976 M.J. Broad
1912 E.S. Markham	1950 B. Nordon	1977 M.J. Broad
1913 P.E. Negretti	1951 J.M. Balch	1978 N.J. Notley
1914 E.S. Markham	1952 E. Holt	1979 A.R. Lewis
1919 E.S. Markham	1953 C.G. Ostler	1980 N.J. Notley
1920 A.E. Phillips	1954 C.G. Ostler	1981 N.J. Notley
1921 J.H. Skelton	1955 C.G. Ostler	1982 N.J. Notley
1922 Maj. J.H. Skelton	1956 C.G. Ostler	1983 N.J. Notley
1923 P.C. Burton	1957 A.E. Potter	1984 J. Warne
1924 J.P. Hall	1958 E. Holt	1985 A.P.O. Cotton
1925 E.S. Markham	1959 B.M. Atkinson	1986 R.A. Latham
1926 O.J. Roy	1960 E. Holt	1987 R.A. Latham
1927 S. Seddon	1961 E. Holt	1988 R.A. Latham
1928 S. Seddon	1962 E. Holt	1989 R.A. Latham
1929 S. Seddon	1963 P.M. Townsend	1990 R.A. Latham
1930 R.E.A. Bott	1964 P.M. Townsend	1991 P.J. Tolley
1931 J.M. Darroch	1965 R. Neill	1992 R.A. Latham
1932 R.E.A. Bott	1966 E. Holt	1993 R.A. Latham
1933 J.M. Darroch	1967 R. Neill	1994 G.J. Maly
1934 I.A. Ewen	1968 I.M. Judge	1995 C.C. Boal
1935 A.G. Snelling	1969 M.J. Broad	1996 R.A. Latham
1936 A.G. Snelling	1970 R.J. Dew	1997 R.A. Latham
1937 R.T. Jones	1971 C.C. Boal	1998 R.A. Latham
1938 W.H. Halstead	1972 A.W. Murphy	

The Captain's Prize
18 hole medal but Captain may vary the format

1911 T. Perkins	1929 W.A. Gray	1949 C. Moxham
1912 A.H. Barron	1930 A.G. Snelling	1950 H.J. Liddiard
1913 W.H. Lynch	1931 J.L. Baucher	1951 A.S. Cramb
1914 J.D. Swinstead	1932 R.D. Henderson	1952 E.R. Brown
1919 G.E. Vaughan	1933 R. Trevor Jones	1953 M.H. Darroch
1920 J.P. Hall	1934 J. Everington	1954 W.F. Blandy
1921 A.E. Canney	1935 G.F. Roberts	1955 J.C. Liddle
1922 J.D. Swinstead	1936 J. Macdonald	1956 M.H. Darroch
1923 A. Sherriff	1937 J. Macdonald	1957 D.F. Smee
1924 F.A.B. Farquharson	1938 J. St. G. Sproule	1958 E.C.A. Bott
1925 E. Keith Robinson	1939 W.H. Halstead	1959 A. Bailey
1926 A.G. Snelling	1946 R.C.C. Green	1960 H.G. Green
1927 R. Worssam	1947 J.A. Fleming	1961 G.W. Murray
1928 E. Keith Robinson	1948 P.A. Strong	1962 H.R. Hewitt

The Captain's Prize – Continued

1963 D.G. Johnson	1975 A.J. Moore	1987 A.P. Coral
1964 A.E. Frost	1976 G.W. Nicklin	1988 B.R. Ransley
1965 I.M. Judge	1977 A.B. Evans	1989 A.C. Taylor
1966 A.E. Frost	1978 D.K.D. Watson	1990 R. Lubbock
1967 D.O. Wood	1979 J.D.R. Jeffery	1991 J. Freeman
1968 D.A.G. Gow	1980 J.D. Crowlesmith	1992 P. Hayes
1969 T.C. Stuart	1981 B.W. Cope	1993 G.J. O'Brien
1970 B. Coral	1982 A.J. McCallum	1994 C.W. Capstick
1971 J. Broad	1983 J.J. Lee	1995 N.R. Cameron
1972 R. O'Dell	1984 M.C. Mealey	1996 C.J. Thornton
1973 E.L. Lewis	1985 R.D. Ransley	1997 B.W. Cope
1974 D.R. Nicklin	1986 R.V. Williams	1998 N.J. Notley

King George V Coronation Challenge Cup
36 hole Scratch Open

1911 O.M. Kerr	Hendon	1959 S/Ldr. W.E. McCrea	Porters Park
1912 J. Livingston	R. Mid-Surrey	1960 E. Holt	Porters Park
1913 J.S. Worthington	not recorded	1961 J. Armour	Berkhamsted
1914 D. Grant	R. Mid-Surrey	1962 H.C. Squirrell	Moor Park
1920 O.C. Bristowe	Stoke Poges	1963 P.M. Townsend	Porters Park
1921 O.C. Bristowe	Stoke Poges	1964 P.M. Townsend	Porters Park
1922 W.I. Hunter	Walmer & Kingsdown	1965 A.W. Holmes	South Herts
1923 F.S. Bond	R. Wimbledon	1966 P.M. Townsend	Porters Park
1924 C.N. Flint	Bushey Hall	1967 S.R. Warrin	Pinner Hill
1925 C.N. Flint	Bushey Hall	1968 D. St. J. Brew	Sandy Lodge
1926 P.L. Smith	Old Fold Manor	1969 J.A. Putt	Oxford City
1927 E.S. Markham	Porters Park	1970 W. Humphreys	R. Mid-Surrey
1928 V.G. Longstaffe	Aldeburgh	1971 J.A. Putt	Frilford Heath
1929 J. Grimditch	Porters Park	1972 S.C. Mason	Goring & Streatley
1930 G.J. Anderson	Muswell Hill		
1931 R.E.A. Bott	Porters Park	1973 A.J. Mason	Berkhamsted
1932 B. Drew	R. Cinque Ports	1974 R.A. Durrant	Moor Park
1933 A.G. Snelling	Porters Park	1975 C. Phillips	Dulwich & Sydenham
1934 G.J. Anderson	Northwood		
1935 No competition		1976 N.J. Notley	Porters Park
1936 R. Pattinson	Derbyshire	1977 J.G. Bennett	Croham Hurst
1937 J. Grimditch	Porters Park	1978 M.T. Seaton	Gog Magog
1938 A.G. Snelling	Porters Park	1979 R.A. Durrant	Moor Park
1939 S. Seddon	Porters Park	1980 M.J. Smyth	Knebworth
1946 L. Perkins	Grim's Dyke	1981 D.G. Lane	Goring & Streatley
1947 L. Perkins	Grim's Dyke		
1948 E. Gibbs	Muswell Hill	1982 Not played (rained off twice)	
1949 P.E. Huddy	Wanstead	1983 N.J. Notley	Porters Park
1950 R.E.A. Bott	Porters Park	1984 J. Earl	Ifield
1951 E.J. Wiggs	Moor Park Artisans	1985 J. Ambridge	West Herts
1952 No competition		1986 C. McKay	Letchworth
1953 E. Holt	Porters Park	1987 W. Henry	Porters Park
1954 G.V. Keith	Mill Hill	1988 R.A. Latham	Porters Park
1955 T. Byrne	Wanstead	1989 W. Bennett	Ruislip
1956 M.H. Darroch	Porters Park	1990 C.C. Boal	Porters Park
1957 B.M. Atkinson	Porters Park	1991 S. Hoffman	Fulwell
1958 P.J. Carter	Porters Park	1992 R. Watts	Stoke Poges
		1993 D. Hamilton	East Herts

1994 S. Webster	Atherstone	1997 J. Knight	Sandford Springs
1995 S. Jarvis	Gog Magog	1998 M. King	Toft Hotel
1996 N. Swaffield	Stourbridge		

The Barron Cup

18 hole Stableford for 5-day members

Presented in 1908 by A.A. Barron to replace Colebrook Cup, which he had won outright. 36 hole medal until 1924. 18 hole medal 1925-53 (with optional second round), then not played for until 1968 when it became competition for 5-day members

1908 E.E. Head	1935 I. Ewen	1978 A.H. Lambert
1909 O.E. Coles	1936 R.E.A. Bott	1979 J. Reid
1910 W.H. Bull	1937 T.I.K. Lloydd	1980 B.J. Thornton
1911 T. Pope	1938 C.N. Mansfield	1981 M. Stoor
1912 A.W. Gourlay	1939 H.E. Medlicott	1982 M. Stoor
1913 P.E. Negretti	1946 D.L. Power	1983 C. Lewis
1914 F.R.M. de Paula	1947 E.C.A. Bott	1984 S.M. Roland
1919 G.E. Vaughan	1948 S. Seddon	1985 A.M. Thornton
1920 D.L. Von Braun	1949 R.H. Baucher	1986 A.P. McMullen
1921 G.E. Vaughan	1950 J. Metcalfe	1987 A.M. Thornton
1922 J.R. Grundy	1951 R.G. Worssam	1988 A.M. Thornton
1923 Maj. A.A. Nathan	1952 A.E. Potter	1989 R.J.C. Scott
1924 Maj. P.C. Burton	1953 P.H. Skelton	1990 N.G. Folland
1925 E.K. Robinson	1968 J.E. Foster	1991 A. Connell
1926 A.G. Snelling	1969 R. Boundry	1992 N. Folland
1927 J.E. Broad	1970 J. Marshall	1993 R. Morgan
1928 A.E. Dodge	1971 R. Brown	1994 I. Kremer
1929 C. Moxham	1972 J.H. Wills	1995 P. Maher
1930 G.F. Roberts	1973 J.H. Wills	1996 P. Williams
1931 W.O. Kennington	1974 M.T. Sotiriou	1997 A. Ralph
1932 Capt. C. McKenzie	1975 N.E. Whittle	1998 M. Boschetti
1933 J.H. Tearle	1976 A.G. Hubbard	
1934 G. McKenzie	1977 J.S. Liddle	

Dearbergh Challenge Cup

36 hole handicap medal

18 hole medal in 1925 & 1939. Played on same day as Richmond Cup from 1954 to 1969

1913 W.H. Lynch	1935 S. Seddon	1958 J. Sprawson
1914 P.R. Harrap	1936 D.S. McClean	1959 B.M. Atkinson
1920 R.F. Foster	1937 J.M. Darroch	1960 T.P. Stephenson
1921 L. McKenzie	1938 W.H.P. Tamplin	1961 D.A.A. Bott
1922 J.R. Grundy	1939 E.F. Cliff	1962 R. Davenport
1923 R.A. Skelton	1946 J.S. Scott-Miller	1963 P.M. Townsend
1924 G.S.A. Wheatcroft	1947 J.S. Scott-Miller	1964 G.A.D. Dailey
1925 E.K. Robinson	1948 J.G. Milner	1965 R. Neill
1926 O.J. Roy	1949 F.W. Glassbrook	1966 A.K. Mercer
1927 E.A. Abram	1950 J.A. Randall	1967 A.J. Taylor
1928 S. Seddon	1951 R.D. Henderson	1968 I.M. Judge
1929 J. Grimditch	1952 J. Darroch	1969 B. Coral
1930 L. Walton	1953 M.H. Darroch	1970 N.F. Lee
1931 A. Sherriff	1954 C.G. Ostler	1971 F.J. Phillips
1932 J.S. Gerber	1955 C.G. Ostler	1972 N. Albrechtsen
1933 T.P. Norris	1956 A.R. Griffith	1973 N. Draper
1934 J. Grimditch	1957 P.M. Harding	1974 J.J. Murray

229

Dearbergh Challenge Cup – Continued

1975 D.M. Lamond	1983 D.C. Griffiths	1991 R. Paffley
1976 A.J. McCallum	1984 J. Connell	1992 A.M. Pountney
1977 A.P. Coral	1985 R.C. Nicklin	1993 D.M. Ward
1978 P.J. Tolley	1986 A.G. Hubbard	1994 A.H. Lambert
1979 G.A.D. Dailey	1987 D.K.D. Watson	1995 G. Wright
1980 N.J. Notley	1988 D. Tomblin	1996 R.A. Latham
1981 E.L. Lewis	1989 A.M. Thornton	1997 A.M. Pountney
1982 D. Tomblin	1990 P.T. Watters	1998 M. Mealey

Whitehead Challenge Trophy

Presented by C.P. Smith and friends in memory of the late Ernest Whitehead.
1921-1930: 18 hole singles Bogey. 1931-1969: fourball Bogey.
From 1970: fourball Stableford

1921 G.F. Roberts	1925 A.L. Chandler	1929 A. Franks
1922 R.K. Cowperthwaite	1926 P. Le Mare	1930 R.E.A. Bott
1923 S. Seddon	1927 S. Seddon	
1924 G.E. Vaughan	1928 A.G. Snelling	

1931 A.E. Dodge & R.J. Fleming	1968 A.J. Winter & V. Humphrey
1932 H. Clayton & H.S. Reeve	1969 E.D. Hurcomb & T.C. Stuart
1933 no record	1970 A.K. Sutcliffe & P. Winship
1934 R.D. Henderson & T.C. Gilson	1971 N. Jenkin & H. Edwards
1935 J. Grimditch & J.E. Grimditch	1972 P.H. Newman & R.G. Wilson
1936 R.E.A. Bott & A.R.M. Harding	1973 P.A. Halsall & P.A. Enright
1937 A.R.M. Harding & D.B. Taunton	1974 P.A. Dew & E.C. Holt
1938 A.R.M. Harding & J.P. Graham	1975 A.B. Higgs & J.F. Reid
1939 R.D. Henderson & R.C.C. Green	1976 D.B. Pollard & A.G. Mills
1946 L. Henderson & G. Boggon	1977 C.C. Boal & M.J. Broad
1947 J.G. Bland & D.M. Keith	1978 A.G. Mills & D.B. Pollard
1948 J.A. Brown & A. Randall	1979 C.C. Boal & M.J. Broad
1949 A.W.H. Baucher & R.H. Baucher	1980 J. Freeman & M. Paterson
1950 J.G. Milner & E.K. Porte	1981 K. Sanderson & L. Winder
1951 E.C. Beck & A.E. Potter	1982 P.J. Tolley & M.J. Broad
1952 P.J. Rayner & L.G. Hulford	1983 M. Wallis & J. Warne
1953 R.G. Wilson & D. Davies	1984 A. Penn & P. Prince
1954 H.W. Singleton & M. Veal	1985 A.B. Higgs & E. Shipway
1955 M.H. Darroch & W.F. Gelson	1986 S. Cox & P. Williamson
1956 J.F. Darroch & R. Parkes	1987 A. Bynoe & A. Matheson
1957 R.H. Baucher & A. Forbes Ilsley	1988 B. Ransley & J. Horrocks
1958 B.H.G. Chapman & W.F. Gelson	1989 A. Bynoe & R. Lubbock
1959 A.R. Griffith & P. Mobsby	1990 M. Mealey & A. Hubbard
1960 R.E.A. Bott & P.D. Orchard-Lisle	1991 M. Mealey & A. Hubbard
1961 P.M. Harding & W.F. Gelson	1992 R. Lewis & R. Tolley
1962 P.M. Harding & W.F. Gelson	1993 D. Slattery & A. McCallum
1963 J.M. Reid & P.M. Townsend	1994 B. Morris & N. Morris
1964 E. Holt & R.N. Glover	1995 M. Broad & N. Draper
1965 R.E.A. Bott & D.A.A. Bott	1996 R. Lewis & R. Tolley
1966 P.B. Mellor & G.N.V. Jenkins	1997 A.J. Lewis & P. Hooper
1967 R. Neill & E.C. Sinclair	1998 A. Hubbard & A.G. Copley

Humble Salver

Singles Knockout, 16 qualify from 18 hole medal
Orginally President's Challenge Salver, became Humble Salver in 1946

1926* S. Seddon	1955 J.B. Cowper	1977 D.M. Lamond
1927 S. Seddon	1956 R.E.A. Bott	1978 A. Bynoe
1928 E.S. Markham	1957 L.A. Swindells	1979 J. Urquhart
1929 E.S. Markham	1958 M.B. Peterson	1980 C.W. Capstick
1930 R.J. Fleming	1959 D. Davies	1981 D. Lewis
1931 C. Moxham	1960 N.J. Youds	1982 A. Cotton
1932 H. Clayton	1961 R.E.A. Bott	1983 D. Lewis
1933 A.R. Baker	1962 N.A. Townsend	1984 C.C. Boal
1934 A.R. Baker	1963 P.M. Townsend	1985 J. Laidler
1935 A.G. Snelling	1964 E. Holt	1986 C.C. Boal
1936 J. Grimditch	1965 I.D.F. McCarroll	1987 N.J. Notley
1937 J. Grimditch	1966 A.K. Mercer	1988 S.A. Masson
1938 R.D. Armstrong	1967 J.M. Reid	1989 R.A. Latham
1946 D. Keith	1968 E.C. Sinclair	1990 C.C. Boal
1947 R.E.A. Bott	1969 A.J. Taylor	1991 D. Tomblin
1948 B. Nordon	1970 J. Van Gelder	1992 D. Palmer
1949 R.A. Fleming	1971 A. Bynoe	1993 A. Pountney
1950 R.A. Fleming	1972 A. Bynoe	1994 R. Capstick
1951 G. Quinn	1973 R.J. Dew	1995 N. Cameron
1952 J.R. Armstrong	1974 P. Dew	1996 R. Latham
1953 T.P. Norris	1975 M. Broad	1997 R.J. Dew
1954 A. Bailey	1976 N. Allanson	1998 R.M. Todd

* First year 18 hole medal only

Benevolent Challenge Trophy

Presented by R.O. Burlison, 1933
18 hole running Stableford
1933-35: Bogey, aggregate of three cards; thereafter Stableford

1933 A.G. Snelling	1960 Mrs. B. Darroch	1980 R.C. Nicklin
1934 D.S. McClean	1961 R.E.A. Bott	1981 Mrs. J. MacIntyre
1935 A.G. Snelling	1962 Mrs. P.A. Strong	1982 P. Williamson
1936 J.G. Milner	1963 Mrs. H.W. Singleton	1983 S.R. Watters
1937 R. Trevor Jones	1964 C.L. Reynolds	1984 J.H. Laidler
1938* W.H. Halstead	1965 R.H. Baucher	1985 P. Winship
1946 J.P. Hall	1966 W.W. Ottewill	1986 M.J. Lamb
1947 G. Usher	1967 E.C. Holt	1987 A.G. Copley
1948 Mrs. H.A. Chapman	1968 T.J. Tyler	1988 R.A. Barnes
1949 B. Nordon	1969 E.C. Holt	1989 M. Boyd
1950 J. Darroch	1970 N.E. Webb	1990 B. Marenbach
1951 R.D. Henderson	1971 E.C. Holt	1991 R. Corner
1952 P.J. Reyner	1972 C.C. Boal	1992 E. Schreier
1953 P.J. Reyner	1973 C.C. Boal	1993 G.A.G. Cutting
1954 C.G. Ostler	1974 I.D. Sweet	1994 N. Draper
1955 Miss P.J. Lane	1975 Mrs. M. Stanbury	1995 Mrs. S. Johns
1956 Miss J. Moxham	1976 N.S. Allanson	1996 G.W. O'Donoghue
1957 P.M. Harding	1977 M.J. Broad	1997 Mrs. J. Francis
1958 Miss A. Henderson	1978 A.J. McCallum	1998 A.G. Mills
1959 E.P. Humphreys	1979 M.J. Broad	

* Ladies and multiple entries permitted

Roberts Challenge Cup

18 hole Stableford (Bogey until 1970)

1935 R.T. Jones	1960 R.S.F. Hennessey	1980 C.C. Boal
1936 M.H. Robinson	1961 H.R. Hofton	1981 J.C. Cox
1937 J. Grimditch	1962 I.M. Judge	1982 D.C. Griffiths
1938 E.T. Benson	1963 I.M. Judge	1983 L.D. Pope
1939 M.A.H. Dick	1964 A.S. Cramb	1984 J. Warne
1940 M.A. Brown	1965 P.J. Phillips	1985 G. Bevan
1946 H.W. Singleton	1966 I.D.F. McCarroll	1986 B. Ransley
1947 H.W. Singleton	1967 M.J. Broad	1987 R.W. Newton
1948 R.H. Baucher	1968 B. Coral	1988 R.C. Nicklin
1949 G. Quinn	1969 P.G. de Havilland	1989 P. Wythe
1950 R.T. Sykes	1970 E.D. Hurcomb	1990 E.L. Lewis
1951 A.E. Potter	1971 A.W. Murphy	1991 J. Duke
1952 R.T. Sykes	1972 A.W. Murphy	1992 A.M. Pountney
1953 D. Davies	1973 G.H. Dudley	1993 M. Peterson
1954 D. Davies	1974 R.A.P. Wehner	1994 N. Draper
1955 J.B. Cowper	1975 C.W. Capstick	1995 P.N. Tolley
1956 C.G. Ostler	1976 A. Lewis	1996 J. Tricker
1957 K.L. Langrish-Smith	1977 D.O. Wood	1997 J. Arora
1958 B.H.G. Chapman	1978 C.C. Boal	1998
1959 R.N. Glover	1979 N.J. Notley	

Maltby Challenge Cup

Presented for best performance in match play against the Professional.
Not played 1958-65. From 1969, best performance v. Captain & Professional

1935 G.F. Roberts	1948 E.C.A. Bott	1955 R.E.A. Bott
1936 G.A. Usher	1949 R.D. Hyde	1956 A.E. Potter
1937 G.A. Usher	1950 H.W. Singleton	1957 J.M. Reid
1938 A.G. Snelling	1952* J.R. Armstrong	1966 M. Boyd
1946 J.M. Reid	1953 J.R. Armstrong	1967 J.A. Randall
1947 J.M. Reid	1954 H.W. Singleton	1968 K.R. Jenkin

1969 J.B. Parrott & J.A. Bunyan	1984 E.L. Lewis & R. Dew
1970 A.T. Burton & C.C. Boal	1985 P.H. Brown & A.G.H. Copley
1971 A.W. Murphy & A.T. Burton	1986 J. Van Gelder & D. Lewis
1972 G.W. Nicklin & D.B. Pollard	1987 C.C. Boal & P.J. Tolley
1973 C.W. Price & C.J. Spacey	1988 J. Hathaway & A. Hubbard
1974 N.J. Notley & S.H. Burton	1989 D.A. Lewis & J. Van Gelder
1975 E.W. Cheadle & D. Lamond	1990 R.J. Dew & E.L. Lewis
1976 J.D.R. Jeffery & J.R. Taylor	1991 R.A. Latham & A.J. McCallum
1977 D.M. Lamond & A.B. Higgs	1992 M. Ward & D. Ward
1978 D.M. Lamond & S.H. Burton	1993 J.H. Laidler & N.F. Lee
1979 D.B. Pollard & G.W. Nicklin	1994 A. Orsich & W.F. Gelson
1980 E.D. Hurcomb & D.B. Pollard	1995 Dr. P.T. Watters & E.V. Stanbury
1981 J.D.R. Jeffery & J.R. Taylor	1996 M. Ward & D. Ward
1982 E.L. Lewis & R. Dew	1997 C.C. Boal & G.A. Uwins
1983 E.L. Lewis & R. Dew	1998

* 1951 not recorded

James Bradbeer Cup
18 hole running Stableford
Presented by G.F. Roberts on Bradbeer's retirement – entrance fees to National Playing Fields Association.
1938-69: Bogey. From 1970: Stableford

1938 E.F. Cliff	1963 I.M. Judge	1982 N.F. Lee
1939 R.E.A. Bott	1964 F.M. Olsen	1983 A. McCallum
1946 B. Nordon	1965 E.A. Judge	1984 M. Mealey
1947 C. McKenzie	1966 A.E. Frost	1985 A.G. Hubbard
1948 F.W. Glassbrook	1967 T.J. Tyler	1986 M. Beresford
1949 F.W. Glassbrook	1968 P.J.R. Marsh	1987 A. Penn
1950 J.R. Armstrong	1969 D. Collier	1988 M. Mealey
1951 R.D. Henderson	1970 J.C. Cogill	1989 D.J. Kimbley
1952 J.M. Balch	1971 F.G. Lee	1990 C.J. Thornton
1953 R.P. Chappell	1972 E.P.S. Thorp	1991 H. Bryce
1954 L.N. Henderson	1973 C.W. Price	1992 W. Gelson
1955 J. Sprawson	1974 C.N. Grant	1993 A. Tolley
1956 P.H. Savery	1975 D.H. Jagger	1994 S. Grierson
1957 D. Davies	1976 M.J. Broad	1995 P. Tomblin
1958 T. Neville	1977 C.W. Capstick	1996 C.M. Smith
1959 A.R. Griffith	1978 P.J. Tolley	1997 P.N. Tolley
1960 R.E.A. Bott	1979 N.J. Notley	1998 R.C. Nicklin
1961 V. Humphrey	1980 C.C. Boal	
1962 I.M. Judge	1981 R.A. Barnes	

Oxhey Salver
Matchplay Knockout for 18-28 Handicap

1947 H. Kendrew	1965 B. Coral	1983 M. de la P. Beresford
1948 S. MacMorran	1966 F. Cusk	1984 J. Connell
1949 H. Kendrew	1967 D.L. Bailey	1985 M.A. Wilson
1950 G.L. Hankey	1968 A.D.W. Sanderson	1986 D.W. Graham
1951 A. Bailey	1969 J. Connell	1987 D. Slater
1952 J.H. Edwards	1970 G.W. Nicklin	1988 unrecorded
1953 J.C. Liddle	1971 H.B. Pickett	1989 J. Connell
1954 J.C. Liddle	1972 P.R.B. Lewis	1990 B. Quinn
1955 G.F. Platt	1973 F.L. Gould	1991 M.A. Wilson
1956 A. Bailey	1974 F.L. Gould	1992 M. Menzies
1957 P. Lynn	1975 J.D.R. Jeffery	1993 A. Grassick
1958 G. Sheffield	1976 K.A. Matheson	1994 A. Grassick
1959 D.O.S. Connolly	1977 D. Llewellyn-Rees	1995 R. Bunce
1960 R. Collier	1978 R. Brown	1996 R. Leach
1961 H.R. Hewitt	1979 B.E. Marenbach	1997 J. Bryce
1962 D.G. Johnson	1980 R. Cowan	1998 C. Lilley
1963 D.B. Moore	1981 M.R. Paterson	
1964 K.E. Whitworth	1982 S. Hutton	

Markham Cup
18 hole medal

1953 J. Everington	1960 J.A. Edwards	1967 A.D.M. Hill
1954 G.F. Platt	1961 R.N. Glover	1968 A.D.M. Hill
1955 J.G. Daniell	1962 J.S. Ross	1969 T.C. Stuart
1956 M.G. Orchard-Lisle	1963 G. Sheffield	1970 W.A. de Podesta
1957 G. Sheffield	1964 R. Collier	1971 G.N.V. Jenkins
1958 R.T. Jones	1965 N.A. Townsend	1972 P. Winship
1959 H.A.C. Edwards	1966 A.J. Taylor	1973 P.J.R. Marsh

233

Markham Cup – Continued

1974 A.J. Taylor	1983 C.C. Boal	1992 M. Wallis
1975 G.F. Platt	1984 R.H. Lubbock	1993 A.R. Smith
1976 G.W.T. O'Donoghue	1985 B.R. Ransley	1994 C.C. Boal
1977 M.J. Broad	1986 M.A. Wilson	1995 J.R. Taylor
1978 J.W. Sainty	1987 J.H. Gunn	1996 R.L. Lewis
1979 E.G.P. Shipway	1988 B. Sandford	1997 D. James
1980 S. Cox	1989 I.R. Eggleden	1998 B. Barnes
1981 S.J. Moore	1990 R.W. Newton	
1982 J.J. Warne	1991 A.K. Davies	

Coral Salver
Winter Foursomes Knockout

1968 W.W. Ottewill & R.A.P. Wehner	1984 J.H. Laidler & J.A. Urquhart
1969 I.M. Judge & W.F. Gelson	1985 J.H. Laidler & J.A. Urquhart
1970 N.P. Broad & A.K. Sutcliffe	1986 D. Roockley & J. Warne
1971 N.F. Lee & A.G. Mills	1987 R. Dew & E.L. Lewis
1972 N.J. Notley & R.J. Nelson-Smith	1988 J. Warne & D. Roockley
1973 R.J. Dew & D.E. Caldwell	1989 P. Lewis & A. Murphy
1974 N.J. Notley & R.J. Nelson-Smith	1990 M. Wallis & J. Warne
1975 H.B. Pickett & J.G. Keller	1991 C.C. Boal & P.R. Robinson
1976 N.J. Notley & R.J. Nelson-Smith	1992 M. Friend & S.A. Masson
1977 J.G. Keller & M.J. Broad	1993 C.C. Boal & D.A. Lewis
1978 C.C. Boal & N.E. Webb	1994 C.C. Boal & D.A. Lewis
1979 N.F. Lee & N.J. Notley	1995 D. Tomblin & P. Tomblin
1980 J. Van Gelder & J.H. Cox	1996 G. Kirby & E. Wilson
1981 A.R. Lewis & P.J. Tolley	1997 P.N. Tolley & G. Brandt
1982 A.P. Coral & R.C. Nicklin	1998 D. Kinnear & A. Wilson
1983 A.P. Coral & R.C. Nicklin	

Sanford Seniors Cup
Knockout for full and 5-day members over 60

1973 E.O. Harris	1982 J. Van Gelder	1991 B.C. Morris
1974 L. Boundy	1983 F.G. Lee	1992 H.R. Harlow
1975 J.A. Randall	1984 L.D. Pope	1993 B.C. Morris
1976 A.D.W. Sanderson	1985 E.G.P. Shipway	1994 M.S. Lavender Jones
1977 D.L. Bailey	1986 R. East	1995 D.M. Aldworth
1978 P.A. Strong	1987 J. Van Gelder	1996 K. King
1979 J. Van Gelder	1988 D. Pope	1997 E. Holt
1980 E.G.P. Shipway	1989 J. Van Gelder	1998
1981 J.A. Randall	1990 P.G. Watson	

Club Championship
Matchplay Knockout – first 8 qualify from Richmond

1976 C.C. Boal	1984 P.J. Tolley	1992 J.K.G. Wright
1977 C.C. Boal	1985 R.A. Latham	1993 C.C. Boal
1978 M.J. Broad	1986 R.A. Latham	1994 G.J. Maly
1979 P.J. Tolley	1987 A.P. Coral	1995 C.C. Boal
1980 C.C. Boal	1988 K.K. Parker	1996 C.C. Boal
1981 D.A. Lewis	1989 P.R. Robinson	1997 C.C. Boal
1982 R.J. Dew	1990 R.A. Latham	1998 R.A. Latham
1983 C.C. Boal	1991 R.A. Latham	

President's Cup
Presented by P.D. Orchard-Lisle
18 hole medal for all medal and trophy winners during year

1991 J. James	1994 P.N. Tolley	1997 C.C. Boal
1992 D. Palmer	1995 P. Tomblin	1998
1993 D. Palmer	1996 N. Cameron	

Porters Park Mid-Amateur
36 hole Scratch Open for over-35s

1993 C.C. Boal, Porters Park	1996 J. Ambridge, Moor Park &
1994 C.C. Boal, Porters Park	M. Ready, Old Fold Manor*
1995 C.C. Boal, Porters Park	1997 C.C. Boal, Porters Park
	1998 D. Hastings, Old Fold Manor

*Trophy shared after tie; play-off not possible

Ladies Captains

1905, '06 Mrs. E. Smyth	1943 Mrs. R.J. Fleming	1971 Mrs. P.H. Newman
1907 Mrs. Martin	1944 Mrs. R.J. Fleming	1972 Mrs. R.A. Johnson
1908, '09 Mrs. E. Smyth	1945 Mrs. R.J. Fleming	1973 Mrs. M.B. Stephenson
1910 Miss G. Kell	1946 Mrs. H.A. Chapman	1974 Mrs. J. MacFarlane
1911-'19 no records	1947 Mrs. J.M. Darroch	1975 Mrs. E. Oliver Harris
1920 Miss M. Sewell	1948 Mrs. R.E.A. Bott	1976 Mrs. J. Howell
1921 Mrs. P. Alliston	1949 Mrs. J.B. Hopkinson	1977 Mrs. E.M. Copley
1922 Mrs. M. Heaton	1950 Mrs. J.B. Hopkinson	1978 Mrs. K. Arthur
1923 Mrs. F.R.M. de Paula	1951 Mrs. B.Q. Robson	1979 Mrs. S. Radcliffe
1924 Mrs. G.E. Vaughan	1952 Mrs. E. Parkes	1980 Mrs. R.W. Connell
1925 Mrs. G.E. Vaughan	1953 Mrs. H.W. Singleton	1981 Mrs. M. Stanbury
1926 Mrs. L.J. Reid	1954 Mrs. C.F.B. Arthur	1982 Mrs. J.M. Horne
1927 Mrs. F.A.B. Farquharson	1955 Mrs. H.K. Wakefield	1983 Mrs. R. Watters
1928 Mrs. H.A. Baucher	1956 Mrs. R.H. Baucher	1984 Mrs. I.G. Sanderson
1929 Mrs. A.E. Dodge	1957 Miss P.J. Lane	1985 Mrs. E.G.P. Shipway
1930 Mrs. A.A. Nathan	1958 Mrs. J.P. Graham	1986 Mrs. M. Thomson
1931 Mrs. R.E.A. Bott	1959 Mrs. F. Vestey Dorée	1987 Mrs. P.J. Rawlings
1932 Mrs. G.F. Roberts	1960 Mrs. A. Bailey	1988 Mrs. M. Williams
1933 Mrs. G.F. Roberts	1961 Mrs. P.M. Reid	1989 Mrs. E.M. Copley
1934 Mrs. R.J. Fleming	1962 Mrs. R.G. Wilson	1990 Mrs. H.D. Wythe
1935 Mrs. R.J. Fleming	1963 Mrs. G. Sheffield	1991 Mrs. L. Beardwell
1936 Mrs. F.R.M. de Paula	1964 Mrs. J.B. Hopkinson	1992 Mrs. M.E. Wilson
1937 Mrs. A.G. Snelling	1965 Mrs. E.D. Broom	1993 Mrs. B. Tattersall
1938 Mrs. E.C. Dix	1966 Mrs. C.R. Glover	1994 Mrs. J.R. Nevitt
1939 Mrs. E. Clifford Turner	1967 Mrs. P. Liddiard	1995 Mrs. Y. Frankland
1940 Mrs. E. Clifford Turner	1968 Mrs. R.H. Baucher	1996 Mrs. S.M. Palmer
1941 Mrs. E. Clifford Turner	1969 Mrs. D.J. Cumming	1997 Mrs. E.M. Hanson
1942 Mrs. E. Clifford Turner	1970 Mrs. P. Power	1998 Mrs. R. Hemmings

Club Championship
Scratch Knockout

1952 Mrs. J.M. Darroch	1959 Miss P.J. Lane	1966 Mrs. D. Johnson
1953 Miss P.J. Lane	1960 Miss P.J. Lane	1967 Miss P.J. Lane
1954 Miss P.J. Lane	1961 Miss P.J. Lane	1968 Miss P.J. Lane
1955 Miss P.J. Lane	1962 Mrs. J. Chapman	1969 Mrs. E.M. Bottomley
1956 Mrs. R.H. Baucher	1963 Miss P.J. Lane	1970 Miss P.J. Lane
1957 Miss P.J. Lane	1964 Mrs. D. Johnson	1971 Miss P.J. Lane
1958 Mrs. Q. Robson	1965 Mrs. B.G.C. Cann	1972 Miss F. Chapman

Club Championship – Continued

1973 Mrs. E.M. Bottomley	1982 Miss N. McCormack	1991 Mrs. R. Watters
1974 Mrs. D. Price	1983 Miss N. McCormack	1992 Mrs. F. Smith
1975 Mrs. S. Westmacott	1984 Mrs. R. Watters	1993 Mrs. R. Watters
1976 Mrs. J. Holdway	1985 Mrs. R. Watters	1994 Mrs. R. Watters
1977 Mrs. M. Hall	1986 Mrs. R. Watters	1995 Mrs. R. Watters
1978 Mrs. M. Hall	1987 Mrs. R Watters	1996 Mrs. F. Smith
1979 Mrs. R. Watters	1988 Mrs. E. Drewery	1997 Ms. A.J. Rooke
1980 Mrs. R. Watters	1989 Mrs. M. Hall	1998 Miss L. Nelson
1981 Mrs. J. Holdway	1990 Mrs. R. Watters	

Kell Cup
Presented by Miss G. Kell
Matchplay Knockout

1911 Miss C. Pennington	1914 Miss M. Smyth	1921 Mrs. A.A. Nathan
1912 Mrs. Stephens	1919 Mrs. A.A. Nathan	1922 Mrs. A.A. Nathan
1913 Mrs. Abady	1920 Mrs. C.L. Richmond	

Mrs. Nathan won this cup outright and presented:

Nathan Cup – *29 handicap and below*

1923 Mrs. F.R.M. de Paula	1954 Mrs. O. Dove	1977 Mrs. S. Westmacott
1924 Mrs. A.E. Dodge	1955 Miss F. Hazeldine	1978 Mrs. B. Harding
1925 Mrs. K. Farquharson	1956 Mrs. J. Chapman	1979 Mrs. J. Horne
1926 Miss Bull	1957 Miss J. Moxham	1980 Mrs. K. Arthur
1927 Mrs. L.J. Reid	1958 Mrs. Q. Robson	1981 Mrs. D. Johnson
1928 Mrs. A. Franks	1959 Miss F. Hazeldine	1982 Mrs. J. Holdway
1929 Mrs. R.E.A. Bott	1960 Mrs. P. Reid	1983 Mrs. M. Hall
1930 Mrs. R.E.A. Bott	1961 Miss J. Moxham	1984 Mrs. R. Watters
1931 Mrs. J. Grimditch	1962 no record	1985 Mrs. M. Stanbury
1932 Mrs. K. Farquharson	1963 Mrs. J. Sheffield	1986 Miss J. Seal
1933 Mrs. B. Clark	1964 Mrs. J.P. Graham	1987 Mrs. K. Arthur
1934 Mrs. R.E.A. Bott	1965 Mrs. J.P. Graham	1988 Mrs. R. Watters
1935 Mrs. B. Harding	1966 Mrs. J.B. Hopkinson	1989 Mrs. M. Thomson
1936 Mrs. J.P. Graham	1967 Mrs. J.P. Graham	1990 Mrs. C. Robinson
1937 Mrs. J.P. Graham	1968 Mrs. S. Westmacott	1991 Mrs. R. Watters
1938 Mrs. S. Everington	1969 Mrs. H.A.C. Edwards	1992 Ms. A.J. Rooke
1939 Mrs. R.E.A. Bott	1970 Mrs. R.G. Wilson	1993 Mrs. L. Beardwell
1948 Miss F. Hazeldine	1971 Mrs. R.G. Wilson	1994 Mrs. J. Bryce
1949 Miss J. Gubbins	1972 Lady Graham	1995 Mrs. J. Dulieu
1950 no record	1973 Mrs. S. Radcliffe	1996 Mrs. A. Prosser
1951 Miss F. Hazeldine	1974 Mrs. K. Arthur	1997 Mrs. L. Beardwell
1952 Mrs. C. Holdsworth	1975 Mrs. M. Stanbury	1998 Mrs. L. Beardwell
1953 Mrs. Q. Robson	1976 Mrs. M. Hall	

Lane Salver
Presented by Miss Pam Lane
36 hole medal – 24 handicap and below

1955 Miss P. Lane	1961 Mrs. Q. Robson	1967 Mrs. N. Graham
1956 Mrs. N. Graham	1962 Mrs. S. Copley	1968 Mrs. V. Baucher
1957 Mrs. J. Platt	1963 Mrs. L. Taylor	1969 Mrs. A. Newman
1958 Mrs. I. Cole	1964 Mrs. P. Reid	1970 Mrs. S. Dorée
1959 Mrs. S. Dorée	1965 Mrs. N. Graham	1971 Mrs. J. MacFarlane
1960 Mrs. V. Baucher	1966 Mrs. S. Copley	1972 Mrs. B. Wilson

Lane Salver – Continued

1973 Mrs. D. Price	1982 Mrs. J. Cooper	1991 Mrs. S. May
1974 Mrs. J. MacFarlane	1983 Mrs. E. Copley	1992 Mrs. A. Davis
1975 Mrs. M. Stanbury	1984 Mrs. M. Stanbury	1993 Mrs. F. Smith
1976 Mrs. A. Wright	1985 Mrs. J. Horne	1994 Mrs. F. Smith
1977 Mrs. J. Horne	1986 Mrs. J. Horne	1995 Mrs. M. Stanbury
1978 Mrs. K. Arthur	1987 Mrs. S. Westmacott	1996 Mrs. A. Prosser
1979 Miss J. Smith	1988 Mrs. M. Stanbury	1997 Miss G. MacLaurin
1980 Mrs. R. Watters	1989 Mrs. P. Clough	1998 Mrs. A. Healy
1981 Mrs. S. Westmacott	1990 Mrs. M. Stanbury	

Humble Salver

Originally The President's Salver, presented by Mr. C.M. Humble
4 lowest medal scores qualify for matchplay knockout off handicap

1926 Mrs. V. Gold	1955 Mrs. Q. Robson	1977 Mrs. J. Horne
1927 Mrs. K. Farquharson	1956 Mrs. J. Chapman	1978 Mrs. A. Wright
1928 Mrs. A.E. Dodge	1957 Mrs. I. Cole	1979 Mrs. M. Hall
1929 Mrs. P. Neill	1958 Mrs. K. Strong	1980 Mrs. M. Stanbury
1930 Mrs. K. Snelling	1959 Mrs. P. Waterfield	1981 Mrs. J. Horne
1931 Miss M. Franks	1960 Mrs. L.M. Hely	1982 Mrs. M. Hall
1932 Mrs. D. Worssam	1961 Miss F. Hazeldine	1983 Mrs. M. Shipway
1933 Mrs. A.E. Dodge	1962 Mrs. B. Broom	1984 Mrs. J. Horne
1934 Miss J. Wheatcroft	1963 Mrs. S. Copley	1985 Mrs. M. Stanbury
1935 Mrs. P.M. Reid	1964 Mrs. L. Taylor	1986 Mrs. E. Drewery
1936 Mrs. A Burdon-Cooper	1965 Mrs. E. Bottomley	1987 Mrs. M. Stanbury
1937 Mrs. M. Steinberg	1966 Mrs. B. Wilson	1988 Mrs. Mary Wilson
1938 Mrs. P.M. Reid	1967 Mrs. L. Taylor	1989 Miss D. McLoughlin
1939 Mrs. Q. Robson	1968 Mrs. J. Chapman	1990 Mrs. C. Robinson
1947 Mrs. J.B. Hopkinson	1969 Mrs. P. Liddiard	1991 Ms. A.J. Rooke
1948 Mrs. J.B. Hopkinson	1970 Mrs. B. Cann	1992 Mrs. Y. Frankland
1949 Mrs. M. Hyde	1971 Mrs. J. MacIntyre	1993 Mrs. V. Honess
1950 Mrs. P.E. Orchard-Lisle	1972 Mrs. J. Sheffield	1994 Mrs. S. Westmacott
1951 Mrs. B. Balch	1973 Mrs. V. Murray	1995 Mrs. P. Clough
1952 Mrs. P. Liddiard	1974 Mrs. J. Chapman	1996 Mrs. J. Capstick
1953 Mrs. E.H. Martin	1975 Mrs. S. Radcliffe	1997 Mrs. A.M. Davis
1954 Mrs. B. Wilson	1976 Mrs. J. MacFarlane	1998 Mrs. L. Beardwell

West Grove Cup

Presented in 1906 by Dr. H.J. Martin; current trophy from 1976
Lowest aggregate score of May & October LGU Medals

1906-'10 no records	1927 Mrs. H.A. Baucher	1947 Mrs. J. Chapman
1911 Miss Sewell	1928 Mrs. J.D. Swinstead	1948 Mrs. N. Graham
1912 Miss M. Smyth	1929 Mrs. R.E.A. Bott	1949 Mrs. Booth
1913 Mrs. E. Smyth	1930 Mrs. J. Grimditch	1950 no record
1914 Mrs. A.E. Dodge	1931 Mrs. R.E.A. Bott	1951 Mrs. B. Harding
1919 Mrs. C.L. Richmond	1932 Mrs. B. Clark	1952 Mrs. C. Holdsworth
1920 Mrs. J.D. Swinstead	1933 Mrs. B. Clark	1953 Mrs. P. Waterfield
1921 Mrs. F.R.M. de Paula	1934 Miss J. Wheatcroft	1954 Miss A. Baucher
1922 Mrs. C.L. Richmond	1935 Mrs. B. Harding	1955 Mrs. J. Chapman
1923 Mrs. R. Foster	1936 Mrs. N. Graham	1956 Miss J. Moxham
1924 Mrs. A.E. Dodge	1937 no record	1957 Miss P.J. Lane
1925 Mrs. C.L. Richmond	1938 Mrs. P.M. Reid	1958 Mrs. E.H. Martin
1926 Mrs. J. Grimditch	1939 Mrs. Goodwin	1959 Mrs. P. Liddiard

West Grove Cup – Continued

1960 Mrs. Q. Robson	1972 Lady Graham	1986 Mrs. B. Harrington-Brown
1961 Mrs. V. Baucher	1973 Mrs. S. Copley	1987 Mrs. M. Hall
1962 Mrs. P. Waterfield	1974 Mrs. S. Farquhar	1988 Mrs. E. Copley
1963 Mrs. Q. Attale	1975 Lady Graham	1989 Mrs. J. Gelson
Mrs. P. Liddiard (tie)	1976 Mrs. J. Howell	1990 Mrs. S. Palmer
1964 Mrs. S. Copley	1977 Mrs. J. Horne	1991 Mrs. M. Nelson
1965 Mrs. B. Harding	1978 Mrs. R. Watters	1992 Mrs. E. Drewery
1966 Mrs. M. Cumming	1979 Mrs. M. Stanbury	1993 Mrs. S. Hawkey
1967 Mrs. I. Cole	1980 Mrs. L. Beardwell	1994 Mrs. A. Prosser
1968 Mrs. V. Baucher	1981 Mrs. R. Gunn	1995 Mrs. S. Hawkey
1969 Mrs. A. Newman	1982 Mrs. D. Johnson	Mrs. J. Bryce (tie)
1970 Mrs. S. Westmacott	1983 Mrs. S. Farquhar	1996 Mrs. C. Sharp
Mrs. E. Bottomley (tie)	1984 Mrs. Myra Wilson	1997 Mrs. E. Cox
1971 Mrs. B. Harding	1985 Mrs. M. Hall	1998 Mrs. E. Drewery

Farquharson Cups
Presented by Mrs. Kathleen Farquharson
18 hole Stableford foursomes

1928 Mrs. R.G. Lane & Mrs. Matheson	1968 Mrs. J. Dean & Mrs. G. Edwards
1929 Mrs. R.E.A. Bott & Miss C.N. Burton	1969 Mrs. J. Dean & Mrs. G. Edwards
1930 Mrs. H.A. Baucher & Mrs. E.B. Roberts	1970 Mrs. J. Arthur & Mrs. K. Arthur
1931 Mrs. J. Grimditch & Mrs. R.G. Lane	1971 Mrs. E. Bottomley & Mrs. P. Bailey
1932 Mrs. R.E.A. Bott & Miss J. Forsyth	1972 Mrs. S. Copley & Miss F. Chapman
1933 Miss K. Garnham & Miss J. Forsyth	1973 Mrs. M. Stephenson & Mrs. B. Broom
1934 Mrs. R.J. Fleming & Mrs. V.W. Fitzgerald	1974 Lady Graham & Mrs. D. Johnson
1935 Mrs. Stevenson & Miss J. Moreland	1975 Mrs. S. Copley & Mrs P. Harris
1936 Mrs. Mead & Mrs. Wills	1976 Mrs. J. Sheffield & Mrs. J. Chapman
1937 Mrs. K. Snelling & Mrs. E. Benson	1977 Mrs. S. Radcliffe & Mrs. M. Thomson
1938 Mrs. R.E.A. Bott & Mrs. K. Snelling	1978 Mrs. A. Wright & Mrs. D. Notley
1939 Mrs. C.W. Beeson & Mrs. H.A. Chapman	1979 Mrs. S. Farquhar & Mrs. P. Clough
1946 Mrs. C. McKenzie & Miss Scott Gilbert	1980 Mrs. D. Johnson & Mrs. S. Thompson
1947 Mrs. J. Chapman & Mrs. N. Burdon-Cooper	1981 Mrs. L. Beardwell & Mrs. M. Shipway
1948 Mrs. B. Harding & Mrs. J.A. Mackie	1982 Mrs. E. Copley & Mrs. B. Harrington-Brown
1949 Mrs. R.E.A. Bott & Mrs. C. McKenzie	1983 Mrs. J. Capstick & Mrs. S. Hathaway
1950 Mrs. V. Baucher & Mrs. R. Brendon	1984 Mrs. S. Farquhar & Mrs. G. Wadey
1951 Mrs. P.E. Orchard-Lisle & Mrs. J. Hopkinson	1985 Mrs. L. Beardwell & Mrs. M. Shipway
1952 Mrs. B. Balch & Mrs. R. Brendon	1986 Mrs. E. Drewery & Mrs. Mary Wilson
1953 Mrs. J. Arthur & Mrs. Q. Robson	1987 Mrs. E. Drewery & Mrs. Mary Wilson
1954 Mrs. B. Harding & Mrs. A. Farrow	1988 Mrs. M. Hall & Mrs. S. Hathaway
1955 Mrs. V. Baucher & Mrs. H.T. Nicholson	1989 Mrs. E. Copley & Mrs. G. Cooper
1956 Mrs. E.A. Judge & Miss J. Moxham	1990 Mrs. L. Beardwell & Mrs. A. Duncan
1957 Mrs. D. Worssam & Mrs. I. Cole	1991 Mrs. P. Clough & Mrs. S. Farquhar
1958 Mrs. A. Dixon & Mrs. A. Potter	1992 Mrs. L. Lambert & Mrs. J. Capstick
1959 Mrs. B. Harding & Mrs. G. Hennessey	1993 Mrs. F. Smith & Mrs. J. Horne
1960 Mrs. V. Baucher & Mrs. B. Walker	1994 Mrs. J. Nevitt & Mrs. M. Havens
1961 Mrs. V. Baucher & Mrs. B. Walker	1995 Mrs. C. Robinson & Mrs. S. Hathaway
1962 Mrs. L. Taylor & Mrs. M. Judge	1996 Mrs. A. Prosser & Mrs. C. Sharp
1963 Mrs. J. Sheffield & Mrs. D. Johnson	1997 Mrs. A. Prosser & Mrs. C. Sharp
1964 Mrs. M. Judge & Mrs. L. Taylor	1998 Mrs. G. Warnes & Mrs. R. Woodley
1965 Mrs. B. Broom & Mrs. M. Stephenson	
1966 Mrs. J. Sheffield & Mrs. A. Otterwill	
1967 Mrs. B. Simmers & Mrs. K. Darroch	

Tatham Cup

Presented by Mrs. Tillyer Tatham
18 hole medal

1911 May Mrs. S.E. Biggs	1933 Mrs. S.D. Clements	1970 Mrs. I.M. Cole
Oct Miss C. Pennington	1934 Miss J. Wheatcroft	1971 Mrs. J. Howell
1912 May Mrs. A.P. Meyer	1935 Mrs. A.G. Snelling	1972 Mrs. E. Harrison
Oct Mrs. E.N. Kent	1936 Mrs. J.P. Graham	1973 Mrs. J. MacFarlane
1913 May Mrs. E. Smyth	1937 Mrs. Bronco Clark	1974 Mrs. A.M. Davis
Oct Mrs. E. Smyth	1938 Mrs. A.G. Snelling	1975 Mrs. A. Newman
1914 May Mrs. H.A. Baucher	1939 Miss Scott Gilbert	1976 Mrs. J. MacIntyre
Oct Miss A.L. Brampton	1946 Mrs. C. McKenzie	1977 Mrs. M. Stanbury
1915 May Mrs. F.R.M. de Paula	1947 Miss J. Ingram	1978 Mrs. J. Horne
1919 Oct Mrs. P. Alliston	1948 Mrs. J.P. Graham	1979 Mrs. R. Watters
1920 Mar Mrs. R. Foster	1949 Mrs. R.D. Hyde	1980 Mrs. J. Horne
Oct Mrs. R. Foster	1950 Mrs. P.E. Orchard-Lisle	1981 Mrs. Myra Wilson
1921 Mar Mrs. P. Alliston	1951 Mrs. J. Sheffield	1982 Mrs. R. Watters
Oct Mrs. A.A. Nathan	1952 Mrs. P. Liddiard	1983 Mrs. M. Stanbury
1922 Mar Mrs. A.A. Nathan	1953 Mrs. J. Sheffield	1984 Mrs. Judith Graham
Oct Mrs. J. Upsdale	1954 Mrs. B.M. Wilson	1985 Mrs. M. Shipway
1923 Mar Lady Peat	1955 Mrs. R. Brendon	1986 Mrs. J. Capstick
Oct Mrs. L.J. Reid	1956 Mrs. J.R.N. Holdsworth	1987 Mrs. E. Cox
1924 Mar Lady Peat	1957 Mrs. R.S.F. Hennessey	1988 Mrs. L. Harris
Oct Mrs. Bayon	1958 Mrs. R.H. Baucher	1989 Mrs. J. Horne
1925 Mar Mrs. Hibberdine	1959 Mrs. B.L. Harding	1990 Mrs. S. Newbury
Oct Mrs. Salaman	1960 Mrs. S. Copley	1991 Mrs. L. Lambert
1926 Mar Mrs. F.R.M. de Paula	1961 Mrs. J.P. Graham	1992 Mrs. M. Hall
Oct Mrs. F.R.M. de Paula	1962 Mrs. J.P. Graham	1993 Mrs. C. Dingley
1927 Mar Mrs. F.R.M. de Paula	1963 Mrs. E.D. Broom	1994 Mrs. M. Stanbury
Oct Mrs. F.R.M. de Paula	1964 Mrs. M. Stephenson	1995 Mrs. S. Johns
1928 Mrs. J.R. Neill	1965 Mrs. B.M. Wilson	1996 Mrs. H. Dennes
1929 Mrs. A.E. Dodge	1966 Mrs. G. Edwards	1997 Mrs. R. Woodley
1930 Mrs. J. Rowley	1967 Mrs. P.A. Strong	1998 Mrs. L. Lambert
1931 Mrs. A.M. Bryer	1968 Mrs. J.B. Hopkinson	
1932 Miss C.M. Burton	1969 Mrs. I.M. Cole	

Swinstead Cup

Presented by Mrs. J.D. Swinstead
Par competition

1930 Mrs. R.G. Lane	1954 Mrs. M.G. Orchard-Lisle	1970 Mrs. A.H. Copley
1931 Mrs. F. Lawrence	1955 Miss F. Hazeldine	1971 Mrs. B. Harding
1932 Mrs. A. Franks	1956 Miss J.M. Moxham	1972 Mrs. K. Arthur
1933 Mrs. A.A. Nathan	1957 Mrs. B. Klean	1973 Lady Graham
1934 Mrs. G.P. Mead	1958 Miss J.M. Moxham	1974 Mrs. J.A. Randall
1935 Mrs. J. Grimditch	1959 Mrs. M. Young	1975 Mrs. A. Burdon-Cooper
1936 Mrs. J.P. Graham	1960 Mrs. S. Copley	1976 Mrs. J. Sheffield
1937 Mrs. W.B. Stephenson	1961 Mrs. R.H. Baucher	1977 Mrs. A. Davis
1938 Miss J. Clements	1962 Miss A.M. Henderson	1978 Mrs. S. Lang
1947 Mrs. M.L. Collis	1963 Mrs. G.V. Stephenson	1979 Mrs. J. Van Gelder
1948 Mrs. J.S. Robson	1964 Mrs. P. Liddiard	1980 Mrs. M. Hall
1949 Miss J. Gubbins	1965 Mrs. E. Bottomley	1981 Mrs. R. Gunn
1950 Mrs. J.A. Mackie	1966 Mrs. A. Newman	1982 Mrs. P. Rawlings
1951 Mrs. G. Quinn	1967 Mrs. D. Johnson	1983 Mrs. J. Anthony
1952 Mrs. H.K. Waterfield	1968 Mrs. A. Newman	1984 Mrs. M. Stanbury
1953 Mrs. S. Dorée	1969 Mrs. M.B. Stephenson	1985 Mrs. J. Anthony

239

1986 Mrs. S. Farquhar	1991 Mrs. S. Hawkey	1996 Miss K. Nelson
1987 Mrs. P. Rawlings	1992 Ms. A.J. Rooke	1997 Mrs. J. Williams
1988 Mrs. J. Nevitt	1993 Mrs. S. Westmacott	1998 Mrs. C.A. Sharp
1989 Mrs. E. Drewery	1994 Mrs. A. Duncan	
1990 Mrs. J. Horne	1995 Mrs. J. Swithenbank	

Barnes Cups

Presented by Mrs. Marguerite Barnes
Handicap Greensomes knockout

1931 Mrs. J. Grimditch & Miss M. Franks	1969 Lady Graham & Mrs. J. Chapman
1932 Miss Martin Smith & Miss P. Martin Smith	1970 Mrs. S. Copley & Mrs. B. Harding
1933 Mrs. F.R.M. de Paula & Miss J. Forsyth	1971 Mrs. S. Copley & Mrs. B. Harding
1934 Mrs. A. Franks & Miss C.M. Burton	1972 Mrs. J. Thorneycroft & Mrs. M. Warren
1935 Mrs. J. Grimditch & Mrs. A. Franks	1973 Mrs. B. Broom & Mrs. M. Stephenson
1936 Miss B. Goddard & partner	1974 Mrs. S. Radcliffe & Mrs. E. Copley
1937 Mrs. K. Farquharson & Mrs. N. Burdon-Cooper	1975 Mrs. M. Stanbury & Mrs. H. Wythe
1938 Mrs. C.C. Arnell & Miss J. Clements	1976 Mrs. M. Stanbury & Mrs. H. Wythe
1947 Mrs. J. Quinn & partner	1977 Mrs. J. Horne & Mrs. J. Capstick
1948 Mrs. S. Pinchard & partner	1978 Mrs. L. Taylor & Mrs. B. Harding
1949 Mrs. N. Graham & Mrs. J. Brown	1979 Mrs. A. Davis & Mrs. R. Watters
1950 Mrs. P.E. Orchard-Lisle & Mrs. S. Copley	1980 Mrs. E. Bottomley & Mrs. J. Cooper
1951 Mrs. N. Graham & Mrs. J. Brown	1981 Mrs. E. Copley & Mrs. S. Radcliffe
1952 Mrs. N. Burdon-Cooper & Mrs. A. Farrow	1982 Mrs. L. Beardwell & Mrs. M. Shipway
1953 Miss P.J. Lane & Mrs. J. Chapman	1983 Mrs. J. Horne & Mrs. R. Watters
1954 Miss P.J. Lane & Mrs. J. Chapman	1984 Mrs. J. Howell & Mrs. M. Thomson
1955 Mrs. J. Chapman & Mrs. V. Baucher	1985 Mrs. S. Westmacott & Mrs. K. Arthur
1956 Mrs. P. Liddiard & Mrs. I. Cole	1986 Mrs. J. Horne & Mrs. R. Watters
1957 Mrs. N. Graham & Mrs. Q. Robson	1987 Mrs. J. Horne & Mrs. R. Watters
1958 Mrs. V. Baucher & Mrs. L. Taylor	1988 Mrs. A. Duncan & Mrs. L. Beardwell
1959 Mrs. O. Dove & Mrs. L.M. Hely	1989 Mrs. R. Connell & Mrs. Y. Frankland
1960 Mrs. V. Baucher & Mrs. B. Walker	1990 Mrs. A. Duncan & Mrs. L. Beardwell
1961 Mrs. J. Chapman & Mrs. S. Copley	1991 Mrs. J. Horne & Mrs. R. Watters
1962 Mrs. G. Parkes & Mrs. E. Simmers	1992 Mrs. F. Smith & Mrs. M. Nelson
1963 Mrs. O. Dove & Mrs. E. Bottomley	1993 Mrs. M. Stanbury & Mrs. H. Wythe
1964 Mrs. B. Broom & Mrs. M. Stephenson	1994 Mrs. E. Drewery & Mrs. M. Hall
1965 Mrs. M. Sims & Mrs. P. Harris	1995 Mrs. D. Moffat & Mrs. J. Ferry
1966 Mrs. S. Dorée & Mrs. J. Hopkinson	1996 Mrs. R. Hemmings & Ms. A.J. Rooke
1967 Mrs. B. Broom & Mrs. M. Stephenson	1997 Mrs. E. Drewery & Mrs. M. Hall
1968 Mrs. B. Broom & Mrs. M. Stephenson	1998

Rushton Cup

Presented by Miss G. Rushton
18 hole medal

1951 Mrs. R. Brendon	1961 Mrs. J. Chapman	1971 Mrs. P. Waterfield
1952 Mrs. P. Liddiard	1962 Mrs. E.W. Parkes	1972 Mrs. S. Westmacott
1953 Mrs. C. Holdsworth	1963 Mrs. M. Thomson	1973 Mrs. V. Murray
1954 Mrs. T. S. Robson	1964 Mrs. J. Arthur	1974 Mrs. B. Broom
1955 Mrs. R.H. Baucher	1965 Mrs. P. Reid	1975 Mrs. S. Dorée
1956 Mrs. P. Liddiard	1966 Mrs. P. Bailey	1976 Mrs. A. Wright
1957 Mrs. M.C. Cole	1967 Mrs. B. Broom	1977 Mrs. J. Horne
1958 Mrs. A.E. Potter	1968 Mrs. L. Taylor	1978 Mrs. R. Watters
1959 Mrs. E.W. Parkes	1969 Mrs. L. Taylor	1979 Mrs. J. Horne
1960 Mrs. J. Hopkinson	1970 Mrs. O. Dove	1980 Mrs. H. Wythe

Rushton Cup – Continued

1981 Mrs. J. Horne	1987 Mrs. E. Cox	1993 Mrs. M. Havens
1982 Mrs. B. Harding	1988 Mrs. J. Howell	1994 Mrs. A. Prosser
1983 Mrs. R. Watters	1989 Mrs. P. Stamford	1995 Mrs. J. Ferry
1984 Mrs. B. Tattersall	1990 Mrs. S. Radcliffe	1996 Mrs. A. Healy
1985 Mrs. E. Cox	1991 Mrs. J. Howell	1997 Mrs. M. Gibson
1986 Mrs. M. Hall	1992 Mrs. D. Samuels	1998 Mrs. L. Beardwell

Doe's Platter

Presented by Mrs. Marjorie Cumming
Knockout, handicaps 30 and over

1969 Mrs. K.E. Whitworth	1979 Mrs. M. King	1989 Mrs. M. Havens
1970 Mrs. R.J. Arthur	1980 Mrs. L. Beardwell	1990 Mrs. V. Honess
1971 Mrs. J. Keele	1981 Mrs. R. Gunn	1991 Mrs. L. Lambert
1972 Mrs. G. Parkes	1982 Mrs. E. de Courcy	1992 Mrs. D. Moffat
1973 Mrs. J. Thurgood	1983 Mrs. P. Edwards	1993 Mrs. R. Graham
1974 Mrs. A. Farrow	1984 Mrs. J. Anthony	1994 Mrs. G. Williams
1975 Mrs. S. Glass	1985 Mrs. V. Roockley	1995 Mrs. D. Liddle
1976 Mrs. J. Horne	1986 Mrs. J. Seale	1996 Mrs. J. Hardy
1977 Mrs. D. O'Gorman	1987 Mrs. M. Dingwall	1997 Mrs. G. Warnes
1978 Mrs. D. O'Gorman	1988 Mrs. D. Samuels	1998 Mrs. R. Woodley

Dixon Plate

Presented by Mrs. Agnes Dixon
Nathan Cup first round losers knockout

1981 Mrs. A. Milne	1987 Mrs. R. Watters	1993 Mrs. M. Nelson
1982 Mrs. H. Wythe	1988 Mrs. M. Stanbury	1994 Mrs. S. Turner
1983 Mrs. M. Stanbury	1989 Mrs. L. Beardwell	1995 Mrs. A. Healy
1984 Mrs. M. Stanbury	1990 not awarded	1996 Mrs. S. Westmacott
1985 Mrs. S. Hathaway	1991 Mrs. C. Robinson	1997 Mrs. J. Bryce
1986 Mrs. Mary Wilson	1992 Mrs. A. Healy	1998

Hopkinson Salver

Presented by Mrs. Joan Hopkinson
Stableford for over-60s

1983 Mrs. E. Harrison	1989 Mrs. E. Ridewood	1995 Mrs. J. Dulieu
1984 Mrs. S. Radcliffe	1990 Mrs. S. Radcliffe	1996 Mrs. J. Bailey
1985 Mrs. C. Newbery	1991 Mrs. J. MacIntyre	1997 Mrs. D. O'Gorman
1986 Mrs. R. Connell	1992 Mrs. E. Hanson	1998 Mrs. J. Howell
1987 Mrs. M. Dingwall	1993 Mrs. P. Clough	
1988 Mrs. J. Howell	1994 Mrs. B. Lynn	

High-Low

Trophies presented by Mrs. R. Connell & Mrs. G. Wadey in 1987
Drawn Foursomes knockout

1982 Mrs. J. Horne & Mrs. S. Williamson	1991 Mrs. J. MacIntyre & Mrs. L. Lambert
1983 Mrs. R. Watters & Mrs. R. Milne	1992 Mrs. J. Van Gelder & Mrs. J. Bryce
1984 Mrs. L. Beardwell & Mrs. Myra Wilson	1993 Mrs. Y. Frankland & Mrs. L. Dytham
1985 Mrs. M. Stanbury & Mrs. Mary Wilson	1994 Mrs. J. MacIntyre & Mrs. J. Bryce
1986 Mrs. R. Connell & Mrs. G. Wadey	1995 Mrs. E. de Courcy & Mrs. M. Mills
1987 Mrs. L. Beardwell & Mrs. J. Van Gelder	1996 Mrs. E. de Courcy & Mrs. D. Liddle
1988 Mrs. S. Hathaway & Mrs. S. May	1997 Mrs. J. Gelson & Mrs. P. Edwards
1989 no record	1998 Mrs. R. Hemmings & Mrs. M. Dingwall
1990 Mrs. S. Palmer & Mrs. S. Newbury	

Business Ladies Cup
18 hole medal

1992 Mrs. E. Drewery	1994 Mrs. S. Hawkey	1996 Mrs. E. Drewery
1993 Mrs. A.M. Davis	1995 Mrs. E. Collyer	1997 Miss V. Fleming
		1998

Tattersall Cup
Presented by Mrs. Brenda Tattersall
18 hole medal

1993 Miss K. Nelson	1995 Mrs. A. Prosser	1997 Mrs. J. Seale
1994 Mrs. M. Hall	1996 Mrs. M. Stanbury	1998

Maltby Cup
Lady Captain and Professional Challenge
1982-87 v. Jack Ramsden. From 1988 v. David Gleeson

1982 Mrs. M. Stanbury & Mrs. H. Wythe	1990 Mrs. S. Farquhar & Mrs. P. Rawlings
1983 Mrs. M. Hall & Mrs. S. Hathaway	1991 Mrs. R. Watters & Mrs. J. Nevitt
1984 Mrs. M. Hall & Mrs. S. Hathaway	1992 Mrs. R. Watters & Mrs. E. Drewery
1985 Mrs. J. Horne & Mrs. M. Stanbury	1993 Mrs. L. Beardwell & Mrs. A. Duncan
1986 Mrs. K. Arthur & Mrs. L. Beardwell	1994 Mrs. L. Beardwell & Mrs. A. Duncan
Mrs. S. Farquhar & Mrs. P. Rawlings	1995 Mrs. L. Beardwell & Mrs. A. Duncan
1987 Mrs. K. Arthur & Mrs. L. Beardwell	1996 Mrs. S. Turner & Mrs. D. Moffat
1988 Mrs. H. Wythe & Mrs. M. Stanbury	1997 Mrs. S. Turner & Mrs. D. Moffat
1989 Mrs. M. Hall & Mrs. S. Hathaway	1998 Mrs. M. Nelson & Miss L. Nelson

Dorothy Johnson Cup
Presented by Mrs. Dorothy Johnson
LGU Medal winners, plus ties, during the year

1973 Mrs. A. Wright	1982 Mrs. J. Horne	1991 Mrs. S. Hathaway
1974 Mrs. S. Farquhar	1983 Mrs. S. Radcliffe	1992 Mrs. P. Cotton
1975 Mrs. H. Wythe	1984 Mrs. R. Connell	1993 Mrs. S. Hawkey
1976 Mrs. M. Stanbury	1985 Mrs. M. Stanbury	1994 Mrs. J. Bryce
1977 Mrs. D. Johnson	1986 Mrs. M. Thomson	1995 Mrs. M. Mills
1978 Mrs. J. Capstick	1987 Mrs. S. Radcliffe	1996 Mrs. A. Prosser
1979 Mrs. P. Clough	1988 Mrs. Myra Wilson	1997 Ms. A.J. Rooke
1980 Mrs. L. Beardwell	1989 Mrs. J. Capstick	1998
1981 Mrs. R. Watters	1990 Mrs. D. Barry	

Golfer of the Year
Presented by Mrs. Rosemary Watters
Points awarded for strokeplay events

1984 Mrs. A.M. Davis	1989 Mrs. E. Drewery &	1995 Ms. A.J. Rooke
1985 Mrs. M. Hall	Mrs. D. Barry	1996 Mrs. J. Dulieu
1986 Mrs. L. Beardwell	1990 Mrs. Myra Wilson	1997 Mrs. A. Prosser
1987 Mrs. L. Beardwell	1991 Mrs. C. Robinson	1998
1988 Mrs. Mary Wilson	1992 Mrs. E. Drewery	
	1993 Ms. A.J. Rooke	
	1994 Mrs. A. Prosser	

Westmacott Plate
Presented by Mrs. Sally Westmacott
Player reducing handicap by greatest margin during the year

1987 Mrs. J. Williams	1991 Mrs. H. Dennes	1995 Mrs. C. Sharp
1988 Mrs. V. Fletcher	Mrs. L. Lambert	1996 Mrs. J. Hardy
1989 Mrs. A. Healy	1992 Mrs. J. Bryce	1997 Miss G. MacLaurin
1990 Mrs. C. Robinson	1993 Miss L. Nelson	1998
	1994 Mrs. J. Gelson	

Ladies Winter League
Presented by Mrs. Sheila Farquhar
Round Robin, qualifying for knockout

1982 Mrs. S. Farquhar	1988 Mrs. J. Richards	1994 Ms. A.J. Rooke
1983 Mrs. M. Kaye	1989 Mrs. L. Beardwell	1995 Mrs. Y. Frankland
1984 Mrs. K. Arthur	1990 Mrs. Y. Frankland	1996 Mrs. M. Nelson
1985 Mrs. M. Hall	1991 Mrs. Myra Wilson	1997 Mrs. A. Prosser
1986 Mrs. M. Stanbury	1992 Mrs. C. Robinson	1998
1987 Mrs. M. Hall	1993 Mrs. C. Robinson	

Mixed Foursomes Challenge Cups
Presented 1905 by A.C. Cory-Wright. Knockout

1905-'07 no record	1958 Mr. & Mrs. H.A. Chapman
1908 Mr. & Mrs. C.M. Humble	1959 Mr. & Mrs. R.G. Wilson
1909 A.E. Colebrook & B.E. Miller	1960 Mr. & Mrs. E.D. Broom
1910 Dr. & Mrs. R.V.B. Smyth	1961 Mr. & Mrs. H.A. Chapman
1911 D. Nicoll & Miss Pennington	1962 Mr. & Mrs. E.A. Judge
1912 Mr. & Mrs. K.N. Stephens	1963 Mr. & Mrs. G.F. Platt
1913 M.B. Smyth & W.R. Beatty Smyth	1964 Mr. & Mrs. T.P. Stephenson
1914 M.B. Smyth & W.R. Beatty Smyth	1965 Mr. & Mrs. J. Van Gelder
1919 Mr. & Mrs. P. Alliston	1966 Mr. & Mrs. J. Van Gelder
1920 Mr. & Mrs. R. Foster	1967 Mr. & Mrs. H.A. Chapman
1921 Mr. & Mrs. A.E. Dodge	1968 Mr. & Mrs. J.F. Darroch
1922 E.J. Outram & Mrs. C.L. Richmond	1969 P.J.R. Marsh & Miss F. Chapman
1923 G.E. Vaughan & Miss Rosenheim	1970 Mr. & Mrs. J.W.G. MacIntyre
1924 R.M. Farquharson & Mrs. Salaman	1971 R.A. Wehner & Mrs. S. Westmacott
1925 Mr. & Mrs. P.C. Burton	1972 Mr. & Mrs. J.A. Randall
1926 R. Woodbridge & Mrs. L.J. Reid	1973 Mr. & Mrs. J.W.G. MacIntyre
1927 Mr. & Mrs. S. Seddon	1974 P.H. Newman & Mrs. D.W. Copley
1928 Mr. & Mrs. R. Worssam	1975 Mr. & Mrs. R.G. Wilson
1929 Mr. & Mrs. R.E.A. Bott	1976 D. Lamond & Mrs. D. Notley
1930 Mr. & Mrs. R.E.A. Bott	1977 J.F. Reid & Mrs. E. Copley
1931 Mr. & Mrs. R.E.A. Bott	1978 P.J.R. Marsh & Mrs. J. Horne
1932 Mr. & Mrs. T.E. Wills	1979 E.A. Foulkes & Mrs. S. Farquhar
1933 R.E.A. Bott & Miss J. Forsyth	1980 J.H. Cox & Mrs. A. Milne
1934 Mr. & Mrs. A.G. Snelling	1981 A. Steel & Mrs. H. Wythe
1935 Mr. & Mrs. R.T. Jones	1982 J.F. Reid & Mrs. E. Copley
1936 Mr. & Mrs. A. Harding	1983 D.A. Lewis & Mrs. J. Van Gelder
1937 Mr. & Mrs. H.A. Chapman	1984 E.D. Hurcomb & Mrs. M. Hall
1938 J.F.M. Douglas & Miss Goddard	1985 H.R. Harlow & Mrs. M. Thomson
1939 Mr. & Mrs. J.M. Darroch	1986 R. Dew & Mrs. A. Lewis
1946 Mr. & Mrs. H.A. Chapman	1987 E.L. Lewis & Mrs. S. Hathaway
1947 Mr. & Mrs. H.A. Chapman	1988 A. Steel & Mrs. H. Wythe
1948 J. Glassbrook & Miss F. Hazeldine	1989 Mr. & Mrs. E. Stanbury
1949 Mr. & Mrs. L.W. Phillips	1990 P.J.R. Marsh & Mrs. J.P. MacIntyre
1950 Mr. & Mrs. R.E.A. Bott	1991 Mr. & Mrs. D. Lewis
1951 Mr. & Mrs. J.M. Balch	1992 Mr. & Mrs. J. Nelson
1952 Mr. & Mrs. J.M. Balch	1993 S. Newbery & Mrs. C. Newbery
1953 Mr. & Mrs. G. Sheffield	1994 N.F. Lee & Mrs. E. Drewery
1954 C. Boyton, jun. & Miss A. Baucher	1995 G. Chivers & Miss V. Fleming
1955 Mr. & Mrs. P.A. Strong	1996 Mr. & Mrs. J. Nelson
1956 B.H.G. Chapman & Miss A.M. Henderson	1997 R.J. Dew & Mrs. S. Turner
1957 R.N. Glover & Miss A. Baucher	1998 P.A. Williams & Ms. L.J. Davis

Nathan Challenge Cups
Mixed Greensomes Knockout
4 pairs qualify from medal

1928	P.C. Burton & Miss C.M. Burton	1967	D. Langrish-Smith & Mrs. M.E. Baynes
1929	E.S. Markham & Mrs. Neill	1968	Mr. & Mrs. H.A.C. Edwards
1930	S. Seddon & Mrs. P.N. Nathan	1969	Mr. & Mrs. R.A. Johnson
1931	Mr. & Mrs. F.A.B. Farquharson	1970	Mr. & Mrs. J.W. MacIntyre
1932	E.S. Markham & Mrs. Neill	1971	G.N.V. Jenkins & Mrs. M. Judge
1933	H.D. Roberts & Miss Farquharson	1972	A. Bailey & Mrs. I.K. Copley
1934	Mr. & Mrs. T.E. Wills	1973	R.G. Wilson & Mrs. S. Westmacott
1935	Mr. & Mrs. R.H. Burdon-Cooper	1974	Mr. & Mrs. R.A. Radcliffe
1936	Maj. & Mrs. W.B. Stevenson	1975	J. Brogden & Mrs. V. Murray
1937	R.E.A. Bott & P.M.T. Bott	1976	Mr. & Mrs. E. Stanbury
1938	Mr. & Mrs. H.A. Chapman	1977	J. Van Gelder & Mrs. K. Arthur
1946	R.D. Henderson & Mrs. J. Ingram	1978	G.A. Uwins & Mrs. J. Horne
1947	F.W. Glassbrook & Miss. F. Hazeldine	1979	G.A. Uwins & Mrs. J. Horne
1948	Mr. & Mrs. G. Quinn	1980	K.R. Jenkin & Mrs. J. Graham
1949	Mr. & Mrs. J.M. Balch	1981	Wing Cdr. & Mrs. Bassingthwaite
1950	R.E.A. Bott & Mrs. G. Rushton	1982	E.A. Foulkes & Mrs. S.L. Farquhar
1951	J.M. Reid & Miss P. Lane	1983	D.M. Lamond & Mrs. D. Notley
1952	J.M. Reid & Miss P. Lane	1984	A.M. Forrest & Mrs. L. Beardwell
1953	Mr. & Mrs. R.G. Wilson	1985	A. Steel & Mrs. H. Wythe
1954	Mr. & Mrs. H.A. Chapman	1986	Mr. & Mrs. E. Stanbury
1955	A.R. Griffiths & Mrs. Q. Robson	1987	P.H. Brown & Mrs. A. Davis
1956	Mr. & Mrs. G.F. Platt	1988	P. Nevitt & Mrs. M. Wilson
1957	Mr. & Mrs. A. Bailey	1989	A.M. Forrest & Mrs. L. Beardwell
1958	T. Neville & Miss A.M. Henderson	1990	Mr. & Mrs. P.J. Robinson
1959	A.J. Taylor & Mrs. Taylor	1991	Mr. & Mrs. P. Healy
1960	A.J. Taylor & Mrs. Taylor	1992	H. Green & Miss A. Waugh
1961	R. Neill & Miss A.M. Henderson	1993	P. Smith & Miss C. Maxwell
1962	T.P. Stephenson & Mrs. Stephenson	1994	G. Fisher & Miss V. Fleming
1963	Mr. & Mrs. R.A. Johnson	1995	Mr. & Mrs. D. Havens
1964	Mr. & Mrs. R.H. Burdon-Cooper	1996	Mr. & Mrs D.M. Holden
1965	Mr. & Mrs. J. Van Gelder	1997	G. Chivers & Mrs. S. Hawkey
1966	R.E.A. Bott & Mrs. D.J. Cumming	1998	Mr. &. Mrs. D.M. Holden

Winter Mixed Foursomes
Knockout, partners drawn

1962	Mrs. Edmonston-Low & P.M. Harding	1978	Mrs. R.V. Watters & J.A. Randall
1963	Mrs. T. Sims & D.A.A. Bott	1979	Mrs. J. Holdway & E.D. Hurcomb
1964	Mrs. B.L. Harding & R.E.A. Bott	1980	Mrs. J. Holdway & J. Connell
1965	Mrs. B.A. Broom & C.W. Greaves	1981	Mrs. J. Holdway & J.A. Randall
1966	Mrs. P. Power & R.E.A. Bott	1982	Mrs. S. Westmacott & A. Steel
1967	Mrs. S. Westmacott & R.E.A. Bott	1983	Mrs. E.M. Copley & D.R. Newbery
1968	Mrs. R.G. Wilson & H.A.C. Edwards	1984	Mrs. M. Hall & J. Van Gelder
1969	Mrs. J.P. MacIntyre & R.A.P. Wehner	1985	Miss J. Seal & P. Winship
1970	Mrs. S. Westmacott & A.K. Sutcliffe	1986	no record
1971	Mrs. R.G. Wilson & H.R. Harlow	1987	Mrs. E. Drewery & J. Tattersall
1972	Mrs. M. Cumming & D. Lamond	1988	Mrs. R.V. Watters & P. Winship
1973	Mrs. E.M. Copley & J.R.H. Kitching	1989	Mrs. A. Healy & R.A. Barnes
1974	Mrs. M. Warren & W.E. Gray	1990	Mrs. J.R. Nevitt & P. Lynn
1975	Mrs. S. Radcliffe & P.A. Mitchell	1991	Mrs. E. Drewery & G. Williams
1976	Mrs. A. Wright & J.C. Holdway	1992	Mrs. R. Watters & D. Findlay
1977	Mrs. J. Holdway & C.W. Capstick	1993	Mrs. R. Watters & P. Healy

Winter Mixed Foursomes – Continued

1994 Mrs. R. Watters & P. Chisholm   1997 Mrs. B. Tattersall & D. Holden
1995 Mrs. A. Healy & S. Newbery   1998
1996 Mrs. E. Hanson & P.T. Watters

Junior Open Challenge Cup
36 hole scratch medal

1952 S.K. Proctor	Moor Park	1971 F. McCathie	Thirsk &
1953 B.H.G. Chapman	Porters Park		N'thallerton
1954 M.M.D. Laidlaw	Chigwell	1972 P.H. Hinton	Enville
1955 R.H. Mummery	R. Ashdown Forest	1973 T.J. Giles	N'hants County
1956 C.W.S. Matts	Moor Park	1974 A. Jackson	Burnham Beeches
1957 K. Hamilton	South Herts	1975 G. Turner	Chelmsford
1958 R.R.W. Davenport	Ashford Manor	1976 A. Rose	John O'Gaunt
1959 D.C. Allen	Welwyn Garden City	1977 N.D. Taee	Pannal
1960 R.W.G. Hayes	Dartford	1978 N. Lucas	Ellesborough
1961 D. Fillary	Bexley Heath	R.J. Mugglestone	Worksop
1962 P.M. Townsend	Porters Park	1979 A. Clark	Old Fold Manor
1963 P.M. Townsend	Porters Park	1980 M. Wharton-Palmer	Robin Hood
1964 P.M. Townsend	Porters Park	1981 A. Tosdevin	Pinner Hill
1965 P. Dawson	Thorpe Hall	1982 N.J. Briggs	Long Ashton
1966 M.G. King	Reading	1983 F. George	Beaconsfield
1967 M.G. King	Reading	1984 P.A. Baker	Lilleshall Hall
1968 W. Humphreys	Royal Mid-Surrey	1985 W. Henry	Porters Park
1969 R.H.N. Sumner	Penwortham	1986 P. Hurring	Cottesmore
1970 P.A. Elson	Coventry	1987 G. Clark	Pinner Hill

Reid Trophy
Inter-club Open Junior Tournament
36 hole scratch team medal

1988 Long Ashton G.C.	1991 Worksop G.C.	1994 Orsett G.C.
1989 Channels G.C.	1992 Worksop G.C.	
1990 Worthing G.C.	1993 not played	

Reid Trophy
Under-14 Boys Open
36 hole scratch medal
Adopted by EGU in 1997

1995 S. Robinson	Seaton Carew	1997 C. Stevenson	Whittington Heath
1996 M. Stam	Royal Liverpool	1998 J. Petrou	Muswell Hill

Darroch Cup
36 hole scratch medal
Not awarded 1961-1964 inclusive

1947 J. Darroch	1958 P.G. de Havilland	1973 C.J. Spacey
1948 M. Darroch	1959 P.G. de Havilland	1974 C.J. Spacey
1949 B.H.G. Chapman	1960 P.M. Townsend	1975 C. Grant
1950 M. Darroch	1965 N.P. Broad	1976 C. Grant
1951 B.H.G. Chapman	1966 R.E.W. Wild	1977 A.R. Lewis
1952 B.H.G. Chapman	1967 L.O. Hughes	1978 D.L. Keller
1953 J. Atkinson	1968 N.E. Webb	1979 D.L. Keller
1954 R.H.L. Baucher	1969 T. Clark	1980 A.P.O. Cotton
1955 N.R. Hyde	1970 N.J. Notley	1981 A.P.O. Cotton
1956 A.S.B. Knight	1971 A.P. Coral	1982 A.P.O. Cotton
1957 P.G. de Havilland	1972 A.P. Coral	1983 N.A. Hathaway

Darroch Cup – Continued

1984 R.L. Lewis	1989 G. White	1994 C. Duke
1985 R.M. Capstick	1990 S. Graham	1995 N. Smith
1986 S.T. Oxenham	1991 J. Duke	1996 N. Smith
1987 G. White	1992 C. Duke	1997 G. Muir
1988 J. Wright	1993 C. Duke	1998 P. Warnes

Neil Elsey Memorial Trophy

1993 N. Smith	1995-97 not played
1994 N. Smith & D. Martin (tie)	1998 M. Moore & A. Dormer

John Roberts Trophy
Most improved player of the year

1992 A. Tolley	1994-96 not awarded	1998
1993 Lorna Nelson	1997 M. Thompson	

Nelson Trophy
Singles Knockout

1993 R. Ellis	1995/6 not played	1998 P. Warnes
1994 W. Piercy	1997 P. Warnes